HUTCHINSON

British
Place-names

Other titles in the Hutchinson Pocket series:

HUTCHINSON POCKET

British Place-names

Adrian Room

Helicon

Copyright © Helicon Publishing Ltd 1995

All rights reserved

Helicon Publishing Ltd
42 Hythe Bridge Street
Oxford OX1 2EP

Printed and bound in Great Britain by
Unwin Brothers Ltd, Old Woking, Surrey

ISBN to come

British Cataloguing in Publication Data

A catalogue record for this book is available
from the British Library

Introduction

Place-names are a regular part of our lives. We live in a place with one name, write or phone to another, and see a third as we drive along a road or travel by train. But what do the names all mean?

It is possible to make an informed guess. *Newcastle* appears to relate to a 'new castle', and *Peterborough* to a 'borough' of someone called Peter. But what of the many names that appear to have no obvious meaning? What about *Leeds*, or *Elgin*, or *Bangor*, or even *London*?

For those, a book like this is needed, which can 'translate' them into something meaningful. But first, of course, their language of origin has to be identified, so that it can be correctly interpreted.

The place-names of Britain have evolved through the languages of its inhabitants. These can be grouped in five stages.

The namers

First, there were the *Celts*, who are Britain's aboriginal people. They spoke a language that has its modern counterparts in modern Welsh and Scottish Gaelic, and in the languages of Cornwall and the Isle of Man. Our earliest place-names are thus Celtic, and are those of the oldest natural features, such as rivers, hills and mountains. Some names are even *pre*-Celtic, and have meanings that cannot be determined. And although it is often possible to deduce the meaning of a Celtic name, it is often hard to determine its original form, or to reconstruct the word that gave it.

The Celts were at the height of their powers in the 4th century BC. Then came the *Romans*, in the 1st century BC. However, although they imported their own language, Latin, the everyday speech of the country remained Celtic, and when the Romans came to name a place, they usually adopted (and adapted) the existing Celtic name. This was often the name of a river, as at *Exeter*, or perhaps of a hill, as at *Manchester*. The names of the Roman settlements at these two places were respectively *Isca* (from the River *Exe*) and *Mamucium* (from a hill called something like *Mam*). The Romans themselves actually gave very few Latin place-names, but one exception is *Pontefract*.

The Romans left Britain in the 5th century AD, and it was then that the

Anof settlement was in eastern and northern England, in the extensive region that came to be known as the Danelaw. Their language was Old Scandinavian (OS), which is related to Old English but clearly different from it. They also frequently had two-part place-names, but instead of OE *-ton* had OS *-by*. Examples of their names are *Formby*, 'Forni's farmstead', *Seathwaite*, 'lake clearing', and *Manthorpe*, 'Manni's outlying farmstead'.

The fifth visitors to Britain were the *Normans*, in the famous year of 1066. The language they spoke was basically a form of French, and it is they who are chiefly responsible for the two-word place-names with a Norman family name as the second word. These are particularly common in the south of England, and are names such as *Keinton Mandeville*, *Shepton Mallet* and *Stanton Fitzwarren*. The family names are those of the Normans who held the manor, with the second word serving to distinguish the place from others identically named. The Normans also gave subjective names such as *Beaulieu*, 'beautiful place', and *Malpas*, 'bad passage'.

The -ing- thing

A large number of OE place-names contain some form of *ing*. Examples are *Nottingham*, *Darlington*, *Hastings*, *Reading* and *Billingborough*. The meaning of *ing* can vary, but it often connects with a personal name, and denotes a place associated with a particular person or with a group of people who are themselves connected with the named person. The meaning is always spelt out in the definitions, but it should be appreciated that 'people', when mentioned, can mean a person's family, or his or her followers, or simply the people that live in the place named after the person. Thus *Fulking*, West Sussex, has a name that relates to the family or followers of a man called *Folca*. Any part of the name after the *ing* denotes the type of settlement, so that *Etchingham*, East Sussex, denotes a homestead (*-ham*) of the family or followers of a man called *Ecci*.

The different types of *ing* are included in List I on p 000.

Sorting the syllables

The second or final component of many OE names can cause problems, especially when it represents one of two similar words with quite different meanings.

The *-ham* that ends many OE names can represent either *hām* (related to modern *hamlet*), meaning 'homestead', 'village', or *hamm* (related to modern *hem*), meaning 'enclosure'. In the later case, this can mean land hemmed in by water, land in the bend of a river, or land on a promontory.

Sometimes it is impossible to tell which sense is meant without an examination of the actual site. And in a few cases it is impossible to be sure at all.

The *-bury* or *-borough* found in several names can similarly represent *burh*, 'fortified place' (modern *borough*), or *beorg*, 'hill' (modern *barrow*). Again, only an examination of the site can determine which.

And the common *-ton* and *-don* can in turn represent either *tūn*, 'farmstead', 'village' (modern *town*), or *dūn*, 'hill' (modern *down*). Once again, only a physical sighting may provide the correct interpretation.

Sources

It is obviously desirable to trace a name back to its earliest recorded forms in order to get an interpretation that is as accurate as possible. Some British place-names were recorded by Ptolemy as early as the 2nd century AD. But mostly it is later writings that give the fullest forms, such as the Venerable Bede's *The Ecclesiastical History of the English People* (8th century) and the many local documents, charts and maps of later years.

It is the *Domesday Book* of 1086, however, that provides the widest coverage of British place-names in medieval times. One must allow for the fact that the French-speaking Norman clerks sometimes had problems with the unfamiliar OE and OS names, producing distortions such as *Straburg* for *Trowbridge* and *Alforda* for *Oakford*. But the names they correctly record are the majority, and have in many cases confirmed an otherwise doubtful derivation.

Reading the rivers

River names, as mentioned, are often the oldest we have. However, there are some river names that are much more recent. Whereas many places are named for their rivers (*Dartmouth*, *Dover*, *Exeter*, *Netheravon*, *Tavistock*), some rivers are named for the places through which they flow. Their names mostly arose in the 16th century and are usually brief versions of the place-name, such as the *Chelt* from *Cheltenham*, the *Rom* from *Romford*, and the *Wid* from *Widford*. Such names are technically known as 'back formations'.

An awareness of such names can help in a correct interpretation of the place-name. *Cambridge*, for example, is not so named because it arose by a bridge over the River Cam. On the contrary, the *Cam* is named for *Cambridge*, which must therefore have some other source for the first part of its name. (It is a river name, but a different one.)

Treading carefully

These and other instances all serve to show that place-names may not be what they seem, so that *Oakham* is not named for its oaks, *Oxted* for its oxen, or *Silverstone* for its silver stones. And although trains stop at *Haltwhistle*, its name is not related to railways!

The Celtic scene

Whereas Old English and Old Scandinavian are dead languages, Welsh and Gaelic are still living. This means that names in Wales, and to a lesser extent Scotland, can often be interpreted literally and accurately, especially for minor places. *Penrhyndeudraeth* thus means 'promontory with two beaches', and *Drumnadrochit* is 'ridge by the bridge'. Even in these names, however, some of the Celtic elements have been slightly anglicized. Nevertheless, the names spell out their meanings fairly clearly and unambiguously, and the barrier is simply the unfamiliar language.

The entries

Each of the 2000-plus entries is presented in three separate 'strands' of information, as follows:

1) The name itself, an identification of the place bearing it (town, village, county, river, etc), the location of the place (usually by county or region), the literal meaning of the name, its composition or 'breakdown' in its language(s) of origin. OE is Old English, OS is Old Scandiavian. All other languages are spelt out in full, *eg* 'Old French', 'Cornish'. An asterisk (*) before a word means that it is hypothetical, *ie* it has not been recorded in independent use or was found in use only at a later date. 'Celtic' is used for a name that is earlier than modern Gaelic or Welsh. In the identification, 'district' is generally used both for a distinct part of a city, such as *Levenshulme* in Manchester, or an administrative division of a county, such as *Tandridge* in Surrey. Many 'districts' in Greater London are in fact associated with a particular borough, although for reasons of space this is not specified. Thus *Holborn* is simply identified as 'district, Greater London', not 'district, Camden, Greater London'.

2) A brief commentary on the name, usually from a geographical (topographical), historical or linguistic aspect. In the case of Celtic names, there will often be a link with a modern Welsh word, as the current Celtic language with which English speakers are likely to be at all familiar. Where a 'hundred' is mentioned, the reference is to the ancient administrative division of a shire or county.

3) Historical records of the name, with year or century of record. In these, the year 1086 always refers to a Domesday Book form. In a few

cases, mainly for Celtic or modern names, this third strand may be absent, either because it cannot be supplied or because the name is too recent to need one. Some of the most modern names of all are the ones devised for administrative districts in the local government boundary changes of 1974 (1975 in Scotland). Most of these were reglo-Saxons arrived.

These were the people who essentially gave not only the English language of today but many English place-names. We now generally refer to their language as Old English (abbreviated OE in this book), and the names that they gave are typically two-part names, often consisting of a personal name or defining word followed by a general term. Examples are *Bickton*, 'Bica's farmstead', *Newport*, 'new market town', and *Woodbury*, 'fortified place by a wood'. Not surprisingly, OE *tūn*, 'farmstead', 'village', frequently occurs as the 'habitation' part of a name, usually represented by *-ton*. But natural features occur as well, one of the most common being *lēah*, 'wood' (modern *lea*), often found as the *-ley* or *-leigh* of a name. It could also mean 'clearing', since a clearing in a wood was often used for a habitation site.

After the Anglo-Saxons came the *Scandinavians*, or Vikings, whose raids began in the 9th century. Their chief area vivals of old regional names, but some were new and artificial creations.

Examples of common OE and OS words and components occurring in place-names will be found in List I on p 000, and of Gaelic and Welsh words in List II. Lists III to VII are informational but more by way of geographical, literary, linguistic or culinary diversion.

Abbots Langley (town, Hertfordshire) 'abbot's long wood', *abbot* + OE *lang*, 'long' + *lēah*, 'wood', 'clearing'. The first word indicates that this particular long wood was granted to the Abbot of St Albans. *Langalege c* 1060, *Abbotes Langele* 1263.

Aberaeron (town, Dyfed) '(place at the) mouth of the (River) Aeron', Welsh *aber*, 'mouth' + river name. The river's name means 'battle' (Old Welsh *aer*), referring to the goddess said to live in its waters. The Medieval Latin form of the name denotes the estuary, not the town, which only became significant in the early 19th century. *Ad ostium Ayron* 1184.

Aberdare (town, Mid Glamorgan) '(place at the) mouth of the (River) Dâr', Welsh *aber*, 'confluence' + river name. The river's name means 'oak' (Old Welsh *dâr*), meaning that these trees grow by it. It is joined here by the Cynon, so that the town stands at a confluence. *Aberdar* 1203.

Aberdeen (city, Grampian) '(place at the) mouth of the (River) Don', Celtic *aber*, 'mouth' + river name. Modern Aberdeen stands on the Dee, and the name thus refers to Old Aberdeen, to the north, which arose at the mouth of the Don. *Aberdon c* 1187, *Aberden c* 1214.

Aberdour (town, Fife) '(place at the) mouth of the (River) Dour', Celtic *aber*, 'mouth' + river name. The river's name means 'waters', from the same root that gave the names of ◊Andover and ◊Dover. *Aberdaur* 1226.

Aberdovey (town, Gwynedd) '(place at the) mouth of the (River) Dovey', Welsh *aber*, 'mouth' + river name. The river name (Welsh *Dyfi*) may derive either from Welsh *du*, 'black', or *dwfn*, 'deep'. The first record names the estuary itself, not the town. *Aberdewi* 12th century, *Aberdivi* 1592.

Aberfeldy (town, Tayside) '(place at the) confluence of Peallaidh', Celtic *aber*, 'confluence' + confluence name. The town stands near the confluence of the Urlar Burn with the Tay. The confluence itself is named *Peallaidh*, after the name of a water sprite (meaning 'pulling one') believed to live here.

Abergavenny (town, Gwent) '(place at the) mouth of the (River) Gavenny', Welsh *aber*, 'mouth' + river name. The river name probably means 'smith' (Modern Welsh *gof*) as a sort of personal nickname. The Welsh name of the town is either *Abergafenni* or *Y Fenni*. The latter has lost the first syllable of the river name. *Abergavenni* 12th century, *Bergeveny* 1255.

Abergele (town, Clwyd) '(place at the) mouth of the (River) Gele', Welsh *aber*, 'mouth' + river name. The river name probably comes from Welsh *gelau*, 'blade', 'spear'. This denotes a river that flows straight and bright, cutting its way to the coast.

Aberlour (town, Grampian) '(place at the) mouth of the Lour (Burn)', Celtic *aber*, 'confluence' + river name. The town stands at the confluence of the Lour Burn and the Spey. The river (or burn) name comes from a root word *labaro-*, 'talkative', as if a 'babbling brook'. The town's formal name is *Charlestown of Aberlour*, after Charles *Grant*, who laid out the original village in 1812. The site was formerly known as *Skirdustan*, 'Drostan's slice'. *Aberlower* 1226.

Abersoch (town, Gwynedd) '(place at the) mouth of the (River) Soch', Welsh *aber*, 'mouth' + river name. The river name means 'drain', 'ditch', denoting one with muddy waters.

Abertillery (town, Gwent) '(place at the) mouth of the Teleri (Brook)', Welsh *aber*, 'confluence' + river name. The town stands at the confluence of the Teleri Brook and the Ebwy Fach ('Little Ebwy', *see* ◊Ebbw Vale). The Teleri Brook bears the name of *Eleri*, a 5th-century female saint. *Teleri* 1332, *Aber-Tilery* 1779.

Aberystwyth (town, Dyfed) '(place at the) mouth of the (River) Ystwyth', Welsh *aber*, 'mouth' + river name. The modern town stands at the mouth of the Rheidol, and the name refers its original site, 1½ miles to the south, in the valley of the Ystwyth. The river name means 'winding'. *Aberestuuth* 1232.

Abingdon (town, Oxfordshire) 'Æbba's hill', OE personal name + *dūn*, 'hill'. The name recorded below relates to a medieval monastery, which stood on flat ground, as Abingdon does today. Perhaps the monks felt that a 'loftier' name was more suitable, so named it after the higher ground to the north, although it is unlikely that the monastery was actually located there. *Abbandune* 968.

Aboyne (village, Grampian) '(place by the River) Aboyne', Gaelic river name. The village is on the Dee but takes its name from the *Aboyne*, a small stream to the north. The name means 'river of the white cow', from *abh*, 'river', *bo*, 'cow', and *fionn*, 'white'. The name is a propitious one, since white cows were believed to bring good luck. *Obyne* 1260

Accrington (town, Lancashire) 'acorn farm', OE *æcern*, 'acorn' + *tūn*, 'farm'. The place was originally on the edge of Rossendale Forest, and acorns from there would have been important for feeding pigs. *Akarinton* 12th century.

Acharacle (village, Highland) 'Thorcuil's ford', Gaelic *ath*, 'ford' + personal name. It is not known who Thorcuil (or Torquil) was. The 'ford' would have been over the River Shiel at the point where it leaves Loch Shiel.

Acocks Green (district, Birmingham, West Midlands) 'Acock's green'. The name comes from that of Richard *Acock*, who owned land here in the 17th century.

Acton (district, Greater London) 'oak farm', OE *āc*, 'oak' + *tūn*, 'farm'. The name is a common one, referring to a farmstead by an oak tree or oak trees. *Acton* 1181.

Addington (district, Greater London) 'estate named after Æddi', OE personal name + *-ing-*, 'named after' + *tūn*, 'estate'. The same personal name, possibly that of the same man, occurs for ◊Addiscombe. *Eddintone* 1086.

Addiscombe (district, Greater London) 'æddi's enclosed land', OE personal name + *camp*, 'enclosed land'. The *-combe* of the name is misleading. *See also* ◊Addington. *Edescamp* 1229.

Adlington (town, Lancashire) 'estate named after Eadwulf', OE personal name + *-ing-*, 'named after' + *tūn*, 'estate'. The personal name means literally 'happy wolf', but has no modern equivalent. *Edeluinton c* 1190.

Ailsa Craig (island, Strathclyde) 'fairy rock', Gaelic *aillse*, 'fairy' + *creag*, 'rock'. The bleak rocky island has associations with fairies and ghosts.

Aintree (district, Liverpool, Merseyside) 'one tree', OS *einn*, 'one' + *tré*, 'tree'. At one time in this suburb of Liverpool there would have been an isolated or 'lonely' tree. *Ayntre c* 1220.

Airdrie (town, Strathclyde) 'high slope', Gaelic *ard*, 'height' + *ruighe*, 'slope'. The name refers to the western spur of the Pentland Hills on which the original settlement developed.

Alcester (town, Warwickshire) 'Roman town on the Alne', Celtic river name + OE *ceaster*, 'Roman settlement'. The river name is of unknown meaning. The Roman name of the settlement was probably *Alauna*, based on the river name. A Roman road (now the A435) runs through the town. *Alencestre* 1138.

Alconbury (village, Cambridgeshire) 'Ealhmund's stronghold', OE personal name + *burh*, 'stronghold'. The *h* of the personal name produced the *c* of the place-name. The Domesday Book record of the name is corrupt. *Acumesberie* 1086, *Alcmundesberia* 12th century.

Aldeburgh (town, Suffolk) 'old stronghold', OE *ald*, 'old' + *burh*, 'stronghold'. The River *Alde* here took its name from the town. *Aldeburc* 1086.

Alderley Edge (town, Cheshire) 'Althrȳth's woodland', OE personal name + *lēah*, 'woodland', 'clearing' + modern *edge*. Althrȳth is a woman's name. The *edge* is the sandstone cliff here. *Aldredelie* 1086.

Aldermaston (village, Berkshire) 'farmstead of the chief', OE *aldor-mann*, 'chief', 'nobleman' + *tūn*, 'farmstead'. The OE word that gave the first part of the name also gave modern *alderman*. It is used here as the title of the chief of a shire. *Ældremanestone* 1086.

Aldershot (town, Hampshire) 'projecting piece of land where alders grow', OE *alor*, 'alder' + *scēat*, 'projecting piece of land'. The town arose only in the 19th century from the army camp based here after the Crimean War. *Halreshet* 1171.

Aldridge (town, West Midlands) 'alder farm', OE *alor*, 'alder' + *wīc*, 'farm', 'dwelling'. The name denotes a farm or settlement among alder trees. *Alrewic* 1086.

Alexandria (town, Strathclyde) 'Alexander's place', personal forename. The name is a modern one, from *Alexander* Smollett of Bonhill (d 1799), local Member of Parliament. The town arose in the 18th century when bleaching and dyeing works were built.

Alford (town, Lincolnshire) 'ford where eels are', OE *ǣl*, 'eel' + *ford*, 'ford'. The town is not on a river, so the 'ford' must be over a stream here. *Alforde* 1086.

Alfreton (town, Derbyshire) 'Ælfhere's farmstead', OE personal name + *tūn*, 'farmstead'. In the record, the clerk seems to have confused *f* with *s*. The letters were similar at that time. *Elstretune* 1086.

Allendale Town (town, Northumberland) 'settlement in the valley of the (River) Allen', river name + OS *dalr*, 'valley' + OE *tūn*, 'settlement'. The river name, that of the *East Allen*, is of Celtic or pre-Celtic origin and unknown meaning. The settlement name was originally the equivalent of *Allenton*, and Scandinavian *dalr* was inserted later. *Alewenton* 1245.

Allerton (district, Liverpool, Merseyside) 'farmstead where alder trees grow', OE *alor*, 'alder' + *tūn*, 'farmstead'. *Allerton*, Bradford, West Yorkshire, has a name of the same origin and meaning. *See also* ◊Northallerton. *Alretune* 1086.

Alloa (town, Central) 'rocky plain', Gaelic *allmhagh*, 'rocky plain'. The name is appropriate for the town, which lies on level ground beside the River Forth. The same word gave the names of ◊Alloway and ◊Alva. *Alveth* 1357.

Alloway (village, Strathclyde) 'rocky plain', Gaelic *allmhagh*, 'rocky plain'. The village lies on level ground on the lower course of the River Doon. *Auleway* 1324.

Alness (town, Highland) '(place on the River) Alness', Celtic river name. The river name is of uncertain meaning. It is related to the *Aln*, which gave the name of ◊Alnwick. *Alune* 1227.

Alnmouth (town, Northumberland) '(place at the) mouth of the (River) Aln', Celtic river name + OE *mūtha*, 'mouth'. This river also gave the name of ◊Alnwick. *Alnemuth* 1201.

Alnwick (town, Northumberland) 'farmstead on the Aln', Celtic river name + OE *wīc*, 'farmstead'. The river name, earlier *Alaunos*, is of uncertain meaning. *Alnewich* 1178.

Alperton (district, Greater London) 'estate named after Ealhbeorht', OE personal name + *-ing-*, 'named after' + *tūn*, 'estate'. The *-ing-* of the original name has become obscured. *Alprinton* 1199.

Alresford (town, Hampshire) 'alder ford', OE *alor*, 'alder' + *ford*, 'ford'. The town is officially known as *New Alresford* to be distinguished from the nearby village of *Old Alresford*, to which the name originally applied. The River *Alre* takes its name from the place. *Alresforda* 701, *Alresforde* 1086.

Alston (town, Cumbria) 'Halfdan's farmstead', OS personal name + OE *tūn*, 'farmstead'. As shown by the first record of the name below, the name originally ended in *-by*, representing OS *bý*, the equivalent of OE *-ton*. *Aldeneby* 1164, *Aldeneston* 1209.

Alton (town, Hampshire) 'farmstead at the river source', OE *Ǣwiell*, 'river source' + *tūn*, 'farmstead'. There are many places of this name, and most have this meaning. Some do not, however, such as Alton, Derbyshire, 'old farmstead', or Alton, Staffordshire, 'Ælfa's farmstead'. *Aultone* 1086.

Altrincham (town, Greater Manchester) 'homestead of Aldhere's people', OE personal name + *-inga-*, 'of the people of' + *hām*, 'homestead'. The name could also mean 'Aldhere's homestead', with the second element *-ing*, 'belonging to'. The original *g* of the name has become softened to a *c*. *Aldringeham* 1290.

Alum Bay (bay, Isle of Wight) 'alum bay'. The bay, well known for its variegated sands, derives its name from the *alum* quarried from the rocks here in the 16th century.

Alva (town, Central) 'rocky plain', Gaelic *allmhagh*, 'rocky plain'. The town's name is of the same origin as that of ◊Alloa and ◊Alloway. *Alweth* 1489.

Alyth (town, Tayside) '(place by the Hill of) Alyth', Gaelic hill name. The town stands at the foot of the Hill of *Alyth* and is named after it. The name is based on Gaelic *aill*, 'rugged bank', 'steep place'.

Amble (town, Northumberland) 'Amma's promontory', OE personal name + *bile*, 'promontory'. The *-ble* of the name is the same as the *Bill* of *Portland Bill*, Dorset. *Ambell* 1204, *Anebell* 1256.

Ambleside (town, Cumbria) 'summer pasture by the river sandbank', OS *á*, 'river' + *melr*, 'sandbank' + *sétr*, 'summer pasture'. The last part of the name denotes a 'shieling', a hill pasture where flocks would be moved in the summer months and temporary shelters set up. The suggestion of *side* is thus misleading. *Ameleseta c* 1095.

Amersham (town, Buckinghamshire) 'Ealhmund's homestead', OE personal name + *hām*, 'homestead'. The *g* in the Domesday Book record represents the *h* of the personal name. *Agmodesham* 1066, *Elmodesham* 1086.

Amesbury (town, Wiltshire) 'Ambre's stronghold', OE personal name + *burh*, 'stronghold'. The 'stronghold' here would have been the nearby Iron Age hill fort known as Vespasian's Camp. *Ambresbyrig c* 880, *Ambresberie* 1086.

Amlwch (town, Gwynedd) '(place) near the swamp', Welsh *am*, 'near' + *llwch*, 'swamp'. The 'swamp' was probably the bay here on the Anglesey coast. It was constructed as a proper harbour in the 18th century. *Anulc* 1254.

Ammanford (town, Dyfed) 'ford over the (River) Amman', Welsh river name + OE *ford*, 'ford'. The river name comes from *banw*, 'pig', denoting a river that 'roots' through the ground. The town's Welsh name is *Rhydaman*, from *rhyd*, 'ford', and the river name.

Ampleforth (village, North Yorkshire) 'ford where sorrel grows', OE *ampre*, 'dock', 'sorrel' + *ford*, 'ford'. The 'ford' would have been over the stream here that is a tributary of the River Rye. *Ampreforde* 1086.

Ampthill (town, Bedfordshire) '(place by the) ant hill', OE *ǣmette*, 'ant' + *hyll*, 'hill'. The name denotes a place infested with ants. The OE word for 'ant' is closer to the dialect name *emmet* than the modern word. *Ammetelle* 1086.

Ancaster (village, Lincolnshire) 'Anna's Roman encampment', OE personal name + *cæster*, 'Roman camp'. The personal name is that of a man. Ancaster lies just west of Ermine Street. *Anecastre* 12th century.

Andover (town, Hampshire) '(place by the) ash tree waters', Celtic river name + word. The first part of the name represents the former river name *Ann*, now *Anton*, meaning 'ash tree stream', from a word related to modern Welsh *onn*, 'ash tree'. The second part is from a word related to modern Welsh *dwfr*, 'water'. Cp ◊Dover. *Andeferas* 955, *Andovere* 1086.

Anfield (district, Liverpool, Merseyside) 'sloping area of ground', Middle English *hange*, 'slope' + OE *feld*, 'open land'. The ground rises here to the northeast of the city centre. *Hongfield* 1642.

Anglesey (island, Gwynedd) 'Ongull's island', OS personal name + *ey*, 'island'. The name has been influenced by *Angle*, as if the island were associated with these people. The island's Welsh name is *Môn*, 'hill', referring to Holyhead Mountain. *Ongulsey* 13th century.

Angmering (village, West Sussex) '(settlement of) Angenmær's people', OE personal name + *-ingas*, 'people of'. The resort of *Angmering-on-Sea* takes its name from the village. *Angemæringum c* 880, *Angemare* 1086.

Angus (district, Tayside) 'Angus's (place)', Celtic personal name. The historic county name is that of a Pictish king who held land here in the 8th century. *Enegus* 12th century.

Annan (town, Dumfries and Galloway) '(place by the River) Annan', Celtic river name. The town takes its name from the river, or more precisely from its valley, *Annandale*, to which the records here refer. The meaning of the river name itself is uncertain. *Anava* 7th century, *Estrahanent* 1124, *Annandesdale* 1179.

Ansdell (district, Lytham St Anne's, Lancashire) '(place named after) Ansdell'. The district takes its name from the painter Richard *Ansdell* (1815-85), who had a large house here called 'Star Hills'.

Anstruther (town, Fife) '(place by) the little stream', Gaelic *an*, 'the', *sruthair*, 'small stream'. The 'little stream' is the Dreel, which enters the sea between Anstruther East and Anstruther West. *Anestrothir* c1205.

Appin (mountainous area, Strathclyde/Highland) 'abbey lands', Celtic word. The name, related to modern Irish *abdhaine*, 'abbacy', refers to land owned here in medieval times by Ligmore Abbey.

Appleby (town, Cumbria) 'apple tree farmstead', OE *æppel*, 'apple tree' + OS *bý*, 'farmstead'. The OE first part of the name probably replaced OS *epli*. *Aplebi* 1130.

Appledore (village, Devon) '(place by the) apple tree', OE *apuldor*, 'apple tree'. The *-dor* of the OE word is a suffix used to form the names of trees. *le Apildore* 1335.

Arbroath (town, Tayside) '(place at the) mouth of the (River) Brothock', Celtic *aber*, 'mouth' + river name. The river name represents Gaelic *brothach*, 'boiling', referring to its fast flow. The old form of the town's name was *Aberbrothock*, as in Southey's poem *The Inchcape Rock* (1802): 'And then they knew the perilous rock, And blest the Abbot of Aberbrothock'.

Ardnamurchan (peninsula, Highland). The origin of the name is obscure. It is almost certainly Gaelic, with the first part representing *ard*, 'height', but the rest of the name remains uncertain. *Art Muirchol* c 700, *Ardnamurchin* 1309.

Ardrishaig (town, Strathclyde) 'height of the brambles', Gaelic *ard*, 'height' + *dris*, 'bramble', 'blackberry'. This is a rather tentative but reasonably plausible origin for the name.

Ardrossan (town, Strathclyde) 'height of the little headland', Gaelic *ard*, 'height' + *rosan*, 'little headland'. The name refers to the lower ground where Saltcoats now stands to the east. *Ardrossan* 1375.

Arfon (district, Gwynedd) '(district) opposite Môn', Welsh *ar*, 'over' + *Môn*, 'Anglesey'. The district is in northwest Wales overlooking Anglesey, whose Welsh name, *Môn*, is here in its mutated form, *Fôn*. The name forms part of the name of ◊Caernarfon.

Argyll (district, Strathclyde) 'coastland of the Gaels', Gaelic *oirthir*, 'coast' + *Ghaidheal*, 'of the Gaels'. The Gaels were originally an Irish race who came to settle in what was Pictish territory in this region. *Arregaithel c* 970.

Arisaig (village, Highland) '(place by the) bay at the river mouth', OS *á*, 'river', *ós*, 'mouth' + *vík*, 'bay'. The *r* of the name represents the genitive ending of *á*, 'river'. The 'river' is a small stream that flows into Loch nan Ceall, as the 'bay'. The name has extended to the whole district.

Armadale (town, Lothian) '(Lord) Armadale's (place)', aristocratic title. The town takes its name from the original landowner here, William Honeyman, Lord *Armadale*, who inherited the estate from his mother in the early 19th century. He took his title from *Armadale*, Sutherland. *Armadale* 1818.

Arnold (town, Nottinghamshire) 'eagles' corner', OE *earn*, 'eagle' + *halh*, 'corner', 'nook of land'. Eagles may at one time have nested in the stream valley here, northeast of Nottingham. *Ernehale* 1086.

Arnside (town, Cumbria) 'Earnwulf's headland', OE personal name + *hēafod*, 'hill', 'headland'. The personal name could also be OS *Arnulfr*. The *-side* is misleading. *Harnolvesheuet* 1184.

Arundel (town, West Sussex) 'hoarhound valley', OE *hārhūne*, 'hoarhound' + *dell*, 'valley'. The plant hoarhound must at one time have grown by the River Arun below the present town. The river name comes from that of the town. Its earlier name was *Tarrant*, related to the ◊Trent. *Harundel* 1086.

Ascot (village, Berkshire) 'eastern cottage', OE *ēast*, 'east' + *cot*, 'shelter', 'cottage'. The name is found fairly widely elsewhere, denoting a place to the east of another. There is sometimes a corresponding *Westcot*. *Estcota* 1177.

Ashbourne (town, Derbyshire) 'stream where ash trees grow', OE *æsc*, 'ash tree' + *burna*, 'stream'. The stream in question is the River Henmore, which was earlier known as the *Ashbourne*. *Esseburne* 1086.

Ashburton (town, Devon) 'farmstead by the ash tree stream', OE *æsc*, 'ash tree' + *burna*, 'stream' + *tūn*, 'farmstead'. The River Yeo here was originally known as the *Ashbourne*. *Essebretone* 1086.

Ashby de la Zouch (town, Leicestershire) 'farmstead by the ash trees of the de la Zuche family', OE *æsc*, 'ash tree' + OS *bý*, 'farmstead' + family name. The first part of the name may be OS *askr*, 'ash tree'. The *de la Zuche* family, from Normandy, were here in the 13th century. *Ascebi* 1086, *Esseby la Zusche* 1241.

Ashdown Forest (heathland, East Sussex) 'hill covered in ash trees', OE *æscen*, 'ashen', 'covered in ash trees' + *dūn*, 'hill' + modern *forest*. The region is now mainly heathland, but there are still some ash trees to be found. *Essendon* 1207.

Ashford (town, Kent) 'ford by the clump of ash trees', OE *æscet, 'ash tree clump' + *ford*, 'ford'. The common name *Ashford* usually means 'ford where ash trees grow', with the first part from OE *æsc*, 'ash tree'. Here, however, early records suggest a word meaning more precisely 'clump of ash trees'. The ford was probably over the East Stour. *Essetesford* 1086.

Ashington (town, Northumberland) 'valley where ash trees grow', OE *æscen*, 'ashen', 'covered in ash trees' + *dūn*, 'valley'. The *-ington* of the name is doubly misleading, since there is no *-ing-* in the original and the *-ton* is really *-don*. *Essenden* 1205.

Ashtead (village, Surrey) 'place where ash trees grow', OE *æsc*, 'ash tree' + *stede*, 'place'. There are still some ash trees left here. *Stede* 1086, *Estede* c 1150.

Ashton-in-Makerfield (town, Greater Manchester) 'farmstead by ash trees in ruined open land', OE *æsc*, 'ash tree' + *tūn*, 'farmstead' + Celtic word + OE *feld*, 'open land'. The Celtic part of the name, meaning 'wall', is related to Latin *maceria*, itself akin to modern English *masonry*. *Makerfield* is an old district name, recorded as *Macrefeld* in 1121. *Eston* 1212.

Ashton-under-Lyne (town, Greater Manchester) 'farmstead by ash trees by the region of elm trees', OE *æsc*, 'ash tree' + *tūn*, 'farmstead' + Celtic word. *Lyne* is an old district name, related to modern Welsh *llyf*, 'elm tree'. *Under* means 'near'. *Haistune* c 1160, *Asshton under Lyme* 1305.

Askern (town, South Yorkshire) 'house by the ash tree', OS *askr*, 'ash tree' + *ærn*, 'house'. The OS word may have replaced an earlier OE *æsc* n the same sense. *Askern* c 1170.

Aspatria (town, Cumbria) '(St) Patrick's ash tree' OS *askr*, 'ash tree' + saint's name. The word order is Celtic, because the Scandinavian settlers here spoke a dialect that reflected the language of Ireland, from where they had come. *Aspatric* c 1160.

Aspull (town, Greater Manchester) 'hill where aspens grow', OE *æspe*, 'aspen' + *hyll*, 'hill'. The 'hill' is the high land on which the town stands, but there are few aspen trees here today. *Aspul* 1212.

Athelney (hamlet, Somerset) 'island of the princes', OE *ætheling*, 'prince' + *ēg*, 'island'. The 'island' is land here that is higher than the surrounding marshes. The 'princes' were the members of a noble Anglo-Saxon family that must have lived here. *Æthelingaeigge* 878, *Adelingi* 1086.

Atherstone (town, Warwickshire) 'Æthelrēd's farmstead', OE personal name + *tūn*, 'farmstead'. The personal name means literally 'noble counsel' and is the same as the familiar *Ethelred*. *Aderestone* 1086, *Atheredestone* 1221.

Atherton (town, Greater Manchester) 'Æthelhere's farmstead', OE personal name + *tūn*, 'farmstead'. The personal name means 'noble army'. *Aderton* 1212.

Attleborough (town, Norfolk) 'Ætla's stronghold', OE personal name + *burh*, 'stronghold'. *Attleborough*, the district of Nuneaton, Warwickshire, has the same personal name but OE *beorg*, 'hill', 'mound'. *Atleburc* 1086.

Auchinleck (town, Strathclyde) 'field of the flat stones', Gaelic *achadh*, 'field' + *leac*, 'flat stone', 'slab of rock'. The same name lies behind that of *Affleck* Castle, Tayside. *Auechinlec* 1239.

Auchterarder (town, Tayside) 'upland of the high water', Gaelic *uachdar*, 'upper' + *ard*, 'high' + *dobhar*, 'water'. The name describes the town's location on high ground north of the River Ruthen. *Vchterardouere c* 1200.

Auchtermuchty (town, Fife) 'upland of the pig place', Gaelic *uachdar*, 'upper' + *muccatu*, 'pig place'. Pigs must have been reared here at one time. *Vchtermuckethin c* 1210.

Audenshaw (town, Greater Manchester) 'Aldwine's copse', OE personal name + *sceaga*, 'copse'. *Shaw* often follows the name of an animal, such as *Ottershaw* or *Hogshaw*, and only rarely a personal name, as here. *Aldwynshawe c* 1200.

Avebury (village, Wiltshire) 'Afa's stronghold', OE personal name + *burh*, 'stronghold'. The 'stronghold' may well have been the Bronze Age burial ground here, rather than a defensive site. *Aureberie* 1086, *Aveberia c* 1180.

Aveley (town, Essex) 'Ælfgȳth's clearing', OE personal name + *lēah*, 'clearing'. The personal name is that of a woman. *Aluitheleam* 1086.

Aviemore (village, Highland) 'big hillface', Gaelic *aghaid*, 'hillface' + *mór*, 'big'. The name is appropriate for the famous skiing centre. *Avimoir* 1654.

Avon (county, England) '(district of the River) Avon', Celtic river name. The county, formed in 1974, took its name from the Bristol *Avon*. The river name is a common one, occurring in all parts of Britain, and is related to modern Welsh *afon* and Irish *abhainn*, 'river'.

Axminster (town, Devon) 'monastery by the (River) Axe', Celtic river name + OE *mynster*, 'monastery', 'large church'. The meaning of the river name is uncertain, but is probably simply 'water'. *Axmouth* takes its name from the same river. *Ascanmynster* late 9th century, *Aixeministra*, 1086.

Aylesbury (town, Buckinghamshire) 'Ægel's stronghold', OE personal name + *burh*, 'stronghold'. There may have been an Anglo-Saxon fort here at some time. *Ægelesburg*, late 9th century, *Eilesberia* 1086.

Aylsham (town, Norfolk) 'Ægel's homestead', OE personal name + *hām*, 'homestead'. The same personal name lies behind ◊Aylesbury. *Ailesham* 1086.

Ayot St Lawrence (village, Hertfordshire) '(place at) Æga's gap named after St Lawrence', OE personal name + *geat*, 'gap', 'pass' + saint's name. The 'gap' is probably the lower terrain between Ayot St Lawrence and Ayot St Peter, which stand on low hills under 2 miles apart. The saints' names, from the dedications of the parish churches, distinguish the two places. *Aiegete c* 1060.

Ayr (town, Strathclyde) '(place by the) Ayr', Celtic river name. The river name is related to those of the *Aar* and *Ahr*, tributaries of the Rhine, meaning simply 'river'. The former name of the place was *Inverayr*, 'mouth of the Ayr'. The record below relates to the river, not the town. *Ar* 1177.

B

Babbacombe (district, Torquay, Devon) 'Babba's valley', OE personal name + *cumb*, 'valley'. Babbacombe lies east of the town centre at a point where the ground slopes fairly steeply down to the beach. *Babba* is a man's name. *Babbecumbe c* 1200.

Bacup (town, Lancashire) 'valley by a ridge', OE *bæc*, 'ridge' + *hop*, 'valley'. The town is in the valley of the River Irwell with high ground to the west. In the record, the first part of the name represents OE *fūl*, 'dirty', 'muddy'. *Fulebachope c* 1200.

Badminton (village, Avon) 'estate named after Baduhelm', OE personal name + *-ing-*, 'named after' + *tūn*, 'estate'. The Domesday Book record has *M* for *B* and may be due to a mishearing. *Badimyncgtun* 972, *Madmintune* 1086.

Bagshot (town, Surrey) 'projecting piece of land frequented by badgers', OE **bagga*, 'badger' + *scēat*, 'projecting land', 'corner'. Names in *-shot* are fairly common in west Surrey and east Hampshire. A well-known example is ◊Aldershot. *Bagsheta* 1164.

Baildon (district, Bradford, West Yorkshire) 'circle hill', OE **bǣgel*, 'circle' + *dūn*, 'hill'. The name can be understood as 'rounded hill', which would suit the outline of Baildon Hill here. *Bægeltune c* 1030, *Beldune* 1086.

Bakewell (town, Derbyshire) 'Badeca's spring', OE personal name + *wella*, 'spring', 'stream'. The town, on the River Wye, is well known for its warm springs. *Badecanwelle* 949, *Badequella* 1086.

Bala (town, Gwynedd) 'outlet', Welsh *bala*, 'outlet'. The town is on the River Dee and takes its name from the point where this leaves Bala Lake. The Welsh name of the lake is *Llyn Tegid*, 'Tegid's lake', from a personal name.

Baldock (town, Hertfordshire) '(place named after) Baghdad', Old French *Baldac*, 'Baghdad'. The unusual name was given by the Knights Templars, who founded the place in the 12th century. *Baldoce c* 1140.

Balham (district, Greater London) 'rounded enclosure', OE **bealg*, 'rounded' + *hamm*, 'enclosure'. The 'enclosure' is the land between the two arms of Falcon Brook. *Bælgenham* 957, *Belgeham* 1086.

Ballahulish (village, Highland) 'homestead on the narrows', Gaelic *baile*, 'homestead' + *caolas*, 'narrows'. The village is at the point where Loch Leven narrows markedly as it flows into Loch Linnhe.

Ballantrae (port, Strathclyde) 'village on the shore', Gaelic *baile*, 'village' + *traigh*, 'shore'. This is not the setting of Stevenson's novel *The Master of Ballantrae*, although he took the name from here.

Balmoral (royal residence, Grampian) 'farmstead in the big clearing', Gaelic *baile*, 'farmstead' + *mór*, 'big' + Celtic word. The Celtic word means 'open space'. Balmoral Castle does not necessarily stand on the exact site of the original 'big clearing'. *Bouchmorale* 1451.

Bamburgh (village, Northumberland) 'Bebbe's stronghold', OE personal name + *burh*, 'stronghold'. The name is that of Queen *Bebbe*, wife of King Æthelfrith of Northumbria, who ruled from 593 to 617. *Bebbanburge c* 710.

Bampton (town, Devon) 'farmstead of the dwellers by the pool', OE *bæth*, 'pool' + *hǽme*, 'dwellers' + *tūn*, 'farmstead'. *Bampton* in Oxfordshire has a name of different meaning, 'farmstead by a tree', with the first part representing OE *bēam*, 'tree'. *Badentone* 1086.

Banbury (town, Oxfordshire) 'Banna's stronghold', OE personal name + *burh*, 'stronghold'. The precise site of the original stronghold is not known. *Banesberie* 1086.

Banchory (town, Grampian) 'place of the peaks', Gaelic *beannachar*, 'mountainous'. The first part of the name represents Gaelic *beinn*, 'peak'. The town is is in a valley surrounded by hills and mountains.

Banff (town, Grampian) '(river of the) little pig', Gaelic river name. The river here is now known as the *Deveron*, but originally had a name representing Gaelic *banbh*, 'little pig'. Such a name referred to the way the river 'rooted' its course to the coast. *Banb c* 1150.

Bangor (town, Gwynedd) 'rod in a wattle fence', Welsh *bangor*, 'upper row of rods in a wattle fence'. Bangor was a monastic settlement, and the name presumably refers to the original wattled construction of the monastic cells. *Benchoer* 634.

Bannockburn (village, Central) '(place by the) Bannock Burn', Celtic river name + OE *burna* 'stream'. The river name comes from the hill called

Bannock, itself meaning 'peaked hill', from a word related to modern Welsh *bannog*, 'elevated', 'horned'. *Bannokburne* 1654.

Banstead (town, Surrey) 'place of beans', OE *bēan*, 'bean' + *stede*, 'place'. At one time the place would have been known for the beans grown here. *Benestede* 1086.

Bardsey Island (island, Gwynedd) 'Bardr's island', OS personal name + *ey*, 'island'. English *island* was added to the name when the meaning of the original was no longer understood.

Bargoed (town, Mid Glamorgan), '(place by the River) Bargoed', Welsh river name. The river name represents *bargod*, 'boundary'. The river marked the border between Glamorganshire and Monmouthshire (now between Mid Glamorgan and Gwent).

Barking (town, Greater London) '(place of) Berica's people', OE personal name + *-ingas*, 'people of'. The personal name is deduced from early records of the name. *Berecingum* 731, *Berchinges* 1086.

Barmouth (town, Gwynedd) '(place at the) mouth of the (River) Mawddach', Welsh *aber*, 'mouth' + river name. Confusingly, the *Bar-* of the name represents *aber*, 'mouth', while the *-mouth* is the river name, which means 'little (river of) Mawdd'. The Welsh name, *Abermo*, is truer to the original. *Abermau* 1284, *Abermowth* 1410.

Barnard Castle (town, Durham) 'Bernard's castle', personal name + *castle*. The town takes its name from the 12th century castle, owned and perhaps even built by the Norman baron, *Bernard* de Balliol. *Castellum Bernardi* 1200.

Barnes (district, Greater London) '(place by the) barn', OE *bere-ærn*, 'barn'. The *s* of the name doubtless refers to the many barns that arose by the original one. The OE word for 'barn' literally means 'barley building'. *Berne* 1086.

Barnet (district, Greater London) 'burnt place', OE *bærnet*, 'land cleared by burning'. Several places of this name are grouped together, including *New Barnet*, *East Barnet* and *Friern Barnet*. The basic name doubtless originally applied to the whole area, as woodland cleared by burning. *Friern* means 'of the brothers', *ie* the Knights of St John of Jerusalem. *Barneto c* 1070.

Barnoldswick (town, Lancashire) 'Beornwulf's farm', OE personal name + *wīc*, 'special place', 'farm'. The farm may well have been a dairy farm. The personal name means 'warrior wolf'. *Bernulfesuuic* 1086.

Barnsley (town, South Yorkshire) 'Beorn's clearing', OE personal name + *lēah*, 'clearing'. The personal name was probably the short form of a longer name such as *Beornmōd*, who gave the name of the otherwise identical *Barnsley*, Gloucestershire. *Berneslai* 1086.

Barnstaple (town, Devon) '(place by the) bearded post', OE *beard*, 'beard' + *stapol*, 'post'. The name probably alludes to a post that had a 'beard' of twigs, like a broom. It could have served to mark the meeting place of the local hundred, or as a landmark for ships at sea. *Beardastapol* late 10th century, *Barnestaple* 1086.

Barra (island, Western Isles) 'hilly island', Celtic word + OS *ey*, 'island'. The first part of the name is related to modern Gaelic *barr*, 'headland'. *Cp* ◊Barrow-in-Furness. *Barru c* 1090, *Barey c* 1200.

Barrhead (town, Strathclyde) 'top of the headland', Gaelic *barr*, 'top', 'headland' + modern English *head*. The name really says the same thing twice. Perhaps English *head* was added to the Gaelic word when the latter was no longer understood. The town lies on Levern Water at the foot of lofty moorland.

Barrow-in-Furness (town, Cumbria) 'promontory island in Furness', Celtic word + OS *ey*, 'island' + district name. *Barrow* is identical in origin to ◊Barra, arising as the name of an island that is now joined to the mainland. *Furness* is the headland on which Barrow is located. The name means 'headland by the buttock-shaped island', from *futh*, 'buttock', here in its genitive form, *futhar*, and *nes*, 'headland'. The reference is to *Futh*, an island now called *Peel Island*, at the tip of the headland, which has a 'slit' or lengthy depression running from north to south. Furness was recorded as *Fuththernessa* in *c* 1150. *Barrai* 1190.

Barry (town, South Glamorgan) '(place of the) hill', Old Welsh *barr*, 'hill'. The name refers properly to the island here rather than the town that arose behind it. *Barry* 1176, *Barri* 1186, *Barrye Island* 1610.

Barton-upon-Humber (town, Humberside) 'outlying grange by the Humber', OE *bere-tūn*, 'barley farm' + river name. Many places called *Barton* arose as a farm that was subsidiary to a more important place, such as a manor or monastery. The name is so common that it frequently has a distinguishing affix, as here. For the river name, *see* ◊Humber. *Bertone* 1086.

Basford (district, Nottingham, Nottinghamshire) 'Basa's ford', OE personal name + *ford*, 'ford'. The ford would have been over the River Leen. *Baseford* 1086.

Basildon (town, Essex) 'Beorhtel's hill', OE personal name + *dūn*, 'hill'. The first *e* of the personal name became *a* under the influence of local dialect. *Berlesduna* 1086, *Bertlesdon* 1194.

Basingstoke (town, Hampshire) 'outlying farmstead of Basa's people', OE personal name + *-inga-*, 'of the people of' + *stoc*, 'outlying farmstead'. The 'outlying farmstead' here originally depended on that at *Basing*, now an eastern extension of Basingstoke itself. *Basingastoc* 990, *Basingestoches* 1086.

Bassenthwaite (lake, Cumbria) '(lake of) Bastun's clearing', Middle English surname + OS *thveit*, 'clearing', 'meadow'. The lake, properly *Bassenthwaite Water*, took its name from the village at its northern end. The record below thus refers to the latter. *Bastunthuait c* 1175.

Bassetlaw (district, Nottinghamshire) 'hill of the dwellers at the burnt place', OE *bærnet*, 'burnt place' + *sǣte*, 'dwellers' + *hlāw*, 'hill'. The present administrative district took the name of a historic wapentake. *Bernesedelaue* 1086.

Bath (city, Avon) '(place at) the (Roman) baths', OE *bæth*, 'pool', 'bath'. The Roman name of Bath was *Aquae Sulis*, 'waters of Sulis', referring to a pagan god. The first record of the name has the OE word in the dative plural, meaning 'at the baths'. *Bathum* 796, *Bade* 1086.

Bathgate (town, Lothian) 'boar wood', Celtic words. The name comprises two Cumbric words related to modern Welsh *baedd*, 'boar', and *coed*, 'wood'. *Batket c* 1160.

Batley (town, West Yorkshire) 'Bata's clearing', OE personal name + *lēah*, 'clearing'. This part of Yorkshire was heavily wooded at one time, as denoted by the many names ending in *-ley* and *-wood*. *Bathelie* 1086.

Battersea (district, Greater London) 'Beadurīc's island', OE personal name + *ēg*, 'island'. The 'island' is higher land by lower marshland, in this case south of the Thames. *Badrices ege*, 11th century, *Patricesy* 1086.

Battle (town, East Sussex) '(place of the) battle', Old French *bataille*, 'battle'. The abbey here was founded by William the Conqueror to commemorate the Battle of Hastings in 1066, which took place at Senlac, to the south (actually 6 miles from Hastings). *La Batailge* 1086.

Bawtry (town, South Yorkshire) '(place by a) tree round as a ball', OE **ball*, 'ball' + *trēow*, 'tree'. The first part of the name could also be an OE personal name such as *Balda*. *Baltry* 1199.

Bayswater (district, Greater London) 'Bayard's water', Middle English surname + *water*. *Water* here means 'watering place', this being on the former River Westbourne. It is possible the first part of the name is not a surname but the word that gave it, *bayard*, 'bay horse'. *Aqua vocata Bayards Watering Place* 1380.

Beachy Head (headland, East Sussex) 'beautiful headland', Old French *beau*, 'beautiful' + *chef*, 'headland' + modern English *head*. The second English word is strictly speaking redundant, and was added when the French name was no longer understood. *Beuchef* 1279.

Beaconsfield (town, Buckinghamshire) 'open land by a beacon', OE *bēacon*, 'beacon' + *feld*, 'open land'. The site of the original beacon or signal fire was probably Beacon Hill, at Penn, some 3 miles away. *Bekenesfelde* 1184.

Beaminster (town, Dorset) 'Bebbe's large church', OE personal name + *mynster*, 'large church'. The original 'large church' was probably on the site of the present 15th-century parish church. *Bebbe* is a woman's name. *Bebingmynster* 862, *Beiminstre* 1086.

Bearsden (town, Strathclyde). The town was originally a village called *New Kilpatrick* ('new St Patrick's church'). When the railway came here in 1863, the station was named *Bearsden* after a large house nearby. The name then passed to the place as a whole.

Beaufort (town, Gwent). The town arose in the 19th century and took its name from the landowner in the late 18th century, the Duke of *Beaufort*. The town's Welsh name is *Cendl*, representing the surname of Edward *Kendall*, the ironmaster who was granted a lease here in 1780.

Beaulieu (village, Hampshire) 'beautiful place', Old French *beau*, 'beautiful' + *lieu*, 'place'. The name is still apt for the location, at the head of the River Beaulieu estuary. The first record of the name is Latin meaning 'beautiful place of the king'. *Cp* ◊Beauly. *Bellus Locus Regis* 1205, *Beulu* c 1300.

Beauly (town, Highland) 'beautiful place', Old French *beau*, 'beautiful' + *lieu*, 'place'. The name alludes to the town's scenic setting near the east coast and is of exactly the same origin as that of ◊Beaulieu. The Latin record below means 'priory of the lovely spot'. *Prioratus de bello loco* 1230.

Beaumaris (town, Gwynedd) 'beautiful marsh', Old French *beau*, 'beautiful' + *marais*, 'marsh'. The Anglesey town is on a low-lying site beside the Menai Straits. The record below is Latin. *Bello Marisco* 1284.

Bebington (town, Merseyside) 'estate named after Bebbe', OE personal name + *-ing-*, 'named after' + *tūn*, 'estate'. The personal name is that of a woman. It could also be *Bebba*, that of a man. *Bebinton c* 1100.

Beccles (town, Suffolk) 'pasture by a stream', OE *bece*, 'stream' + *lǣs*, 'pasture'. The 'stream' here is the River Waveney. *Becles* 1086.

Beckenham (town, Greater London) 'Beohha's homestead', OE personal name + *hām*, 'homestead'. The second part of the name may represent OE *hamm*, 'enclosure'. The *-n-* is the genitive ending of the personal name. *Bacheham* 1086.

Becontree (district, Greater London) 'Beohha's tree', OE personal name + *trēow*, 'tree'. The 'tree' marked the meeting place of the local hundred. The second record of the name shows a popular attempt to interpret it. *Beuentreu* 1086, *Beacon Tree Heath* 1805.

Bedale (town, North Yorkshire) 'Bēda's corner of land', OE personal name + *halh*, 'nook of land'. The 'corner of land' was that in the curve of Bedale Beck here. The personal name is the same as that of the Venerable Bede. *Bedale* 1086.

Bedford (town, Bedfordshire) 'Bīeda's ford', OE personal name + *ford*, 'ford'. The 'ford' would have been over the River Ouse here. The county name, *Bedfordshire*, is first recorded in the 11th century. *Bedanford* 880, *Bedeford* 1086.

Bedlington (town, Northumberland) 'estate named after Bēdla', OE personal name + *-ing-*, 'named after' + *tūn*, 'estate'. The personal name is conjectural, and could equally be *Bētla*. *Bedlingtun c* 1050.

Bedwas (town, Mid Glamorgan) 'birch tree grove', Old Welsh *betguas*, 'birch grove'. The town arose in the 19th century.

Bedworth (town, Warwickshire) 'Bēda's enclosure', OE personal name + *worth*, 'enclosure'. The personal name is the same as that of the Venerable Bede. *Bedeword* 1086.

Beer (village, Devon) '(place by the) grove', OE *bearu*, 'grove'. A place-name formed from a single word. *Cp* ◊Bere Regis. *Bera* 1086.

Beeston (town, Nottinghamshire) 'farmstead where bent grass grows', OE **bēos*, 'bent grass' + *tūn*, 'farmstead'. 'Bent grass' is a type of reed or rush used for both pasture and thatching. *Bestune* 1086.

Beith (town, Strathclyde) '(place by the) birch tree', Gaelic *beith*, 'birch'. The name simply means 'place where birches grow'.

Belford (village, Northumberland) 'ford by the bell-shaped hill', OE *belle*, 'bell' + *ford*, 'ford'. The 'hill' is presumably the one called *Bellshill* to the south. The 'ford' is over a small stream here that joins the Elwick Burn about a mile away. *Beleford* 1242.

Bellingham (town, Northumberland) 'homestead of the dwellers at the bell-shaped hill', OE *belle*, 'bell' + *-inga-*, 'of the people of' + *hām*, 'homestead'. The name is pronounced 'Bellinjam'. *Bellingham* 1254.

Belper (town, Derbyshire) 'beautiful retreat', Old French *beau*, 'beautiful' + *repaire*, 'retreat'. Another name of the same origin, though less obviously so, is that of *Bearpark*, Durham. *Beurepeir* 1231.

Belvoir (village, Leicestershire) 'beautiful view', Old French *bel*, 'beautiful' + *vedeir*, 'view'. The Vale of Belvoir is a broad valley to the west of Grantham. *Belveder* 1130.

Bembridge (town, Isle of Wight) '(place) inside the bridge', OE *binnan*, 'inside' + *brycg*, 'bridge'. The town is on a peninsula that at one time must have been reached by a bridge across the entrance to what is now Bembridge Harbour. *Bynnebrygg* 1316.

Benllech (village, Gwynedd) '(place by the) headstone', Welsh *penllech*, 'headstone'. The name refers to the headstone of a nearby cromlech.

Ben Nevis (mountain, Highland) 'mountain of the (River) Nevis', Gaelic *beinn*, 'mountain' + river name. The mountain takes its name from the nearby river, whose own name represents *nemess*, 'spiteful'. Both the river and its valley have a 'malicious' reputation. *Gleann Nibheis*, 16th century.

Bentley (district, Doncaster, South Yorkshire) 'clearing where bent grass grows', OE *beonet*, 'bent grass' + *lēah*, 'clearing'. 'Bent grass' (bent) was used both for feeding livestock and for thatching. The name is common elsewhere. *Benedleia* 1086.

Bere Regis (village, Dorset) '(place by the) grove held by the king', OE *bearu*, 'grove' + Latin *regis*, 'of the king'. The first word of the name could also represent OE *bǣr*, 'woodland pasture'. The second word implies that the place was a crown demesne (manor held by the king) in Norman times. *Bere* 1086, *Kyngesbyre* 1264.

Berkeley (village, Gloucestershire) 'clearing in birch trees', OE *beorc*, 'birch' + *lēah*, 'clearing'. The same two words could also give a sense '(place by a) birch wood'. *Berclea* 824, *Berchelai* 1086.

Berkhamsted (town, Hertfordshire) 'homestead by a hill', OE *beorg*, 'hill' + *hām-stede*, 'homestead'. The town lies in a gap in the Chiltern Hills. *Beorhthanstædæ* 10th century, *Berchehamstede* 1086.

Berkshire (county, England) 'hilly place', Celtic word + OE *scīr*, 'shire'. The first part of the name is related to modern Welsh *bre*, 'hill'. It is possible that the original reference was to a single hill, perhaps one near Hungerford. *Berrocscire* 893.

Bermondsey (district, Greater London) 'Beornmund's island', OE personal name + *ēg*, 'island'. The 'island' would have been the higher dry ground beside the lower marshy bank of the Thames. The name was gradually 'smoothed' to the third record below, but local people restored the original. *Vermundesei c* 712, *Bermundesye* 1086, *Barmsey* 1617.

Berwick-upon-Tweed (town, Northumberland) 'barley farm on the Tweed', OE *bere-wīc*, 'barley farm' + Celtic river name. The OE word that literally means 'barley farm' came to be used for the outlying part of an estate. As such it is more often found today as the name of a village rather than a town. The river name may mean 'strong one'. *Berewich* 1167, *Berewicum super Twedam* 1229.

Bethesda (town, Gwynedd) 'house of mercy', Hebrew biblical name. The town arose round a Calvinistic Methodist Bethesda Chapel established in 1820 on a site known as *Y Wern Uchaf*, 'the upper marshland'. Most such 'chapel' names in Wales are of villages.

Bethnal Green (district, Greater London) 'green of Blītha's corner of land', OE personal name + *halh*, 'corner of land' + *grēne,* 'green'. The apparent personal name may actually be a stream name, as *Blīthe*, 'gentle one'. The 'green' is the village green. *Blithehale* 13th century, *Blethenalegrene* 1443.

Betws-y-Coed (village, Gwynedd) 'prayer house in the wood', Welsh *betws*, 'prayer house' + *y*, 'the' + *coed*, 'wood'. Welsh *betws* was adopted from Middle English *bed-hūs*, 'prayer house'. (The OE word that meant 'prayer' gave modern *bead*, as these are used for 'telling' prayers in a rosary.) *Betus* 1254, *Bettws y Coed* 1727.

Beverley (town, Humberside) '(place by the) beaver stream', OE *beofor*, 'beaver' + **licc*, 'stream'. The conjectural word *licc*, known only in this place-name, became confused with the more common OE *lēah*, 'clearing', and this gave the *-ley* of the present name. *Beverlic c* 1025, *Bevreli* 1086.

Bewdley (town, Hereford and Worcester) 'beautiful place', Old French *beau*, 'beautiful' + *lieu*, 'place'. The name is of the same origin as

◊Beaulieu, and the town, like that place, is on a river, in this case the Severn. *Beuleu* 1275, *Bellum Locum* 1308.

Bexhill (town, East Sussex) 'box wood', OE **byxe*, 'box' + *lēah*, 'wood'. The second part of the name has misleadingly become associated with OE *hyll*, 'hill'. *Bixlea* 772, *Bexelei* 1086.

Bexleyheath (district, Greater London) 'heath by a box wood', OE **byxe*, 'box' + *lēah*, 'wood' + Modern English *heath*. The second word of the name was added when the district became larger than the original village of *Bexley*, named in the first record below. (The second relates to the present place.) The original heath existed to the north of this, and vestiges of it remain in the playing fields beside the A207. *Byxlea* 774, *Bexley Heath* 1868.

Bicester (town, Oxfordshire) 'fort of the warriors', OE *beorn*, 'warriors' + *ceaster*, 'Roman fort'. The first part of the name may be the OE personal name *Beorn*. *Bernecestre* 1086.

Bickley (district, Greater London) 'clearing with bees' nests', OE **bīc*, 'bees' nest' + *lēah*, 'clearing'. The first part of the name could also be an OE personal name *Bica*. *Byckeleye* 1279.

Biddulph (town, Staffordshire) '(place) by the quarry', OE *bī*, 'by' + **dylf*, 'diggings'. The 'diggings' were probably stone quarries, which still exist here. *Bidolf* 1086.

Bideford (town, Devon) 'ford over the (River) Bȳd', Celtic river name + OE *ford*, 'ford'. The meaning of the river name is unknown. The river here now is the *Torridge* (*see* ◊Torrington). *Bedeford* 1086.

Bigbury-on-Sea (village, Devon) 'Bica's stronghold', OE personal name + *burh*, 'stronghold'. The coastal resort has adopted the name of the village of *Bigbury*, 2 miles inland, and the record relates to this. *Bicheberie* 1086.

Biggar (town, Strathclyde) 'triangular plot of barley', OS *bygg*, 'barley', + *geiri*, 'triangular plot'. The second part of the name is related to English *gore*, as in Kensington *Gore*. *Bigir* 1170.

Biggleswade (town, Bedfordshire) 'Biccel's ford', OE personal name + *wæd*, 'ford'. The personal name is a conjectural one. The 'ford' would have been over the River Ivel. The Domesday Book record of the name has *P* for *B*. *Pichelesuuade* 1086, *Bicheleswada* 1132.

Billericay (town, Essex) 'dyehouse', Medieval Latin **bellerica*, 'tan-house'. The name long proved a mystery, and this origin was proposed in 1983 by a member of the English Place-Name Society. The conjectural

Latin word is found in the botanical name of the plant myrtolan, *Terminalia bellerica*, used for tanning and dyeing. *Byllyrica* 1291.

Billinge (town, Merseyside) '(place by the) ridge', OE hill name. The hill name means 'sharp ridge', and derives from **billing*, a word related to modern *billhook*. *Billing* 1202.

Billingham (town, Cleveland) 'homestead of Bill's people', OE personal name + -*inga*-, 'of the people of' + *hām*, 'homestead'. The first part of the name could also represent OE **billing*, 'ridge', as for ◊Billinge, so that the sense is 'homestead by the ridge'. *Billingham c* 1050.

Billingshurst (town, West Sussex) 'Billing's wooded hill', OE personal name + *hyrst*, 'wooded hill'. It is possible the first part of the name may be OE **billing*, 'sharp ridge' (from a word that gave modern *billhook*). *Bellingesherst* 1202.

Bilston (district, Wolverhampton, West Midlands) 'farmstead of the dwellers by the ridge', OE *bill*, 'ridge' + *sǣte*, 'dwellers' + *tūn*, 'farmstead'. The OE word here rendered 'ridge' also meant 'sword'. Such a ridge would have been a sharp one. *Bilsetnatun* 996, *Billestune* 1086.

Bingley (town, West Yorkshire) 'clearing of Bynna's people', personal name + -*inga*-, 'of the people of' + *lēah*, 'clearing'. It is possible that the first part of the name is actually OE **bing*, 'hollow'. *Bingelei* 1086.

Birkenhead (town, Merseyside) 'headland with birch trees', OE *birce*, 'birch' + *hēafod*, 'headland'. The *c* of the OE word became *k* under Scandinavian influence. The record relates to the headland, not the town. It is not clear precisely which headland is meant. *Bircheveth c* 1200.

Birmingham (city, West Midlands) 'homestead of Beorma's people', OE personal name + -*inga*-, 'of the people of' + *hām*, 'homestead'. The name of Britain's second largest city is typical of many small villages. The personal name is a shortened form of *Beornmund*, as for ◊Bermondsey. *Bermingeham* 1086.

Bishop Auckland (town, Durham) 'bishop's rock on the (River) Clyde', OE *biscop* + Celtic word + river name. The second half of the name contains a Celtic word related to modern Welsh *allt*, 'rock', and the river name *Clyde*, borrowed from Scotland, as the old name of the *Gaunless* (an OS name meaning 'unprofitable'). The first half denotes ownership by the Bishop of Durham. *Alclit c* 1040.

Bishop's Castle (town, Shropshire) 'bishop's castle', OE *biscop*, 'bishop' + *castel*, 'castle'. The place was founded in 1154 by the *Bishop* of Hereford. *Bissopes Castell* 1269.

Bishop's Stortford (town, Hertfordshire) 'bishop's ford by the tongues of land', OE *biscop*, 'bishop' + *steort*, 'tongue of land' + *ford*, 'ford'. The 'tongues of land' are between streams. The first half of the name denotes ownership by the Bishop of London. The River *Stort* here takes its name from that of the town. *Storteford* 1086.

Bishop's Waltham (town, Hampshire) 'bishop's woodland estate', OE *biscop*, 'bishop' + *wald*, 'woodland' + *hām*, 'estate'. The place was originally *Waltham* but added the first word to denote its possession by the *Bishop* of Winchester. *Waltham* 904, 1086.

Blaby (district, Leicester, Leicestershire) 'Blár's farmstead', OS personal name + *bý*, 'farmstead'. The Domesday Book record has *d* for *b*. *Bladi* 1086, *Blabi* 1175.

Blackburn (town, Lancashire) '(place by the) black stream', OE *blæc*, 'black' + *burna*, 'stream'. The name denotes a stream with dark-coloured water. The stream here is actually called the *Blackwater*. *Blacheburne* 1086.

Blackheath (district, Greater London) 'black heath', OE *blæc*, 'black' + *hǣth*, 'heath'. A 'black heath' is one that is dark-coloured. The record has an added OE *feld*, 'open land'. *Blachehedfeld* 1166.

Black Mountains (hills, Powys/Gwent) 'black mountains'. The hills generally appear dark when viewed from the eastern and southern sides.

Blackpool (town, Lancashire) 'black pool', OE *blæc* + **pull*, 'pool'. The town arose by a peaty-coloured pool about half a mile from the sea. *Pul* c 1260, *Lepole, commonly called Black-poole* 1637.

Blackrod (town, Greater Manchester) 'black clearing', OE *blæc*, 'black' + **rodu*, 'clearing'. The second part of the name is more commonly found as *-royd*, eg *Ackroyd*, 'oak clearing', *Murgatroyd*, 'Margaret's clearing'. The clearing would have been 'black' or dark because of the thick foliage of the trees and bushes rather than from the colour of the ground. *Blacherode* c 1189.

Blaenau Ffestiniog (town, Gwynedd) 'heights of Ffestiniog', Welsh *blaenau*, 'heights' + place-name. The 'heights' are the headwaters of the River Dwyryd. The town is 3 miles north of, and named after, *Ffestiniog*, 'defensive position', from Welsh *ffestin*, 'fastness' with the adjectival suffix *-iog*.

Blaenavon (town, Gwent) 'head of the river', Welsh *blaen*, 'height', 'head' + *afon*, 'river'. The town stands on the upper reaches of the Afon Lwyd ('grey river').

Blair Atholl (village, Tayside) 'plain of Atholl', Gaelic *blàr*, 'plain' + place-name. *Atholl* represents Gaelic *ath*, 'again', and *Fotla*, a poetic name for Ireland, linked with *Fodla*, an Irish goddess. The name amounts to 'New Ireland', and was given by the Gaels when they came from Ireland to settle here in the 5th century. *Athochlach c* 970, *Athfoithle c* 1050.

Blairgowrie (town, Tayside) 'Gabran's plain', Gaelic *blàr*, 'plain' + district name. The place was originally *Blair*, then added the district name to be distinguished from nearby *Blair Atholl*. The second part of the name represents that of *Gabran*, a 6th-century king who held the territory here. *Blare* 13th century, *Blair in Gowrie* 1604.

Blakeney (village, Norfolk) 'black island', OE *blæc*, 'black' + *ēg*, 'island'. The 'island' is the area of higher ground in marshes here, which must have been dark-coloured. *Blakenye* 1242.

Blandford Forum (town, Dorset) '(place with a) market by a ford where gudgeon are', OE *blǣge*, 'gudgeon' + *ford*, 'ford' + Latin *forum*, 'market'. The first part of the name represents the genitive plural (*blǣgna*) of the OE word for 'gudgeon' (or *blay*, a fish still found in the Stour here). *Forum* was added to distinguish this Blandford from others nearby, such as *Blandford St Mary*, on the same river. *Blaneford* 1086, *Blaneford Forum* 1297.

Blaydon (town, Tyne and Wear) '(place by the) black hill', OS *blár*, 'black' + OE *dūn*, 'hill'. A 'black' hill is one that is cold, cheerless or exposed. *Bladon* 1340.

Bletchley (town, Buckinghamshire) 'Blæcca's clearing', OE personal name + *lēah*, 'clearing'. The town is near Whaddon Chase, a former forest, where several clearings would have been needed to establish new settlements. *Blechelai* 12th century.

Bloomsbury (district, Greater London) 'de Blemund's manor', family name + OE *burh*, 'stronghold', 'manor'. The Anglo-Norman *de Blemund* family were here in the 13th century. *Blemondesberi* 1291.

Bloxham (village, Oxfordshire) 'Blocc's homestead', OE personal name + *hām*, 'homestead'. The personal name is found only in places beginning *Blox-*, such as *Bloxholm*, Lincolnshire, and *Bloxwich*, West Midlands. *Blochesham* 1086.

Blubberhouses (hamlet, North Yorkshire) 'houses by the bubbling (spring)', Middle English *bluber*, 'bubbling' + OE *hūs*, 'house'. The name does not have anything to do with modern *blubber*. *Bluberhusum* 1172.

Blyth (town, Northumberland) '(place by the River) Blyth', OE river name. The town stands at the mouth of the river, whose own name represents OE *blīthe*, 'gentle', 'pleasant' (modern *blithe*). *Blida* 1130.

Boat of Garten (village, Highland) 'ferrying place by the cornfield', English *boat* + Gaelic place-name. The first word translates Gaelic *coit*, literally 'little boat', as the first word of the Gaelic name, *Coit Ghairtean*. The 'ferrying place' is over the River Spey.

Bodmin (town, Cornwall) 'dwelling by church land', Old Cornish **bod*, 'dwelling' + **meneghi*, 'church land'. Old Cornish *meneghi* is a derivative of *managh*, 'monk'. *Bodmine c* 975, 1086.

Bognor Regis (town, West Sussex) 'Bucge's shore honoured by the king', OE personal name + *ōre*, 'shore' + Latin *regis*, 'of the king'. *Bucge* is a woman's name. OE *ōra* also denoted a low hill, and this may apply here, rather than 'shore'. The Latin second word honours George V, who convalesced nearby in 1929. *Bucganora c* 975.

Boldon (town, Tyne and Wear) '(place by the) rounded hill', OE **bol*, 'ball-shaped', 'rounded' + *dūn*, 'hill'. The 'rounded hill' in question is presumably the one below which the town lies. *Boldun c* 1170.

Bollington (town, Cheshire) 'farmstead on the (River) Bollin', river name + OE *tūn*, 'farmstead'. The origin of the river name is uncertain. *Bolynton* 1270.

Bolsover (town, Derbyshire) 'Boll's ridge', OE personal name + **ofer*, 'ridge'. The personal name may be *Bull*. The 'ridge' is a hillside spur to the east of the town. *Belesovre* 1086, *Bolesoura* 12th century.

Bolton (town, Greater Manchester) 'settlement with a (special) building', OE **bothl-tūn*, 'building settlement'. OE *bōthl* meant a special building of some kind, and *Bolton*, a name found elsewhere, probably denoted the residential part of a settlement, as distinct from outlying buildings. *Boelton* 1185.

Bo'ness (town, Central) 'promontory of Beornweard's farmstead', OE personal name + *tūn*, 'farmstead' + *næss*, 'promontory'. The name is an abbreviation of *Borrowstounness*, in which, what could have been *Bernardston,* was assimilated to the word *burrowstown*, 'municipality'.

Berwardeston c 1335, *Burnstounnes* 1532, *Borrowstownness, or Bo'ness* 1868.

Bonnyrigg (town, Lothian) 'bannock-shaped ridge', OE *bannuc*, 'bannock' + *hrycg*, 'ridge'. A bannock is a round flat cake, here used to describe the contours of the ridge. The name has been assimilated to Scottish *bonny*, as for *Bonnybridge* and other places. *Bannockrig* 1773.

Boothferry (district, Humberside) '(district of) Boothferry (Bridge)', family name + OS *ferja*, 'ferrying place'. The district name comes from *Boothferry Bridge*, a bridge over the Ouse at a point where there was earlier only a boat crossing. This took its name from the nearby village of *Booth*, earlier *Boothby*, itself named after a family who came from some other *Boothby*, a place-name meaning 'farmstead with booths', *ie* with shelters. *Booth's Ferry* 1651.

Bootle (town, Merseyside) '(special) building', OE *bōtl*, 'building'. The OE word that gave the name was used for a special or prominent building of some kind. It may not have been a residence, and could even have been an outlying building. The Domesday Book record has acquired an extra *l*. *Boltelai* 1086.

Borehamwood (residential district, Hertfordshire) '(place by the) wood of the homestead on a hill', OE **bor*, 'hill' + *hām*, 'homestead' + *wudu*, 'wood'. The original *Boreham* gave its name to a wood which in turn gave the name of the residential district. The first record thus relates to the original settlement, the second to the wood, the third to the development. *Borham* 1188, *Burhamwode* 13th century, *Boreham Wood* 1868.

Boroughbridge (town, North Yorkshire) 'bridge by the stronghold', OE *burh* 'stronghold' + *brycg*, 'bridge'. The 'stronghold' was that of nearby *Aldborough* ('old stronghold'), the Roman settlement of *Isurium Brigantum*. The 'bridge' is over the River Ure. *Burbrigg* 1220.

Borrowdale (river valley, Cumbria) 'valley of the fort river', OS *borg*, 'fort' + *á*, 'river' + *dalr*, 'valley'. *Borrow* was the earlier name of the upper *Derwent* here, probably referring to a Romano-British hill fort at the location now known as Castle Craig. *Borgordale c* 1170.

Boscastle (village, Cornwall) 'Boterel's castle', Old French family name + OE *castel*, 'castle'. The *Boterel* family were here in the 14th century. *Boterelescastel* 1302.

Bosham (village, West Sussex) 'Bōsa's promontory', OE personal name

+ *hamm*, 'promontory'. The village is on land that projects into Chichester Harbour. *Bosanhamm* 731, *Boseham* 1086.

Boston (town, Lincolnshire) 'Bōtwulf's stone', OE personal name + *stān*, 'stone'. The church here (the 'Boston Stump') is dedicated to St *Botolph*, but it is unlikely that *Bōtwulf* represents his name. The 'stone' would have marked a boundary or meeting place. *Botulustan* 1130.

Bothwell (town, Strathclyde) 'shelter by the spring', Middle English *bothe*, 'shelter' + OE *wella*, 'well', 'spring'. The name probably refers to a sheltered site for fishing here on the Clyde. *Botheuill c* 1242.

Botley (town, Hampshire) 'Bōta's clearing', OE personal name + *lēah*, 'clearing'. The first part of the name could also represent OE *bōt*, 'advantage', 'benefit' (modern *to boot*), meaning a clearing where timber could be obtained. *Botelie* 1086.

Bourne (town, Lincolnshire) '(place by the) stream', OE *burna*, 'spring', 'stream'. The town is near the source of the *Bourne* Eau. *Brune* 1086.

Bournemouth (town, Dorset) '(place at the) mouth of a stream', OE *burna*, 'stream' + *mūtha*, 'mouth'. The 'stream' is the *Bourne*, which now runs through the Pleasure Gardens. The town arose only in the 19th century, and the record below refers to the stream mouth. *Bournemowthe* 1407.

Bournville (district, Birmingham, West Midlands), 'town by the (River) Bourne'. The district arose from the model estate built in 1879 for employees at Cadbury's chocolate factory. The first part of the name comes from the *Bourne* stream here, and the latter from modern French *ville*, 'town'.

Bourton-on-the-Water (town, Gloucestershire) 'farm by a fortified place by a river', OE *burh-tūn*, 'farm by a fortified place' + modern *water*. The 'fortified place' is the nearby Iron Age encampment of Salmondsbury Fort. The 'water' is the River Windrush, which flows through the town. The added three words distinguish this Bourton from *Bourton-on-the-Hill*, to the north. *Burchtun* 714, *Bortune* 1086, *Bourton super aquam* 1601.

Bovey Tracey (town, Devon) 'de Tracy's (place by the River) Bovey', river name + family name. The river name is pre-English and of uncertain meaning. The Anglo-Norman *de Tracy* family were here in the 13th century. *Bovi* 1086, *Bovy Tracy* 1276.

Bowes (town, Durham) '(place by the) bends', OE *boga*, 'bend'. The name is said to refer to a former arched bridge over the River Greta here. *Bogas* 1148.

Bowland (district, Lancashire) 'district of bends', OE *boga*, 'bend' + *land*, 'land', 'district'. The name, that of a historic district and forest, relates to a region in a *bend* of the River Ribble. *Boelanda* 1102.

Bowling (district, Bradford, West Yorkshire) 'place by a hollow', OE *bolla*, 'hollow' + *-ing*, 'belonging to'. The name relates to a depression or 'dip' here, or to a number of such depressions. *Bollinc* 1086.

Brackley (town, Northamptonshire) 'Bracca's clearing', OE personal name + *lēah*, 'clearing'. The area is still well wooded and there are sawmills nearby. *Brachelai* 1086.

Bracknell (town, Berkshire) 'Bracca's corner of land', OE personal name + *halh*, 'nook of land'. The *n* represents the genitive ending of the personal name. *Braccan heal* 942.

Bradford (city, West Yorkshire) '(place at the) broad ford', OE *brād*, 'broad + *ford*, 'ford'. A fairly common name, as a 'broad ford' over a river is a suitable place for a settlement to develop. The one here would have been over the rather small Bradford Beck. *Bradeford* 1086.

Bradford-on-Avon (town, Wiltshire) '(place at the) broad ford over the (River) Avon', OE *brād*, 'broad', + *ford*, 'ford' + Celtic river name. As for ◊Bradford, West Yorkshire, the name relates to a river crossing that was a suitable place for a settlement to develop. The suffix, naming the river crossed (*see* ◊Avon), was added to distinguish this Bradford from others. *Bradanforda be Afne c* 900, *Bradeford* 1086.

Bradwell-on-Sea (village, Essex) '(place by a) broad stream', OE *brād*, 'broad' + *wella*, 'spring', 'stream'. The village is on the River Blackwater. The suffix was added later to distinguish this Bradwell from others and also serves as a commercial pointer. *Bradewella* 1194, *Bradwell-next-the-Sea* 1868.

Braemar (village, Grampian) 'upper (part of) Marr', Gaelic *braigh*, 'upper' + district name. The origin of *Marr* is uncertain. It may be a tribal or personal name. *The Bray of Marre* 1560.

Braintree (town, Essex) 'Branca's tree', OE personal name + *trēow*, 'tree'. The tree would have been a prominent one on land owned by Branca or even a 'built' tree in the form of a cross. The River *Brain* here was named from the place. *Branchetreu* 1086.

Bramhall (town, Greater Manchester) 'corner of land where broom grows', OE *brōm*, 'broom' + *halh*, 'corner of land'. The *Bram-* of this name is the *Brom-* of names such as ◊Bromyard. *Bramale* 1086.

Brampton (town, Cumbria) 'farmstead where broom grows', OE *brōm*, 'broom' + *tūn*, 'farmstead'. The name is a fairly common one, and sometimes has a distinguishing affix, as for *Chapel Brampton* and *Church Brampton*, Northamptonshire. *Cp* ◊Braunton. *Brampton* 1169.

Brandon (town, Suffolk) 'hill where broom grows', OE *brōm*, 'broom' + *dūn*, 'hill'. The name is found elsewhere, as for the town in Co Durham. *Bromdun* 11th century, *Brandona* 1086.

Braunstone (district, Leicester, Leicestershire) 'Brant's farmstead', OE personal name + *tūn*, 'farmstead'. The personal name is conjectural. *Brantestone* 1086.

Braunton (town, Devon) 'farmstead where broom grows', OE *brōm*, 'broom' + *tūn*, 'farmstead'. A name of exactly the same origin as that of ◊Brampton. *Brantona* 1086.

Bray (village, Berkshire) '(place by) marshland', Old French *bray*, 'mud', 'marsh'. The village is in a bend of the Thames. The Old French word is not known in any other place-name. *Brai* 1086.

Brechin (town, Tayside) 'Brychan's (place)', Celtic personal name. The same personal name gave that of ◊Brecon. *Brechin c* 1145.

Breckland (district, Norfolk) 'broken land', English dialect *breck*, 'broken' + *land*. The name implies that the land was difficult to cultivate, so had to be broken up.

Brecknock (district, Powys) '(district based on) Brecon'. The name is an Anglicized form of *Brycheinioc*, an early form of ◊Brecon.

Brecon (town, Powys) 'Brychan's (place)', Celtic personal name. *Brychan* was a 5th-century Welsh prince. His name also gave that of the district and historic county of *Brecknock*, formed from Welsh *Brycheinioc*, the personal name with the territorial suffix *-ioc*. The town's Welsh name is *Aberhonddu*, 'mouth of the Honddu'. *Brecheniauc* 1100, *Bregnok* 1409.

Brent (borough, Greater London) '(borough of the River) Brent', Celtic river name. The borough was created in 1965 by the amalgamation of the former boroughs of Wembley and Willesden. *See* ◊Brentford.

Brentford (district, Greater London) 'ford over the (River) Brent', Celtic river name + OE *ford*, 'ford'. The river name means 'holy one'. The London borough of ◊Brent is named from the river. *Breguntford* 705.

Brentwood (town, Essex) 'burnt wood', OE **berned*, 'burnt' + *wudu*, 'wood'. The name implies that the place arose by a wood destroyed by burning. The first record is Latin. *Boscus arsus* 1176, *Brendewode* 1274.

Bridgend (town, Mid Glamorgan) '(place) by a bridge', OE *brycg*, 'bridge' + *ende*, 'end'. *End* here denotes a place close to the named object. The sense is thus not 'end of the bridge' but 'land close to the bridge'. The Welsh name includes the river: *Pen-y-bont ar Ogwr*, 'head of the bridge over the Ogmore'. *Byrge End* 1535.

Bridge of Allan (town, Central) '(place by the) bridge over the (River) Allan'. The word order is that of the Gaelic original, *ie* 'bridge of Allan' rather than 'Allan bridge'. The town is south of the Strath Allan.

Bridgnorth (town, Shropshire) 'northern (place by the) bridge', OE *brycg*, 'bridge' + *north*, 'north'. The place was originally *Bridge*, with *north* added to show that the place was at a bridge over the Severn further north than the earlier one, at Quatford to the southeast. *Brug* 1156, *Brugg Norht* 1282.

Bridgwater (town, Somerset) '(place at) Walter's bridge', OE *brycg*, 'bridge' + personal name. The personal name is that of the Norman lord of the manor here. *Brugie* 1086, *Brigewaltier* 1194.

Bridlington (town, Humberside) 'estate named after Berhtel', OE personal name + *-ing-*, 'named after' + *tūn*, 'estate'. The personal name is based on OE *beorht*, 'bright'. *Bretlinton* 1086, *Burlington* 1771.

Bridport (town, Dorset) 'Bredy port', OE place-name + *port*, 'market town'. *Bredy*, a former borough here, is named for the River *Bride*, itself a Celtic name meaning 'gushing', related to modern Welsh *brydio*, 'to boil'. Bridport itself is on the River *Brit*, named after it. *Brideport* 1086.

Brierfield (town, Lancashire) 'field of briars'. The name is of 19th-century origin and was doubtless adapted from that of nearby *Briercliffe*, 'bank where briars grow', from OE *brē*, 'briar', and *clif*, 'bank'.

Brigg (town, Humberside) '(place by the) bridge', OE *brycg*, 'bridge'. The 'bridge' is that of the River Ancholme. The town was earlier *Glanford Brigg*, the first word of which means 'ford of revelry', from OE *glēam*, 'revelry', 'games', and *ford*, 'ford'. The ford would have been an assembly point for merrymaking or sport. *Glanford Brigg* 1235, 1896.

Brighouse (town, West Yorkshire) 'houses by the bridge', OE *brycg*, 'bridge' + *hūs*, 'house'. The form of OE *brycg* here has been influenced by its OS equivalent, *bryggja*. The record below shows the plural 'houses'. *Brighuses* 1240.

Brightlingsea (town, Essex) 'Beorhtrīc's island', OE personal name + *ēg*, 'island'. The -*ing*- of the name means that the personal name may really be *Beorhtling*, where it serves as a diminutive or 'pet' suffix (as in modern *duck* and *duckling*). The 'island' no longer exists as such, but the coastal town is still almost surrounded by the River Colne. *Brictriceseia* 1086, *Brihtlenggesseya* 1212.

Brighton (town, East Sussex) 'Beorhthelm's farmstead', OE personal name + *tūn*, 'farmstead'. The present name became established as a 'smoother' form of the original after the town developed as a watering place in the 18th century. *Bristelmestune* 1086, *Brightelmstone* 1771, *Brighton*, or *Brighthelmston* 1868.

Bristol (city, Avon) 'assembly place by the bridge', OE *brycg*, 'bridge' + *stōw*, 'assembly place'. The original assembly place may have been where Bristol Bridge is now, at the point where the M4 crosses the Floating Harbour. The final *l* came through Norman French influence. *Brycg stowe* 11th century, *Bristou* 1086, *Bristoll* 1200.

Brixham (town, Devon) 'Brioc's homestead', OE personal name + *hām*, 'homestead'. The second part of the name could also represent OE *hamm*, 'enclosure'. *Briseham* 1086, *Brikesham* 1205.

Brixton (district, Greater London) 'Beorhtsige's stone', OE personal name + *stān*, 'stone'. The 'stone' was probably a natural rock used to mark the meeting place of a hundred. *Brixges stan* 1062, *Brixiestan* 1086.

Broadstairs (town, Kent) 'broad stairs', OE *brād*, 'broad' + *stǣger*, 'stairway'. The 'stairs' were cut in the cliff here at some time in the 15th century to give access to the sea. *Brodsteyr* 1435.

Broadway (town, Hereford and Worcester) '(place at the) broad way', OE *brād*, 'broad' + *weg*, 'way'. The 'broad way' is not the town's present main road but the older one that runs south up the valley to the village of Snowshill. *Bradanuuege* 972, *Bradeweia* 1086.

Brockenhurst (village, Hampshire) 'Broca's wooded hill', OE personal name + *hyrst*, 'wooded hill'. The first part of the name could also represent OE *brocen*, 'broken', referring to undulating terrain. The Domesday Book record has omitted a syllable. *Broceste* 1086, *Brocheherst* 1158.

Brockworth (town, Gloucestershire) 'enclosure by the brook', OE *brōc*, 'brook' + *worthign*, 'enclosure'. The 'brook' in question is Horsbere Brook. *Brocowardinge* 1086

Brodick (town, Strathclyde) 'broad bay', OS *breithr*, 'broad' + *vík*, 'bay'. The town is a port in the Isle of Arran. Its Gaelic name is *Traigh a' Chaisteil*, 'beach of the castle', alluding to Brodick Castle, which dates from at least the 14th century. *Brathwik* 1306, *Bradewik* 1450.

Bromley (borough, Greater London) 'clearing where broom grows', OE *brōm*, 'broom' + *lēah*, 'clearing'. The name usually has this meaning. However, *Bromley*-by-Bow, also in Greater London, means 'clearing where brambles grow', from OE *bræmbel*, 'bramble'. *Bromleag* 862, *Bronlei* 1086.

Bromsgrove (town, Hereford and Worcester) 'Brēme's grove', OE personal name + *græfe*, 'grove'. This is one of the few names beginning *Brom-* where the meaning is not 'broom'. *Bremesgrefan* 804, *Bremesgrave* 1086.

Bromyard (town, Hereford and Worcester) 'enclosure where broom grows', OE *brōm*, 'broom' + *geard*, 'enclosure'. The OE word that gave the second part of the name is the source of modern *yard*. *Bromgeard c* 840, *Bromgerde* 1086.

Broughty Ferry (district, Dundee, Tayside) 'ferry of the bank', Gaelic *bruach*, 'bank' + English *ferry*. The name refers to a former ferry across the River Tay from a bank here to the point where Tayport stands today. *Brochty* 1595.

Brownsea (island, Dorset) 'Brūnoc's island', OE personal name + *ēg*, 'island'. The name is now usually *Brownsea Island*, adding *island* to a word that already means this. *Brunkeseye* 1241, *Branksea* (now generally called "Brownsea") 1893.

Brown Willy (hill, Cornwall) 'hill of the swallows', Cornish *bronn*, 'breast', 'hill' + *gwennili*, 'swallows'. The hill is a granite tor on Bodmin Moor. The *gw* of *gwennili* has here become *w* through mutation. *Brunwenely* 1239, *Brounwellye hill* 1576.

Broxburn (town, Lothian) '(place by the) stream where badgers are', OE *brocc*, 'badger' + *burna*, 'stream'. The town has the same name as *Broxbourne*, Hertfordshire. *Broxburne* 1638.

Bruton (town, Somerset) 'farmstead on the (River) Brue', Celtic river name + OE *tūn*, 'farmstead'. The river name means 'brisk', related to modern Welsh *bryw*, 'lively'. *Briwetone* 1086.

Brynmawr (town, Gwent) 'big hill', Welsh *bryn*, 'hill' + *mawr*, 'big'. The original name of the location here was *Gwaun-helygen*, 'moorland of the willows', but this was apparently changed to something more appropriate for a growing settlement. *Bryn-mawr* 1832.

Buckfastleigh (town, Devon) 'clearing near Buckfast', OE place-name + *lēah*, 'clearing'. *Buckfast* is a village to the north. Its name means 'place of shelter for bucks', from OE *bucc*, 'buck' (male deer) + *fæsten*, 'fastness', 'place of shelter'. *Leghe Bucfestre* 13th century.

Buckingham (town, Buckinghamshire) 'land in the river bend of Bucca's people', OE personal name + *-inga-*, 'of the people of' + *hamm*, 'land in river bend'. The town lies in a bend of the River Ouse. The county name, *Buckinghamshire*, is first recorded in the 11th century. *Buccingahamme* early 10th century, *Bochingeham* 1086.

Bude (town, Cornwall) '(place of the River) Bude', river name. It is assumed that the name is that of the stream here, although that is first recorded in 1587 as *Bedewater*. Its meaning and origin are uncertain. *Bude* 1400.

Budleigh Salterton (town, Devon) 'salt works at Budleigh', OE place-name + *salt-ærn*, 'building where salt is made'. The main part of the name is the second word. This then added the name of nearby *Budleigh*, 'Budda's clearing', from an OE personal name and *lēah*, 'clearing'. The *-ton* was added later. *Cp* ◊Salcombe. *Saltre* 1210, *Salterne in the manor of Buddeleghe* 1405, *Salterton* 1667.

Builth Wells (town, Powys) 'cow pasture with wells', Welsh *buellt*, 'cow pasture' + English *wells*. The second word of the name was added in the 18th century when the chalybeate springs here began to attract visitors from England. *Buelt* 10th century.

Bungay (town, Suffolk) 'island of Būna's people', OE personal name + *-inga-*, 'of the people of' + *ēg*, 'island'. The 'island' is the location of the town in a loop of the River Waveney. *Bunghea* 1086.

Buntingford (town, Hertfordshire) 'ford where buntings are', Middle English *bunting*, 'bunting' + *ford*, 'ord'. The birds would have frequented the ford over the River Rib here. *Buntingeford* 1185.

Burford (town, Oxfordshire) 'ford by the fortified place', OE *burh*, 'fortified place' + *ford*, 'ford'. The precise site of the original 'fortified place' is uncertain but the town is set in a hilly location. The 'ford' would have been over the River Windrush. *Bureford* 1086.

Burgess Hill (town, West Sussex) '(place by) Burgeys' hill', family name + *hill*. The *Burgeys* family were here in the 13th century. *Burges Hill* 1597.

Burnham-on-Crouch (town, Essex) 'homestead on a stream by the (River) Crouch', OE *burna*, 'stream' + *hām*, 'homestead' + river name. The 'stream' is one to the north of the town which flows into the *Crouch*. The river name is of uncertain origin and not recorded before the 16th century. It may represent OE *crūc*, 'cross'. *Burneham* 1086.

Burnham-on-Sea (town, Somerset) 'enclosure by a stream by the sea', OE *burna*, 'stream' + *hamm*, 'enclosure' + modern *on sea*. The 'stream' here is the River Brue. This is one Burnham that does not have OE *hām*. Cp ◊Burnham-on-Crouch. *Burnhamm c* 880, *Burneham* 1086.

Burnley (town, Lancashire) 'clearing by the (River) Brun', OE river name + *lēah*, 'clearing'. The river name means either 'brown' (*brūn*) or simply 'stream' (*burna*). *Brunlaia* 1124.

Burntisland (town, Fife) 'burnt island'. The name is said to refer to a fire on a small island to the west of the present town where some fishermen's huts were destroyed in the early 16th century. *Bruntisland c* 1600.

Burry Port (town, Dyfed) 'port by the sand dunes', English dialect *burrow* + *port*. The first word of the name represents the local word *burrows*, referring to the sand dunes here. The word is a development of OE *beorg*, 'mound', 'hill'.

Burslem (town, Staffordshire) 'Burgweard's estate in Lyme', OE personal name + Celtic place-name. The first part of the name may be OE *burhweard*, 'fort keeper'. *Lyme* is a district name, probably meaning 'region of elms'. Cp ◊Ashton-under-Lyne. *Barcardeslim* 1086, *Borewardeslyme* 1242.

Burton Latimer (town, Northamptonshire) 'fortified farmstead of the le Latimer' family', OE *burh-tūn*, 'fortified farmstead' + family name. The *le Latimer* family held the manor here in the 13th century. The *Burton* of ◊Burton-upon-Trent has a slightly different meaning. *Burtone* 1086, *Burton Latymer* 1482.

Burton-upon-Trent (town, Staffordshire) 'farmstead of the fortified place on the (River) Trent', OE *burh-tūn*, 'farmstead of the fortified place' + river name. The river name was added to distinguish this Burton from the many others. The river name probably means 'trespasser', referring to its liability to flood. Cp ◊Stoke-on-Trent. *Byrtun* 1002, *Bertone* 1086, *Burton* 1771.

Bury (town, Greater Manchester) '(place by the) fort', OE *burh*, 'fort'. Grammatically, the name represents OE *byrig*, the dative case of *burh*, meaning 'at the fort'. *Biri* 1194.

Bury St Edmunds (town, Suffolk) 'St Edmund's town', OE *burh*, 'town', 'borough' + saint's name. The town is named after *St Edmund*, 9th-century king of East Anglia, whose remains were buried here. The name as recorded was revived in modern use for the administrative district of ◊St Edmundsbury. *Sancte Eadmundes Byrig* 1038.

Bushey (town, Hertfordshire) 'enclosure by a thicket', OE **bysce*, 'bush', 'thicket' + *hæg*, 'enclosure'. The first part of the name could also be OE **byxe*, 'box' (the tree). *Bissei* 1086.

Buttermere (lake, Cumbria) 'lake with good pasture', OE *butere*, 'butter' + *mere*, 'lake'. The name denotes a lake surrounded by rich pastures, where cows will graze and produce good milk for making butter. *Butermere* 1230.

Buxton (town, Derbyshire) '(place by a) rocking stone', OE **būg-stān*, 'rocking stone'. There must have been a 'rocking stone' (logan stone) here at one time, but its location has not been identified. The town arose on the site of a Roman spa called *Aquae Arnemetiae*, 'waters of Arnemetia' (a Roman goddess). *Buchestanes c* 1100.

Byfleet (village, Surrey) '(place) by the stream', OE *bī*, 'by' + *flēot*, 'stream'. The 'stream' here is the River Wey, which more directly gave the name of ◊Weybridge. *Biflete* 933, *Biflet* 1086.

C

Caerleon (town, Gwent) 'camp of the legion', Welsh *caer*, 'fort' + Latin *legio, legionis*, 'legion'. The town is the site of the Roman camp of *Isca Legionis*, the first word of which represents the River *Usk*. The Roman Second Legion was stationed here in AD 75. *Castra Legionis c* 150, *Caerleion* 1086.

Caernarfon (town, Gwynedd) 'fort in Arfon', Welsh *caer*, 'fort' + *yn*, 'in' + Welsh place-name. *Arfon* means 'opposite Anglesey', from Welsh *ar*, 'over', and *Fôn*, the mutated form of *Mon*, 'Anglesey'. The town stands on the Menai Strait overlooking Anglesey. *Kairarvon* 1191, *Kaer yn Arvon* 1258.

Caerphilly (town, Mid Glamorgan) 'Ffili's fort', Welsh *caer*, 'fort' + personal name. The identity of Ffili is unknown. The Welsh form of the name, *Caerffili*, is increasingly common. *Kaerfili* 1271.

Cairngorms (mountains, Highland/Grampian) 'blue rock', Gaelic *carn*, 'rock' + *gorm*, 'blue'. The name is properly that of *Cairn Gorm*, the highest peak of the mountain mass.

Caistor (town, Lincolnshire) 'Roman fort', OE *cæster*, 'Roman fort'. The fort in question may have been the one known as *Bannovalium*, 'strong horn'. *Castre* 1086.

Caithness (district, Scotland) 'promontory of the Cat (people)', Celtic tribal name + OS *nes*, 'promontory'. The tribal name means 'cats', but it is not known why or how the people came to be so called. *Kathenessia c* 970.

Caldy (island, Dyfed) 'cold island', OS *kald*, 'cold' + *ey*, island'. The island is exposed to southwest winds, which sweep over it unchecked. Its Welsh name is *Ynys Pyr*, 'Pyr's island', after a 6th-century saint. *Caldea c* 1120.

Caledonian Canal (canal, Highland) 'canal of Caledonia', Latin district name. *Caledonia* was the Roman name of Scotland, with *Cal-* based on a

Celtic root word meaning 'hard', 'strong' (Welsh *caled*, 'hard', 'severe'). The canal was built only in the 19th century.

Callander (town, Central) '(place by the) turbulent stream', Celtic river name. The river here now is the *Teith*, but the town's name may derive from an earlier name for it, related to that of the *Calder* in England. The word is related to modern Welsh *caled*, 'severe', 'harsh'. *Kalentare* 1504.

Callington (town, Cornwall) 'farmstead by the bare hill', OE *calu*, 'bare hill' + *tūn*, 'farmstead'. The 'bare hill' is Kit Hill, which dominates the town. The *-ing-* of the name was not in the original. *Calwe-* in the first record below is OE *calwe*, the dative form of *calu*, meaning 'at the bare hill'. *Calwetone* 1086, *Calwinton* 1187, *Calyton* 1306.

Calne (town, Wiltshire) '(place on the River) Calne', river name. The town takes its name from the pre-English name, of unknown meaning, of the river now called Marden Brook. *Calne* 955, 1086.

Camberley (town, Surrey) '(place named after) Cambridge', place-name. The town arose in the early 19th century and was originally called *Cambridge Town*, after the Duke of *Cambridge*. The name was changed in 1877, however, to avoid confusion with Cambridge itself. The *-ley* matches other local names, such as Frimley, Eversley and Yatesley.

Camberwell (district, Greater London) '(place by the) well', OE *wella*, 'well', 'spring'. The origin of the *Camber-* is uncertain. It may be a blend of OE *cran*, 'crane' (the bird) and *burna*, 'stream'. *Cambrewelle* 1086.

Camborne (town, Cornwall) 'crooked hill', Cornish *camm*, 'crooked' + *bronn*, 'breast', 'hill'. The 'crooked hill' is probably Camborne Beacon, to the south of the town. *Cameron* 1182, *Cambron c* 1230.

Cambrian Mountains (mountains, Wales) 'mountains of Cambria', Roman district name. The name is based on the Roman name for Wales, *Cambria*, itself from the Welsh people's name for themselves, in modern terms *Cymry* ('compatriots').

Cambridge (city, Cambridgeshire) 'bridge on the (River) Granta', Celtic river name + OE *brycg*, 'bridge'. The river here is now known as both *Cam* and *Granta*. The change from *Granta* to *Cam* in the town's name is due to Norman influence. (For the origin of *Granta*, *see* ◊Grantchester.) *Grontabricc c* 745, *Cantebrigie* 1086.

Cambuslang (town, Strathclyde) 'river bend of the ship', Gaelic *camas*, 'bay', 'crooked channel' + *long*, 'ship'. The name aptly describes the town's location on a bend of the Clyde. *Camboslanc* 1296.

Camden Town (district, Greater London) 'Camden's town', family title + place-name. The district is named after Charles Pratt, Earl *Camden*, who came into possession of the manor of Kentish *Town* here in the late 18th century. The Earl's title comes from *Camden* Place, Chislehurst.

Camelford (town, Cornwall) '(place by a) ford over the (River) Camel', Celtic river name + OE *ford*, 'ford'. The river name derives from a word related to Cornish *cam*, 'crooked', referring to its course. *Camelford* 13th century.

Campbeltown (town, Strathclyde) 'Campbell's town', family name + OE *tūn*, 'town'. The name is that of Archibald *Campbell*, Earl of Argyle, who was granted land here in 1667. The previous name of the place was *Lochhead*, 'head of the loch'.

Campsie Fells (hills, Central/Strathclyde) 'hills of Campsie', Gaelic hill name. The range of hills takes its name from one of them, itself meaning 'crooked fairy (hill)', from *cam*, 'crooked', and *sìth*, 'fairy'. *Fells* represents OS *fjall*, 'hill'.

Cannock (town, Staffordshire) 'hillock', OE *cnocc*, 'hillock'. The 'hillock' is probably Shoal Hill, to the west of the town. *Chenet* 1086, *Canoc* 12th century.

Canterbury (city, Kent) 'fortified town of the people of Kent', Celtic place-name + OE *-ware*, 'dwellers' + *burh*, 'fortified town'. The Roman name of Canterbury was *Durovernum*, 'walled town by the alder marsh'. *Cantwaraburg c* 900, *Canterburie* 1086.

Canvey Island (island, Essex) 'island of Cana's people', OE personal name + *-inga-*, 'of the people of' + *ēg*, 'island'. Modern *island* was added to the OE word that already meant this, as the *-ey* of the main name. *Caneveye* 1255.

Capel Curig (village, Gwynedd) 'Curig's chapel', Welsh *capel*, 'chapel' + Welsh personal name. *Curig* was the son of Ilid, a 7th-century Welsh saint, and the chapel here is dedicated to him.

Cardiff (city, South Glamorgan) 'fort on the (River) Taff', Welsh *caer*, 'fort' + Celtic river name. The river name derives from the same word that gave the name of the ◊Thames. It probably means simply 'water', 'river'. *Kairdiff* 1106.

Cardigan (town, Dyfed) 'Ceredig's land', Welsh personal name + suffix *-ion*. The town took its name from *Ceredigion*, that of the district here. The

-ion suffix means 'territory'. The Welsh name of Cardigan is *Aberteifi*, 'mouth of the Teifi'. *Cereticiaun* 12th century, *Kerdigan* 1194.

Carisbrooke (village, Isle of Wight) '(place by) Cary brook', Celtic river name + OE *brōc*, 'brook'. There is no river or stream named *Cary* here now, and its meaning is uncertain. It may be the same name as that in ◊Castle Cary. *Caresbroc* 12th century.

Carlisle (city, Cumbria) 'castle of (the place belonging to) Lugovalos', Celtic *cair*, 'castle' + personal name. *Lugovalos* means 'strong as Lugos', this being the name of a Celtic god. The evolution of the name from Roman times is illustrated by the records below. The present spelling may have arisen by association with Norman French *isle*, 'island'. *Luguvalium* 4th century, *Luel* 9th century, *Carleol* c 1106.

Carmarthen (town, Dyfed) 'fort of Maridunum', Old Welsh *cair*, 'fort' + Celtic place-name. *Maridunum* means 'seaside fort', from the Celtic elements *mari-*, 'maritime', and *duno-*, 'fort'. The Roman camp here was *Moridunum*, which also gave the Welsh name of the town, *Caerfyrddin*. By the 12th century *Myrddin* in this name (with *m* mutated to *f*) came to be taken as a personal name, as if meaning 'Myrddin's fort'. This in turn was Latinized as *Merlinus*, giving the name of *Merlin* the magician. *Maridunum* 4th century, *Cair Mirdin* 1130.

Carnforth (town, Lancashire) 'ford where cranes are', OE *cran*, 'crane' + *ford*, 'ford'. Early records of the name show it to be the same as *Cranford* elsewhere. *Chreneforde* 1086.

Carshalton (district, Greater London) 'farm by the spring where cress grows', OE *cærse*, 'watercress' + *ǣwiell*, 'spring' + *tūn*, 'farm'. The original name of the place (in modern terms) was *Alton*, with the 'cress' element added later. *Alton* in Hampshire is still famous for its watercress. *Aultone* 1086, *Cresaulton* 1235.

Carstairs (village, Strathclyde) 'castle of Tarres', Middle English *castel*, 'castle' + personal name. It is not known who *Tarres* was. *Casteltarres* 1170.

Cartmel (village, Cumbria) 'sandbank by rocky ground', OS **kartr*, 'rocky ground' + *melr*, 'sandbank'. The village is on an elevated site above Morecambe Bay. *Cartmel* 12th century.

Castlebay (town, Western Isles) '(town) on the bay of the castle'. The town, on the island of Barra, is named for *Castle Bay*, itself named for the medieval fortress here. The Gaelic name of the town is *Baile Mhic Néill*, 'town of the MacNeils'.

Castle Bromwich (district, Birmingham, West Midlands) 'farm where broom grows with a castle', Middle English *castel*, 'castle' + OE *brōm*, 'broom' + *wīc*, 'farm'. The 'castle' here survives as a 12th-century 'motte and bailey' defence. The first word distinguishes this Bromwich from ◊West Bromwich. *Bramewice* 1168, *Castelbromwic* 13th century.

Castle Cary (town, Somerset) 'castle by the (River) Cary', Middle English *castel*, 'castle' + Celtic river name. The first word of the name refers to the former Norman castle here. The river name, which may be pre-Celtic, is of uncertain origin and meaning. *Castelkary* 1237.

Castle Combe (village, Wiltshire) 'valley with a castle', OE *castel*, 'castle' + *cumb*, 'valley'. The place was originally named for its valley alone. The first word was added when a Norman castle was built here. *Come* 1086, *Castelcumbe* 1270.

Castle Douglas (town, Dumfries and Galloway) 'Douglas's castle'. The town is named after Sir William *Douglas*, who bought the village of Carlingwerk, as it then was, in 1789, and developed it. *Carlingwerk*, still the name of the loch here, means 'work of the hag', OS *kerling*, 'hag', and *verk*, 'work'. The reference is to some local legend.

Castleford (town, West Yorkshire) 'ford by the Roman fort', OE *cæster*, 'Roman camp' + *ford*, 'ford'. The Roman name of the fort here was *Lagentium*, of uncertain origin. *Ceaster forda* late 11th century.

Castle Point (district, Essex). The name was devised for the administrative district formed in 1974. It refers to to two prominent local features: Hadleigh *Castle* and Canvey *Point*.

Castle Rising (village, Norfolk) '(settlement of) Risa's people with a castle', Middle English *castel*, 'castle' + OE personal name + *-ingas*, 'people of'. It is possible the second word may begin with OE *hrīs*, 'brushwood', so that the meaning would be 'dwellers by the brushwood'. The *castle* was the Norman one here. *Risinga* 1086, *Castel Risinge* 1254.

Caterham (town, Surrey) 'homestead by Cadeir', Celtic hill name + OE *hām*, 'homestead'. *Cadeir*, meaning 'chair', is the name of a hill here. The *-ham* of the name could also come from OE *hamm*, 'enclosure'. *Catheham* 1179.

Catford (district, Greater London) 'ford where wild cats are', OE *catt*, 'cat' + *ford*, 'ford'. The ford here would have been over the Ravensbourne. *Catford* 1254.

Catterick (village, North Yorkshire), '(place by the) waterfall', Latin *cataracta*, 'waterfall'. The Latin name apparently arose due to a misunderstanding of an earlier Celtic name meaning '(place of) battle ramparts', from a base word related to modern Welsh *cad*, 'battle'. *Katouraktonion* c 150, *Catrice* 1086.

Caversham (district, Reading, Berkshire) 'Cāfhere's homestead', OE personal name + *hām*, 'homestead'. The second part of the name could equally be OE *hamm*, 'enclosure'. *Caueresham* 1086.

Cerne Abbas, (village, Dorset) '(place by the River) Cerne with an abbey', Celtic river name + Latin *abbas*, 'abbot'. The river name comes from a word related to English *cairn*, and denotes a stony bed. The second word of the name refers to the Benedictine abbey built here in the 10th century. *Cernel* 1086, *Cerne Abbatis* 1288.

Chadderton (town, Greater Manchester) 'farmstead by (the hill called) Cadeir', OE hill name + OE *tūn*, 'farmstead'. The hill was probably the one nearby called *Hanging Chadder*. The name means literally 'chair', from a word related to modern Welsh *cadair* in this sense. *Chaderton* c 1200.

Chagford (town, Devon) 'ford where gorse grows', OE **ceacga*, 'gorse' + *ford*, 'ford'. The first part of the name is represented in modern dialect *chag*, 'broom', 'gorse'. The 'ford' would have been over the River Teign here. *Chageford* 1086.

Chalfont St Giles (town, Buckinghamshire) 'spring where calves are, named after St Giles', OE *cealf*, 'calf' + **funta*, 'spring' + saint's name. The second half of the name, from the dedication of the church, distinguishes this Chalfont from *Chalfont St Peter*. *Celfunte* 1086, *Chalfund Sancti Egidii* 1237.

Chandler's Ford (district, Eastleigh, Hampshire) 'Chaundler's ford', family name + OE *ford*, 'ford'. The *Chaundler* family are known to have been in the area since the 14th century, although the place-name is not recorded before 1759. The 'ford' took a Roman road over Monks Brook.

Chapel-en-le-Frith (town, Derbyshire) 'chapel in the sparse woodland', Middle English *chapele*, 'chapel' + Old French *en le*, 'in the' + OE *fyrhth*, 'sparse woodland'. The 'chapel' of the name is the one built here in the 13th century, dedicated to St Thomas Becket. *Capella de le Frith* 1272.

Chard (town, Somerset) 'house in rough ground', OE *ceart*, 'rough round' + *ærn*, 'house'. The name has lost the second element of the original. *Cerdren* 1065, *Cerdre* 1086.

Charing Cross (district, Greater London) 'bend with a cross', OE **cerring*, 'turn', 'bend' + Middle English *cros*, 'cross'. The 'bend' was either in the Roman road here, as it made a turn to the west, or in the course of the Thames. The second word refers to the 'Eleanor Cross' set up here in memory of Queen Eleanor after her death in 1290. (A modern replica stands in the forecourt of Charing Cross Station.) *Cyrring c* 1000, *La Charryngcros* 1360.

Charlbury (town, Oxfordshire) 'fortified place named after Ceorl', OE personal name + *-ing-*, 'named after' + *burh*, 'fortified place'. The original *–ing-* of the name has disappeared. *Ceorlingburh c* 1000.

Charmouth (town, Dorset) '(place at the) mouth of the (River) Char', Celtic river name + OE *mūtha*, 'mouth'. The river name means 'stony', and is of the same origin as that of the *Cerne* at ◊Cerne Abbas. *Cernemude* 1086.

Charnwood Forest (forest, Leicestershire) 'wood in rocky countryside', Celtic **carn*, 'rocky land' + OE *wudu*, 'wood'. *Forest* was added to denote the former status of the wood as a hunting preserve. *Cernewoda* 1129.

Chatham (town, Kent) 'homestead by the wood', Celtic word + OE *hām*, 'homestead'. The first part of the name is related to modern Welsh *coed*, 'wood'. *Cp* ◊Cheadle. *Cetham* 880, *Ceteham* 1086.

Chatteris (town, Cambridgeshire) 'Ceatta's ridge', OE personal name + **ric*, 'ridge', 'raised strip'. It is possible that the first part of the name may mean 'wood', from a Celtic word related to modern Welsh *coed* in this sense. *Cæateric* 974, *Cietriz* 1086.

Cheadle (town, Greater Manchester) '(place by the) wood', Celtic word + OE *lēah*, 'wood'. The first part of the name is related to modern Welsh *coed*, 'wood'. The OE word, also meaning 'wood', was added to this when it was no longer understood. *Cedde* 1086, *Chedle c* 1165.

Cheam (district, Greater London) 'homestead by the tree stumps', OE **ceg*, 'tree stump' + *hām*, 'homestead'. The two parts of the name have blended into one. *Cegham* 967, *Ceiham* 1086.

Cheddar (town, Somerset) 'ravine', OE **cēodor*, 'ravine'. The reference is to Cheddar Gorge. *Ceodre c* 880, *Cedre* 1086.

Chelmsford (city, Essex) 'Cēolmǣr's ford', OE personal name + *ford*, 'ford'. The town gave the name of the *Chelmer*, the river on which it stands. The name of the Roman town here was *Caesaromagus*, 'Caesar's market'. *Celmersfort* 1086.

Chelsea (district, Greater London) 'landing place for chalk', OE *cealc*, 'chalk' + *hȳth*, 'landing place'. It is possible the first part of the name represents OE *cælic*, 'cup', 'chalice', referring to some natural feature here. *Celchyth* 789, *Chelchede* 1086.

Cheltenham (town, Gloucestershire) 'river meadow by (a hill called) Celte', OE or pre-Celtic **celte*, 'hill slope' + OE *hamm* 'river meadow'. The hill name must relate to Cleeve Hill, which overlooks the town. The 'river meadow' is one by the *Chelt*, whose own name comes from that of the town. *Celtanhomme* 803, *Chinteneham* 1086.

Chepstow (town, Gwent) 'market place', OE *cēap*, 'market' + *stōw* 'place'. The town is near enough to England to have an English name. Its Welsh name is *Cas-Gwent*, 'castle in Gwent'. Its name was recorded in 1224 as *Strigull*, a name of unknown meaning. *Chepstowe* 1308.

Chertsey (town, Surrey) 'Cerot's island', Celtic personal name + OE *ēg*, 'island'. The 'island' is the higher ground by the Thames on which the town stands. *Cerotaesei* 731, *Certesy* 1086.

Cherwell (district, Oxfordshire) '(district of the River) Cherwell', OE river name. The administrative district takes its name from the river, whose own name probably means 'winding stream', from OE **cearr*, 'winding', and *wella*, 'stream'. Cp ◊Charing Cross.

Chesham (town, Buckinghamshire) 'river meadow by a heap of stones', OE *ceastel*, 'heap of stones' + *hamm*, 'river meadow'. The 'heap of stones' was the circle of stones on which the parish church was built. *Cæstæleshamme* 1012, *Cestreham* 1086.

Cheshire (county, England) 'district of Chester', OE place-name + *scīr*, 'district'. The name is effectively *Chestershire*, and was actually recorded as such in a text dated 1326. *Cestre Scire* 1086.

Cheshunt (town, Hertfordshire) 'spring by a Roman camp', OE *ceaster*, 'Roman camp' + **funta*, 'spring'. Although the name apparently indicates a former Roman camp here, none is known. *Cestrehunt* 1086.

Chessington (district, Greater London) 'Cissa's hill', OE personal name + *dūn*, 'hill'. The personal name is the same as that for ◊Chichester.

The -*ington* of the name is misleading. *Cisendone* 1086.

Chester (city, Cheshire) 'Roman town', OE *ceaster*, 'Roman camp'. The first name recorded below relates to the location of the place on the River ◊Dee. The second name means 'city of the legions', referring to the Roman town here. The first part of this later disappeared to leave the basic OE word. *Deoua c* 150, *Legacæstir* 735, *Cestre* 1086.

Chesterfield (town, Derbyshire) 'open land near a Roman town', OE *ceaster*, 'Roman town' + *feld*, 'open land'. The name of the Roman settlement here is unknown. *Cesterfelda* 955, *Cestrefeld* 1086.

Chester-le-Street (town, Durham) 'Roman fort on the Roman road', OE *ceaster*, 'Roman fort' + French *le*, 'the' + OE *strǣt*, 'Roman road'. The second part of the name was added to distinguish this Chester from ◊Chester itself. The Roman encampment here was known as *Conganis*, a name of uncertain origin. *Cestria c* 1160, *Cestra in Strata* 1400.

Chesterton (village, Cambridgeshire) 'farmstead by a Roman fort', OE *ceaster*, 'Roman fort' + *tūn*, 'farmstead'. The Roman fort here was known as *Durobrivae*, as was the one at ◊Rochester. *Cestretone* 1086.

Cheviot Hills (hills, England/Scotland). The pre-English name is of unknown origin and meaning. *Chiuiet* 1181.

Chichester (city, West Sussex) 'Cissa's Roman town', OE personal name + *ceaster*, 'Roman town'. *Cissa* was one of the sons of Ælla, first king of the South Saxons. The Roman town was called *Noviomagus*, 'new market'. (The same name gave that of *Nijmegen*, in the Netherlands). *Cisseceastre* 895, *Cicestre* 1086.

Chigwell (town, Essex) 'Cicca's stream', OE personal name + *wella*, 'spring', 'stream'. There is no obvious stream here now, although the River Roding runs to the west of the town. *Cingheuuella* 1086, *Chiggewell* 1187.

Chiltern Hills (hills, Oxfordshire/Hertfordshire) 'hill slope', OE or pre-English **celte*, 'hill slope'. The same basic word lies behind the name of ◊Cheltenham. *Ciltern* 1009.

Chingford (town, Greater London) 'shingle ford', OE **cingel*, 'shingle' + *ford*, 'ford'. The 'shingle ford' would have been over the *Ching*, itself named for the town. *Cingefort* 1086, *Chingelford c* 1243.

Chippenham (town, Wiltshire) 'Cippa's river meadow', OE personal name + *hamm*, 'river meadow'. The 'river meadow' would have been in the bend of the Avon here. The same personal name occurs for ◊Sydenham. *Cippanhamme c* 900, *Chipeham* 1086.

Chipping Campden (town, Gloucestershire) '(place by a) valley with enclosures with a market', OE *cēping*, 'market' + *camp*, 'enclosed land' + *denu*, 'valley'. Three other towns have added *Chipping* similarly: *Norton*, Oxfordshire, 'north farmstead', *Ongar*, Essex, 'pasture land', and *Sodbury*, Avon, 'Soppa's fortified place'. *Campedene* 1086, *Chepyng Campedene* 1287.

Chislehurst (district, Greater London) 'gravelly wooded hill', OE *cisel*, 'gravel' + *hyrst*, 'wooded hill'. It is not certain which the original 'gravelly wooded hill' was, although Chislehurst itself is on raised terrain in a still wooded area. *Cyselhyrst* 973.

Chiswick (district, Greater London) 'cheese farm', OE **cīese*, 'cheese' + *wīc*, 'farm'. A name of identical origin, but different form, is ◊Keswick. *Ceswican c* 1000.

Chorley (town, Lancashire) 'clearing of the churls', OE *ceorl*, 'churl', 'peasant' + *lēah*, 'wood'. 'Churls' were freemen, ranking above serfs, who were slaves. *Cp* ◊Chorleywood. *Cherleg* 1246.

Chorleywood (town, Hertfordshire) '(place by a) wood by a clearing of the churls', OE *ceorl*, 'churl', 'peasant' + *lēah*, 'wood' + Middle English *wode*, 'wood'. The original place *Chorley* here gave its name to a wood which then gave the name of the present development. The basic name is exactly the same as that of ◊Chorley, Lancashire. *Cherle* 1278, *Charlewoode* 1524, *Chorley Wood* 1868.

Chorlton cum Hardy (district, Manchester, Greater Manchester) 'Cēolfrith's farmstead with the hard island', OE personal name + *tūn*, 'farmstead' + Latin *cum*, 'with' + OE *heard*, 'hard' + *ēg*, 'island'. The name combines two formerly separate villages. A 'hard island' is an area of firm or stony raised land. The records below are for the separate places. *Cholreton* 1243, *Hardey* 1555.

Christchurch (town, Dorset) 'church of Christ', OE *Crist*, 'Christ' + *cirice*, 'church'. The earlier name of the place was *Twynham*, 'between the rivers' (*ie* Stour and Avon), from OE *betwēonan*, 'between', and *ēa*, 'river' (here in the dative plural, *ēam*). *Christecerce c* 1125.

Chudleigh (town, Devon) 'Ciedda's clearing', OE personal name + *lēah*, 'clearing'. The first part of the name could also represent OE *cēod*, 'hollow', so that the meaning is 'clearing in a hollow'. *Ceddelegam c* 1150.

Chulmleigh (town, Devon) 'Cēolmund's clearing', OE personal name + *lēah*, 'clearing'. This name is identical to the place-name that gave the surname *Cholmondeley*, conventionally pronounced 'Chumley'. *Chalmonleuga* 1086.

Church (town, Lancashire) '(place at the) church', OE *cirice*, 'church'. The original church here probably stood on or near the site of the present St James's Church. *Chirche* 1202.

Church Stretton (town, Shropshire) 'village on a Roman road with a church', OE *strǣt*, 'Roman road' + *tūn*, 'village' + *cirice*, 'church'. The first word distinguishes this Stretton from the neighbouring villages of *All Stretton* and *Little Stretton*. The 'church' is the 12th-century St Lawrence's Church here. *Stratun* 1086, *Chirchestretton* 1337.

Cinderford (town, Gloucestershire) 'cinder ford', OE *sinder*, 'cinders' + *ford*, 'ford'. A 'cinder ford' is one built up with cinders or slag from iron smelting. It would have been over the small stream here that flows through the Forest of Dean to the Severn. *Sinderford* 1258.

Cirencester (town, Gloucestershire) 'Roman town (called) Corinium', Celtic place-name + OE *ceaster*, 'Roman town'. The name of the Roman station is of unknown meaning. The Celtic root word behind it also gave the name of the River *Churn* here. *Korinion c* 150, *Cirenceaster c* 900, *Cirecestre* 1086.

Clackmannan (town, Central) 'stone of Manau', Gaelic *clach*, 'stone' + district name. The 'stone' is a glacial rock in the town centre. *Manau* is the name of the district here. *Clacmanan* 1147.

Clacton-on-Sea (town, Essex) 'estate named after Clacc', OE personal name + *-ing-*, 'named after' + *tūn*, 'estate'. The original *-ing-* of the name has disappeared. The *-on-Sea* is partly commercial, but also distinguishes this Clacton from *Great Clacton* and *Little Clacton*. *Claccingtune c* 1000, *Clachintune* 1086.

Clapham (district, Greater London) 'homestead by the hillock', OE **clopp*, 'hillock' + *hām*, 'homestead'. The 'hillock' is the rising ground on which Clapham lies south of the Thames. *Cloppaham c* 880, *Clopeham* 1086.

Clare (town, Suffolk) '(place by the River) Clare', Celtic river name. The river here now is the Stour, but it must earlier have had a name meaning 'bright', from a Celtic word related to modern Welsh *claer*, 'bright'. The same word gave the name of *Highclere*, Hampshire. *Clara* 1086.

Clay Cross (town, Derbyshire) 'Clay's cross'. The name is first recorded only in 1734, and apparently derives from a local family named *Clay*, who presumably lived by a *cross* or crossroads.

Clayton-le-Moors (town, Lancashire) 'farmstead on clayey soil in the moors', OE *clǣg*, 'clay' + *tūn*, 'farmstead' + French *en le*, 'in the' + *mōr*, 'moor'. The 'moors' are the higher ground between Accrington and Great Harwood. French *en*, 'in', has disappeared. *Cleyton* 1243, *Clayton super Moras* 1284.

Cleckheaton (town, West Yorkshire) 'high farmstead by a hill', OS *klakkr*, 'hill' + OE *hēah*, 'high' + *tūn*, 'farmstead'. The original name was simply *Heaton*. *Hetun* 1086, *Claketon* 1285.

Cleethorpes (town, Humberside) 'hamlets near Clee', OE place-name + OS *thorp*, 'hamlet'. *Clee* was the collective name of three hamlets here, from OE *clǣg*, 'clay', referring to the soil. They were Hole ('hollow place'), Clee (now Old Clee) and Itterby ('outer farm'), all now swallowed up in Grimsby and Cleethorpes itself. *Cleethorpes* is recorded no earlier than the 17th century.

Clerkenwell (district, Greater London) 'well where students come', Middle English *clerc*, 'student' + OE *wella*, 'well'. The first part of the name (which gave modern *clerk*) is here in the plural (*clercen*). The students must have used the well as a congenial meeting place in summer months. *Clerkenwell c* 1150.

Clevedon (town, Avon) '(place by the) hill of the cliffs', OE *clif*, 'cliff' + *dūn*, 'hill'. There are several hills here, and the cliffs behind the town rise quite high. *Clivedon* 1086.

Cleveland (county, England) 'district of cliffs', OE *clif*, 'cliff' + *land*, 'land', 'district'. The county, formed in 1974, takes its name from the *Cleveland* Hills here. *Clivelanda c* 1110.

Cleveleys (town, Lancashire) '(place named after) Cleveley', family name. The name is not recorded before the 20th century, but is perhaps that of a family who originally owned a manor here. They themselves may have come from the village of *Cleveley*, some 10 miles to the east, northwest of Garstang.

Clitheroe (town, Lancashire) 'hill of loose stones', OE **clider*, 'loose stones' + *hōh*, 'hill'. The second part of the name may represent OS *haugr*, with the same meaning. The 'loose stones' would have been the crumbling limestone on which the 12th-century castle was built. *Cliderhou* 1102.

Clovelly (village, Devon) 'cleft in the (hill resembling a) wheel rim', OE *clofa*, 'cleft' + *felg*, 'felly', 'wheel rim'. The name describes a semicircular hill, shaped like the rim of a wheel, with Clovelly in a 'cleft' in it. *Cloveleia* 1086.

Clwyd (county, Wales) '(district of the River) Clwyd', Celtic river name. The county is named for the river here, which enters the sea west of Rhyl. Its own name is the Welsh word for 'hurdle', presumably as hurdles were used to ford it or make a causeway across. The record below is of the river name. *Cloid fluvium* 1191.

Clyde (river, Strathclyde) 'cleansing one', Celtic river name. The name denotes a river that 'washes' as it flows, from a root word indirectly related to English *clean*. *Clota c* 110.

Clyst Honiton (village, Devon). For the origin of this name, *see* ◊Honiton.

Coalbrookdale (village, Shropshire) '(place in the) valley of the cold brook', OE *cald*, 'cold' + *brōc*, 'brook' + modern *dale*, 'valley'. The small river here is actually called the *Coalbrook*. *Caldebrok* 1250, *Colebrookdale* 1868.

Coalville (town, Leicestershire) 'coal(-mining) town'. The name is a modern one, given to the mining settlement that developed round a house called *Coalville* House in the early 19th century.

Coatbridge (town, Strathclyde) 'bridge by (a place called) Coats', OE *cot*, 'shelter' + modern *bridge*. *Coats* was the name of a group of cottages by the Monkland Canal here. *Bridge* was added subsequently. *Coittis* 1584.

Cobham (town, Surrey) 'Cofa's homestead', OE personal name + *hām*, 'homestead'. The first part of the name could also represent OE *cofa*, 'hut', 'shelter'. *Covenham* 1086.

Cockermouth (town, Cumbria) '(place at the) mouth of the (River) Cocker', Celtic river name + OE *mūtha*, 'mouth'. The river name means 'crooked', from a word related to modern Welsh *crwca* in this sense. *Cokyrmoth c* 1150.

Colchester (town, Essex) 'Roman town on the (River) Colne', pre-English river name + OE *ceaster*, 'Roman town'. The river name is of uncertain meaning. It may be simply 'water'. The Roman town here was *Camulodunum*, 'fort of Camulos' (a Celtic war god). Latin links means that the first part of the name may represent a shortened form of *colonia*, 'colony'. *Cp* ◊Lincoln. *Colneceastre* early 10th century, *Colecestra* 1086.

Coleford

Coleford (town, Gloucestershire) '(place by the) coal ford', OE *col*, 'char-coal' + *ford*, 'ford'. A 'coal ford' is one where charcoal would have been carried across a river or a stream, as here. *Coleforde* 1282.

Coleshill (town, Warwickshire) '(place by the) hill on the (River) Cole', Celtic river name + *hyll*, 'hill'. The origin and meaning of the river name are uncertain. *Colleshyl* 799, *Coleshelle* 1086.

Colne (town, Lancashire) '(place by the River) Colne', pre-English river name. The town takes its name from the *Colne* Water. Its own name is of uncertain meaning, but is identical to that of the river that gave the name of ♢Calne. *Calna* 1124.

Colwyn Bay (town, Clwyd) '(place by the River) Colwyn on the bay', Welsh river name + English *bay*. The stream here takes its name from Welsh *colwyn*, 'puppy', alluding to its small size. *Bay* was added in 1866, when the resort developed, to distinguish it from the original village of *Colwyn* (now Old Colwyn). The record refers to this. *Coloyne* 1334.

Colyton (town, Devon) 'farmstead by the (River) Coly', Celtic river name + OE *tūn*, The river name may mean 'narrow', from a word related to modern Welsh *cul* in this sense. *Cp* ♢Kyles of Bute. *Culintona* 946, *Colitone* 1086.

Congleton (town, Cheshire) 'farmstead by the round-topped hill', OE **cung*, 'round-topped hill', *hyll*, 'hill' + *tūn*, 'farmstead'. One of the hills round the town, it is not clear which, must have been known as *Conkhill*, 'round-topped hill'. *Cogeltone* 1086, *Congulton* 13th century.

Conisbrough (town, South Yorkshire) 'king's fortification', OS *konungr*, 'king' + OE *burh*, 'fortification'. The defence here was held by King Harald III (killed 1066), but the name was recorded before his time so must refer to some earlier king. *Cunugesburh c* 1003, *Coningesburg* 1086.

Coniston Water (lake, Cumbria) 'lake by Coniston', OS/OE place-name + *water*. The lake is named after the village of *Coniston* at its northern end. The village name means 'king's manor', 'royal estate', from OS *konungr*, 'king', and OE *tūn*, 'manor'.

Consett (town, Durham) 'headland of (a hill called) Conek', Celtic hill name + OE *hēafod*, 'headland'. The Celtic (or pre-Celtic) hill name means simply 'hill', denoting the one on which the town stands. The first record has *n* miscopied as *v*. *Covekesheued* 1183, *Conekesheued* 1228.

Conwy (town, Gwynedd) '(place on the River) Conwy', Celtic river name. The river name probably means 'famous'. The former name of the town was *Aberconwy*, 'mouth of the Conwy', denoting its location. This was revived for the modern administrative district. *Conovium* 4th century, *Conguoy* 12th century, *Aberconuy*, 12th century, *Conway* 1771.

Corbridge (town, Northumberland) '(place by the) bridge near Corchester', place-name + OE *brycg*, 'bridge'. The town takes its name from a shortened form of the nearby Roman station of *Corstopitum*, now known as *Corchester*, with the 'bridge' that crosses over the Tyne here. The meaning of the Roman name is uncertain. *Corebricg c* 1050.

Corby (town, Northamptonshire) 'Kori's farmstead', OS personal name + *bý*, 'farmstead'. The name of *Corby Glen*, Lincolnshire, 25 miles to the northwest, is identical in origin. *Corbei* 1086.

Corfe Castle (village, Dorset) '(place in the) cutting with a castle', OE **corf*, 'cutting', 'pass' + *castel*, 'castle'. The 'cutting' is the gap in the Purbeck Hills here. The second word refers to the Norman castle. *Corf* 955, *Corffe Castell* 1302.

Cornwall (county, England) '(territory of the) Cornovii Britons', Celtic tribal name + OE *walh*, 'Briton', 'Welshman'. The *Cornovii* lived both here and in the West Midlands and Scotland in pre-English times. Their name means 'peninsula people'. OE *walh*, plural *walas*, was used by the Anglo-Saxons for someone who spoke a Celtic language, unlike themselves. *Cp* ◊Wales. *Cornubia c* 705, *Cornwalas* 891, *Cornualia* 1086.

Corringham (town, Essex) 'homestead of Curra's people', OE personal name + *-inga-*, 'of the people of' + *hām*, 'homestead'. The personal name is conjectural, as is often the case. *Currincham* 1086.

Corsham (town, Wiltshire) 'Cosa's homestead', OE personal name + *hām*, 'homestead'. The personal name could also be *Cossa*. The *r* in the present name is probably the result of Norman influence. Otherwise the name is identical to that of ◊Cosham. *Coseham* 1001, *Cosseham* 1086.

Cosham (town, Hampshire) 'Cossa's homestead', OE personal name + OE *hām*, 'homestead'. The *-ham* of the name could also represent OE *hamm*, 'enclosure'. *Coseham* 1086.

Cotswolds (hills, Gloucestershire) 'Cōd's high forest land', OE personal name + *wald*, 'high forest land'. The Cotswold village of *Cutsdean*, 'Cōd's valley', was named after the same man. *Codesuualt* 12th century.

Coulsdon (district, Greater London) 'Cūthrǣd's hill', OE personal name + *dūn*, 'hill'. The *r* of the personal name became *l* under Norman influence.

Cudredesdune 967, *Colesdone* 1086.

Coventry (city, West Midlands) 'Cofa's tree', OE personal name + *trēow*, 'tree'. A named 'tree' was often the meeting place of the local hundred. However, Coventry was not the centre of a hundred, so here it must have served some other function. *Couentre* 1043, *Couentreu* 1086.

Cowbridge (town, South Glamorgan) '(place by the) cows' bridge'. The name denotes a bridge over the River Ddaw that cows would have crossed on their way to market. The town's Welsh name is *Y Bont-faen*, 'the stone bridge', but there was formerly another bridge here called *Pont y fuwch*, 'cow bridge'.

Cowes (town, Isle of Wight) '(place by sandbanks resembling) cows', OE *cū*, 'cow'. The reference is to the two sandbanks off the mouth of the Medina here, individually named in a text dated 1413 as *Estcowe* and *Westcowe* but now known jointly as *The Cows*. *Cowes* 1771.

Crail (town, Fife) 'rocky place', Gaelic *carr*, 'rock' + *all*, 'rock'. The name has blended two words meaning 'rock', the second now obsolete. *Caraile* (no date).

Cramlington (town, Northumberland) 'farmstead of the dwellers at the cranes' stream', OE *cran*, 'crane' + *wella*, 'stream' + -*inga*-, 'of the people of' + *tūn*, 'farmstead'. This is a possible but not definitive explanation of the name. *Cramlingtuna c* 1130.

Cranbrook (town, Kent) 'brook where cranes are', OE *cran*, 'crane' + *brōc*, 'brook'. A stream near the town is actually called *Crane Brook*. *Cranebroca* 11th century.

Cranleigh (town, Surrey) 'clearing where cranes are', OE *cran*, 'crane' + *lēah*, 'clearing'. The name is found elsewhere, often in the form *Cranley*. *Cranlea* 1166.

Craven (district, North Yorkshire) 'place of garlic', Celtic word. The name comes from a Celtic word related to modern Welsh *craf*, 'garlic'. *Crave* 1086.

Craven Arms (town, Shropshire) '(place by the) Craven Arms (inn)'. The town takes its name from the inn built here in the early 19th century. The inn's own name comes from the Earls of *Craven*, who held the manor of Stokesay near here in the early 17th century.

Crawley (town, West Sussex) 'wood where crows are', OE *crāwe*, 'crow' + *lēah*, 'wood'. The name is found elsewhere, mainly in the south of England. *Crauleia* 1203.

Crayford (district, Greater London) '(place by a) ford over the (River) Cray', Celtic river name + OE *ford*, 'ford'. The river name means 'fresh', 'clean', from a word related to modern Welsh *crai* in this sense. *Creiford* 1199.

Crediton (town, Devon) 'farmstead on the (River) Creedy', Celtic river name + OE *tūn*, 'farmstead'. The river name means 'winding one'. *Cridiantune* 930, *Chritetona* 1086.

Crewe (town, Cheshire) '(place by a) fish trap', Celtic word. The name refers to a basket for catching fish, from a word related to modern Welsh *cryw*, 'creel', 'weir'. This would have been in one of the small streams here. *Creu* 1086.

Crewkerne (town, Somerset) 'house by the hill', Celtic **crug*, 'hill' + OE *ærn*, 'house'. The reference is to one of the hills that surround the town. *Crucern* 9th century, *Cruche* 1086.

Criccieth (town, Gwynedd) 'captives' mound', Welsh *crug*, 'mound' + *caeth*, 'captive'. The name alludes to the Norman castle here, built in the 13th century on a headland (the 'mound'). The second half of the name properly comes from Welsh plural *caith*, 'captives', 'bondsmen'. *Crukeith* 1273.

Cricklewood (district, Greater London) 'curved wood', Middle English *crikeled*, 'curved' + *wode*, 'wood'. The wood here would have had a *crickled* or irregular edge. *Le Crikeldwode* 1294.

Cromarty (town, Highland) 'crooked place by the sea', Old Gaelic *crumb*, 'crooked', Old Irish *bath*, 'sea'. The coastline here is irregular or 'crooked'. The second part of the name was probably influenced by Gaelic *àrd*, 'high'. *Crumbathyn* 1264.

Cromer (town, Norfolk) 'lake where crows are', OE *crāwe*, 'crow' + *mere*, 'lake'. The 'lake' would have been inland from the sea here. *Crowemere* 13th century.

Crook (town, Durham) '(place in a) corner of land', OS *krókr*, 'crook'. The 'crook' would have been a bend in the river here, a tributary of the Wear. The name could equally have come from OE **crōc* in the same sense. The Domesday Book record shows that the name was originally *Crookton*, with OE *tūn*, 'farmstead'. *Cruketona* 1086, *Crok* 1304.

Crosby (town, Merseyside) 'village with a cross', OS *krossa-bý*, 'village with a cross'. Most places of this name are in the north of England, and are often distinguished from one another by additional words. The village of

Little Crosby, north of this Crosby (which is properly *Great Crosby*) still has six original Viking crosses. *Crosebi* 1086.

Crowborough (town, East Sussex) 'hill where crows are', OE *crāwe*, 'crow' + *beorg*, 'hill'. The 'hill' is the elevated site of the town. The record has *n* as a miscopying of *u*. *Cranbergh* 1292.

Crowland (town, Lincolnshire) 'area of land by a (river) bend', OE **crūw*, 'bend' + *land*, 'land'. The original 'bend' by the River Welland here has been obscured through land reclamation. *Cruwland* 8th century, *Croiland* 1086.

Crowthorne (town, Berkshire) 'thorn tree where crows are', OE *crāwe*, 'crow' + *thorn*, 'thorn tree'. The name is first recorded, as now, in 1607, when it relates to an isolated tree at a road junction. The town arose only in the 19th century.

Croydon (town, Greater London) 'valley of wild saffron', OE *croh*, 'wild saffron' + *denu*, 'valley'. The 'wild saffron' would have been used for dyeing and medicinal purposes. OE *croh* is related to modern *crocus*. *Crogedene* 809, *Croindene* 1086.

Cuckfield (town, West Sussex) 'Cuca's open land', OE personal name + *feld*, 'open land'. The name has probably been influenced by *cuckoo*. *Kukefeld c* 1095.

Cullompton (town, Devon) 'farmstead on the (River) Culm', Celtic river name + OE *tūn*, 'farmstead'. The river name means 'winding stream', from a word related to modern Welsh *clwm*, 'knot'. The Domesday Book record has truncated the name. *Columtune c* 880, *Colump* 1086.

Cumberland *See* ◊Cumbria.

Cumbernauld (town, Strathclyde) '(place at the) confluence', Gaelic *comar-an-allt*, 'meeting of the streams'. The record relates to the original confluence. *Cumbenald* 13th century.

Cumbria (county, England) '(territory of the) Cymry', Celtic tribal name. The present county and the historic *Cumberland* have a name of identical origin, from the *Cymry*, the Cumbrian Britons. The tribal name is the same as that of the Welsh people for themselves, meaning 'fellow countrymen'. The records relate to both names. *Cumbria* 8th century, *Cumbra land* 945.

Cwmbran (town, Gwent) 'valley of the (River) Brân', Welsh *cwm*, 'valley' + river name. The river name means 'raven', Welsh *brân*, either referring to its dark waters or serving as a personification. *Bran* exists as a Welsh personal name. The town arose in the 19th century.

D

Dacorum (district, Hertfordshire) '(hundred) of the Danes', Latin *Dacorum*, 'of the Danes'. The name refers to a hundred on the English side of the Danelaw boundary, *ie* one in an Anglo-Saxon region having a Danish overlord. The name is the genitive plural of Latin *Daci*, a name used in error for the Danes in medieval times. (It really means 'Dacians'.) *Danais* 1086, *de hundredo Dacorum* 1196.

Dagenham (district, Greater London) 'Dæcca's homestead', OE personal name + *hām*, 'homestead'. The *n* represents the genitive ending of the personal name. *Dæccanhaam c* 690.

Dalbeattie (town, Dumfries and Galloway), 'field by the birch trees', Gaelic *dail*, 'field' + *beith*, 'birch'. There are still birches here. *Dalbat* 1469.

Dalkeith (town, Lothian) 'field by a wood', Celtic words. The two words that comprise the name are respectively related to modern Welsh *dôl*, 'meadow', and *coed*, 'wood'. The area round the town is still well wooded. *Dolchet* 1144.

Dalston (district, Greater London), 'Dēorlāf's farmstead', OE personal name + *tūn*, 'farmstead'. This name has exactly the same origin as that of ◊Darlaston. *Derleston* 1294.

Dalton-in-Furness (town, Cumbria), 'farmstead in a valley in Furness', OE *dæl*, 'valley' + *tūn*, 'farmstead' + district name. For the origin of the district name, *see* ◊Barrow-in-Furness. *Daltune* 1086, *Dalton in Fournais* 1332.

Darlaston (district, Walsall, West Midlands) 'Dēorlāf's farmstead', OE personal name + *tūn*, 'farmstead'. This name has exactly the same origin as that of ◊Dalston, except here the personal name is better preserved. *Derlaveston* 1262.

Darlington (town, Durham) 'estate named after Dēornōth', OE personal name + *-ing*, 'named after' + *tūn*, 'estate'. The *n* of the personal name became *l* under Norman influence. *Dearthingtun c* 1009.

Dartford (town, Kent) 'ford over the (River) Darent', Celtic river name + OE *ford*, 'ford'. The river name means 'river of oak trees', from a base word related to modern Welsh *derw*, 'oak'. It is unusual for a ford to be named after the river it crosses. *Tarentefort* 1086.

Dartmoor (moor, Devon) 'moor (in the valley) of the (River) Dart', Celtic river name + OE *mōr*, 'moor'. The river name means 'river of oak trees'. *Cp* ◊Dartford. *Dertemora* 1182.

Dartmouth (town, Devon) '(place at the) mouth of the (River) Dart', Celtic river name + OE *mūtha*, 'mouth'. For the meaning of the river name, *see* ◊Dartmoor. *Dertamuthan* 11th century.

Darwen (town, Lancashire) '(place on the River) Darwen', Celtic river name. The river name means 'river where oak trees grow', from a word related to modern Welsh *derwen*, 'oak'. *Cp* ◊Dartford, ◊Derwent Water. *Derewent* 1208.

Datchet (town, Berkshire), Celtic name. The name is probably of Celtic origin although of uncertain meaning. *Deccet*, 10th century, *Daceta* 1086.

Daventry (town, Northamptonshire) '(place at) Dafa's tree', OE personal name + *trēow*, 'tree'. A 'tree' like this was often the meeting place of a hundred. But Daventry was not the centre of a hundred, so the word has some other sense. Dafa may have erected a cross or crucifix here. *Daventrei* 1086.

Dawley (town, Shropshire) 'Dalla's clearing', OE personal name + *lēah*, 'clearing'. The town forms the central area of Telford. *Dalelie* 1086.

Dawlish (town, Devon) '(place by the) Dawlish (Water)', Celtic river name. The *Dawlish* Water, on which the town stands, has a name meaning 'dark stream', from words related to modern Welsh *du*, 'black', and *glais*, 'stream', seen also in the personal name *Douglas*. *Douelis* 1086.

Deal (town, Kent) '(place at the) hollow', OE *dæl*, 'hollow', 'valley'. There is hardly a hollow here now, so there have presumably been changes in the local topography. The Domesday Book record is prefixed by Latin *ad*, 'at'. *Addelam* 1086, *Dela* 1158.

Dee (river, Cheshire/Merseyside), 'holy one', Celtic *deva*, 'goddess'. The river was originally seen as a benevolent goddess, from a word related to English *deity*. *Deoua c* 150.

Delyn (district, Clwyd) '(district of the rivers) Dee and Alun'. The name of the modern administrative district was devised as a blend of two of its rivers, the ◊Dee and the *Alun*, with the latter's name adjusted to *Alyn*, as in the neighbouring district of *Alyn and Deeside*. Welsh *delyn* also happens to be the mutated form of *telyn*, 'harp', the instrument associated with Wales.

Denbigh (town, Clwyd) 'little fort', Welsh *din*, 'fort' + *bych*, 'little'. The 'little fort' would have stood where the ruins of the 12th-century castle stand now. *Cp* the identical name of ◊Tenby. *Dinbych* 1269.

Dent (town, Cumbria), river name. The origin of the name is uncertain. It may derive from an old name of the River ◊Dee here. The town is in a valley called *Dentdale*. *Denet* 1202.

Deptford (district, Greater London) 'deep ford', OE *dēop*, 'deep' + *ford*, 'ford'. The town is at the confluence of the Thames and the Ravensbourne, and the 'deep ford' would have been over the latter. *Depeforde* 1293.

Derby (city, Derbyshire) 'farmstead where deer are kept', OS *djúr*, 'deer' + *bý*, 'farmstead'. This OS name replaced the earlier OE one of *Northworthy*, 'northern enclosure'. The county name *Derbyshire* is first recorded in the 11th century. *Northworthige c* 1000, *Derby* 1086.

Derwent Water (lake, Cumbria) 'lake of (the River) Derwent', Celtic river name + *water*. The lake is named for the river, whose own name means 'river where oak trees grow'. There are several rivers of the name, others being in Derbyshire, Durham and on the North Yorkshire-Humberside border. *Cp* ◊Dartmoor.

Desborough (town, Northamptonshire) 'Dēor's stronghold', OE personal name + *burh*, 'stronghold'. The *r* of the personal name has disappeared in the modern form of the name. *Dereburg* 1086, *Deresburc* 1166.

Devizes (town, Wiltshire) '(place on the) boundaries', Old French *devise*, 'boundary'. The 'boundaries' are those of two hundreds, Potterne and Cannings, that passed through the former Devizes Castle. *Divises* 11th century.

Devon (county, England) '(territory of the) Devonians', OE tribal name. The OE name for the people here was *Defnas*. This evolved from the earlier Celtic name, *Dumnonii*, meaning 'deep ones' (modern Welsh *dwfn*, 'deep'), probably referring to their mining activities. The county name *Devonshire* is first recorded in the 9th century. *Defena*, late 9th century.

Devonport (district, Plymouth, Devon) 'Devon port'. The district was originally known as *Plymouth Dock* when it arose in the 17th century. In 1824 the present name was adopted, implying that the place would be one of the county's leading ports.

Dewsbury (town, West Yorkshire) 'Dewi's stronghold', Old Welsh personal name + OE *burh*, 'stronghold'. The personal name is the equivalent of English *David*. *Deusberia* 1086.

Didcot (town, Oxfordshire) 'Dudda's cottage', OE personal name + *cot*, 'cottage'. The same personal name lies behind the name of ◊Dudley. *Dudecota* 1206.

Dingwall (town, Highland) 'parliament field', OS *thing*, 'parliament' + *vǫllr*, 'field'. The name refers to the regular assembly held here to administer justice and discuss public matters. *Dingwell* 1227.

Disley (town, Cheshire) '(special) clearing', OE *lēah*, 'clearing'. The first part of the name is uncertain. It may represent OE **dystels*, 'mound', 'heap'. *Destesleg c* 1251.

Diss (town, Norfolk) '(place at the) ditch', OE *dīc*, 'ditch', 'dyke'. There must have been an ancient ditch or dyke here at one time. *Dice* 1086.

Dodworth (town, South Yorkshire) 'Dod's enclosure', OE personal name + *worth*, 'enclosure'. The personal name may be *Dod* or *Dodda*. *Dodesuuorde* 1086.

Dolgellau (town, Gwynedd) 'cells in the river bend', Welsh *dôl*, 'loop', 'bend' + *cell*, 'cell'. There must formerly have been monastic cells here at the confluence of the Aran and Wnion. The second part of the name represents plural *cellau*, 'cells'. *Dolkelew* 1254.

Don (river, South Yorkshire/Humberside) 'water', 'river', Celtic river name. The word that gave the name is seen behind the names of rivers elsewhere in Europe, such as the *Don* in Russia and the *Danube* in western Europe.

Doncaster (town, South Yorkshire), 'Roman town on the (River) Don', Celtic river name + OE *ceaster*, 'Roman town'. The Roman town here was called *Danum*, from the river name. For its origin, *see* ◊Don. *Doneceastre* 1002, *Donecastre* 1086.

Dorchester (town, Dorset) 'Roman town of Durnovaria', Celtic placename + OE *ceaster*, 'Roman town'. The name of the Roman settlement may have meant 'place of fist-sized pebbles', from a word related to modern Welsh *dwrn*, 'fist'. The *Dor-* is all that remains of the original. *Dornwaraceaster* 864, *Dorecestre* 1086.

Dorking (town, Surrey) '(settlement of) Deorc's people', OE personal name + *-ingas*, 'people of'. The personal name is from the OE word that gave modern *dark*. *Dorchinges* 1086.

Dorset (county, England) '(territory of the) people round Dorn', Celtic place-name + OE *sǣte*, 'people', 'settlers'. *Dorn* is a short form of *Dornwaraceaster*, the OE name of ◊Dorchester. *Dornsætum* late 9th century.

Dover (town, Kent) '(place by the River) Dour', Celtic river name. The river name means simply 'waters', from a word related to modern Welsh *dwfr*, 'water'. *Dubris* 4th century, *Dofras c* 700, *Dovere* 1086.

Downham Market (town, Norfolk) 'homestead by a hill with a market', OE *dūn*, 'hill' + *hām*, 'homestead' + Middle English *market*, 'market'. The second word was added both to distinguish this Downham from others and to indicate the important presence of a market, which was already here in the 11th century. *Dunham* 1086, *Forum de Dunham c* 1110, *Mercatus de Dunham* 1130.

Droitwich (town, Hereford and Worcester) '(place at) dirty saltworks', OE *drit*, 'dirt' + *wīc*, 'saltworks'. The place was originally *Wich*, then added the defining first part to distinguish it from other saltworks, notably those at ◊Middlewich, ◊Nantwich and ◊Northwich. *Wich* 1086, *Drihtwych* 1347.

Dronfield (town, Derbyshire) 'open land frequented by drones', OE *drān*, 'drone' + *feld*, 'open land'. The *drones* would have been wild male honey-bees. The name is unusual. *Dranefeld* 1086.

Dudley (town, West Midlands) 'Dudda's clearing', OE personal name + *lēah*, 'clearing'. The same personal name gave the name of ◊Didcot. *Dudelei* 1086.

Dufftown (town, Grampian) 'Duff's town'. The town was founded in 1817 by James *Duff*, 4th Earl of Fife, and named after him. *Cp* ◊Macduff.

Dukinfield (town, Greater Manchester) 'open land where ducks are', OE *dūce*, 'duck' + *feld*, 'open land'. The ducks may have been domestic, although most birds and animals in place-names are wild. The *-in-* of the name represents the genitive plural ending of *dūca*, as *dūcena*, 'of ducks'. *Dokenfeld* 12th century.

Dulverton (town, Somerset) 'farmstead by the hidden ford', OE *dīegal*, 'hidden' + *ford*, 'ford' + *tūn*, 'farmstead'. The town is on the edge of Dartmoor, where a ford could well be obscurely located or 'hidden'. *Dolvertune* 1086.

Dulwich (district, Greater London) 'marshy meadow where dill grows', OE *dile*, 'dill' + *wisc*, 'marshy meadow'. The herb dill has long been cultivated for medicinal use. The second part of the name has been influenced by OE *wīc*, 'dwelling'. *Dilwihs* 967.

Dumbarton (town, Strathclyde) 'fort of the Britons', Gaelic *dùn*, 'fort' + *Breatann*, 'Briton'. This was a stronghold of the Strathclyde Britons from the 5th century. The Britons themselves called it *Alclut*, 'rock of the Clyde', referring to Dumbarton Rock. *Cp* ◊Bishop Auckland. *Dumbrethan* late 13th century.

Dumfries (town, Dumfries and Galloway) 'woodland stronghold', Gaelic *dùn*, 'stronghold' + *preas*, 'copse', 'thicket'. The 'stronghold' here was a fort that probably stood in the centre of the oldest part of the town. The second part of the name is related to Welsh *prys*, 'bush', 'wood'. *Dunfres* c 1183.

Dunbar (town, Lothian) 'fort on the height', Gaelic *dùn*, 'fort' + *barr*, 'height'. The 'height' where the 'fort' stood is the rocky headland above the harbour where the ruins of Dunbar Castle now are. *Dynbaer* 709.

Dunblane (town, Central) 'Blaan's hill', Gaelic *dùn*, 'hill' + personal name. The personal name is that of the bishop who had a monastery here in the 6th century. He is better known as St *Blane*. *Dumblann* c 1200.

Dundee (city, Tayside), 'Daig's fort', Gaelic *dùn*, 'fort' + personal name. The 'fort' would have been where Dundee Castle once stood. It is not known who *Daig* was. *Dunde* c 1180.

Dunfermline (town, Fife), '(special) hill', Gaelic *dùn*, 'hill' + unknown word(s). The definitive part of the name has never been satisfactorily explained. *Dumfermelyn* 11th century, *Dumferlin* 1124.

Dungeness (headland, Kent) 'headland by Denge (Marsh)', OE placename + *næss*, 'headland'. The headland takes its name from *Denge Marsh*, whose own name means 'marsh of the valley district', from OE *denu*, 'valley', **gē*, 'district', and *mersc*, 'marsh'. *Dengenesse* 1335.

Dunkeld (town, Tayside) 'fort of the Caledonians', Gaelic *dùn*, 'fort' + tribal name. The 'Caledonians' were the Picts who occupied this region, which later became Perthshire. *Duncalden* 10th century.

Dunmow (town, Essex) 'meadow on the hill', OE *dūn*, 'hill' + **māwe*, 'meadow'. The town is officially *Great Dunmow*, as distinct from the nearby village of *Little Dunmow*, whose name refers to the same hill. *Dunemowe* 951, *Dommauua* 1086.

Dunoon (town, Strathclyde) 'fort by the river', Gaelic *dùn*, 'fort' + *abh*, 'river'. The second part of the name represents *obhainn*, the adjectival form of *abh*. The 'river' is the Clyde. *Dunnon c* 1240, *Dunhoven* 1270.

Duns (town, Borders) '(place by the) hills', Gaelic *dùn*, 'hill'. The name could equally represent OE *dūn*, 'hill'. Either way, an English plural *s* has been added. The town stands at the foot of *Duns Law*.

Dunstable (town, Bedfordshire) 'Dunna's post', OE personal name + *stapol*, 'post'. The 'post' probably marked a boundary, or served as a marker or 'waypost'. Dunstable stands at the intersection of two Roman roads, Watling Steet and the Icknield Way. The Roman camp here was called *Durocobrivis*, 'fort with bridges', presumably referring to some sort of bridge-like structure, since there is no river here. *Dunestaple* 1123.

Durham (city, Durham) 'island with a hill', OE *dūn*, 'hill' + OS *holmr*, 'island'. The 'island' is the high rock (the 'hill') in the bend of the River Wear here. The *n* of *dūn* became *r* under Norman influence. *Dunholm c* 1000.

Dursley (town, Gloucestershire) 'Dēorsige's clearing', OE personal name + *lēah*, 'clearing'. The personal name means literally 'animal victory' (or 'deer victory'), implying a successful hunter. *Dersilege* 1086.

Dyfed (county, Wales) '(territory of the) Demetae', Celtic tribal name. The meaning of the tribal name is uncertain. A link with Irish *diomaite*, 'apart from', has been suggested, referring to people who lived away from their native Ireland on the southwest peninsula of Wales. *Demetae c* 150.

Dymchurch (town, Kent) 'church of the judge', OE *dēma*, 'judge' + *cirice*, 'church'. It is possible the first part of the name represents the OE personal name *Dema*. *Deman circe c* 1100.

E

Ealing (town, Greater London) '(place of) Gilla's people', OE personal name + *-ingas*, 'people of'. Despite the proximity of the Thames, the name has no connections with eels, as sometimes proposed. *Gillingas c* 698.

Easington (town, Durham) 'estate named after Ēsa', OE personal name + *-ing-*, 'named after' + *tūn, 'estate'*. There are several places of the name, but not always with this meaning. Easington, Oxfordshire, has the same personal name but ends in OE *dūn*, 'hill'. *Esingtun c* 1050.

Eastbourne (town, East Sussex) '(place at the) eastern stream', OE *ēast*, 'east' + *burna*, 'stream'. The place was originally *Bourne*, but later added *east* to be distinguished from *Westbourne*, West Sussex. *Burne* 1086, *Estbourne* 1310.

East Dereham (town, Norfolk) 'eastern deer enclosure', OE *ēast*, 'east' + *dēor*, 'deer' + *hamm*, 'enclosure'. The final part of the name could equally be OE *hām*, 'homestead'. The town is over 20 miles *east* of the village of *West Dereham*. *Derham* 1086, *Estderham* 1428.

East Grinstead (town, West Sussex) 'eastern green place', OE *ēast*, 'east' + *grēne*, 'green' + *stede*, 'place'. A 'green place' is grassy pastureland. The town is some 20 miles *east* of the village of *West Grinstead*. *Grenesteda* 1121, *Estgrenested* 1271.

East Kilbride (town, Strathclyde) 'eastern church of (St) Brigid', OE *ēast*, 'east' + Gaelic *cill*, 'church' + saint's name. The place was originally *Kilbride*, but later added *East* for distinction from *West Kilbride*. *Kellebride* 1180.

Eastleigh (town, Hampshire) 'eastern clearing', OE *ēast*, 'east' + *lēah*, 'clearing'. The town developed only in the 19th century, so the records below relate to the original location. It is not certain where the corresponding 'western clearing' was. *East lea* 932, *Estleie* 1086.

East Molesey (town, Surrey) 'eastern island of Mūl', OE *ēast* + personal name + *ēg*, 'island'. The 'island' here is a raised area in marshland by the

River *Mole*, which gets its name from *Molesey*. The place is *east* of *West Molesey*. *Muleseg* 672, *Molesham* 1086.

Eastwood (town, Nottinghamshire) 'eastern clearing', OE *ēast*, 'east' + OS *thveit*, 'clearing'. Historic records of the name show that the *wood* was not in the original. It may have arisen by association with the many names locally in *-ley*, from OE *lēah*, 'wood', 'clearing'. *Estewic* 1086, *Estweit* 1165, *Eastwait alias Eastwood* 1608.

Ebbw Vale (town, Gwent) 'valley of the (River) Ebwy', Celtic river name + English *vale*. The river name may mean 'horse river', from a word related to modern Welsh *ebol*, 'colt'. This could denote a river where horses regularly worked or drank. *Vale* was added when the town developed in the 19th century. The record relates only to the river. *Eboth* 1101.

Ecclefechan (town, Dumfries and Galloway) 'little church', Celtic words. The name comprises words related to modern Welsh *eglwys*, 'church' (Latin *ecclesia*), and *bychan*, 'little'. *See also* ◊Eccles.

Eccles (town, Greater Manchester) 'church', Celtic word. The Celtic word, a borrowing of Latin *ecclesia*, denotes a Romano-British Christian church. *Cp* ◊Eccleston. *Eccles c* 1200.

Eccleston (town, Lancashire) 'farmstead by a church', Celtic word + OE *tūn*, 'farmstead'. For the first part of the name, which is found elsewhere, *see* ◊Eccles. *Aycleton* 1094.

Edenbridge (town, Kent) 'Eadhelm's bridge', OE personal name + *brycg*, 'bridge'. The River *Eden* here gets its name from the place, not the other way round. *Eadelmesbregge* 12th century.

Edgbaston (district, Birmingham, West Midlands) 'Ecgbald's farmstead', OE personal name + *tūn*, 'farmstead'. The Domesday Book record below has an incorrect version of the personal name. The *E* has been miscopied as *C*, and *d* as the two letters *el*. *Celboldestone* 1086, *Egbaldestone* 1184.

Edgware (district, Greater London) 'Ecgi's wear', OE personal name + *werr*, 'weir'. The 'weir' would have been a fishing enclosure in what is now Edgware Brook. *Ægces wer c* 975.

Edinburgh (city, Lothian) 'fort of Eidyn', Celtic place-name + OE *burh*, 'fort'. The name is popularly associated with *Edwin*, 7th-century king of Northumbria. But it was recorded before his time. *Eidyn* may mean 'fort on a slope', referring to Castle Rock. In the first record, *Din* is the Celtic word for 'fort' that was later replaced by OE *burh*. *Din Eidyn* c 600, *Edenburge* 1126.

Edmonton (town, Greater London) 'Eadhelm's farmstead', OE personal name + *tūn*, 'farmstead'. The personal name is the same as the one that gave ◊Edenbridge. *Adelmetone* 1086.

Egham (town, Surrey) 'Ecga's homestead', OE personal name + *hām*, 'homestead'. The personal name means 'sword' (literally 'edge'), from OE *ecg*, as in modern *Egbert*. *Egeham* 933, 1086.

Egremont (town, Cumbria) 'pointed hill', Old French *aigre*, 'sharp' + *mont*, 'hill'. There is no obvious 'pointed hill' here, but the reference must be to the site of the former Norman castle. The name was probably imported by the Normans from *Aigremont*. *Egremont* c 1125.

Elgin (town, Grampian) 'little Ireland', Gaelic place-name + diminutive suffix *-in*. The main part of the name represents *Ealg*, an early Gaelic name for Ireland. The name would have been given by Scots who had emigrated from Ireland, denoting a 'home from home'. (*Cp New England* in America.) *Elgin* 1136.

Elland (town, West Yorkshire) 'land by the river', OE *ēa*, 'river' + *land*, 'land'. The name probably refers to a stretch of specially cultivated land by the River Calder here. *Elant* 1086.

Ellesmere (town, Shropshire) 'Elli's lake', OE personal name + *mere*, 'lake'. The lake in question is the one known as The Mere to the east of the town. The Domesday Book record has the *r* as *l*. *Ellesmeles* 1086, *Ellesmera* 1172.

Ellesmere Port (town, Cheshire) 'port by (the) Ellesmere (Canal)'. The name is a modern one, given in the early 19th century to the town that had arisen at the junction of the Ellesmere Canal and the Mersey.

Elmbridge (district, Surrey) '(district of the) bridge over the (River) Emel', Celtic river name + OE *brycg*, 'bridge'. The *Emel* is the former name of the *Mole* (*see* ◊East Molesey), perhaps meaning 'misty'. The 'bridge' was probably where Albany Bridge takes the A244 over the river today. The name as a whole is an old hundred name, revived for the modern administrative district.

Ely (city, Cambridgeshire) 'district where eels are', OE *ǣl*, 'eel' + **gē*, 'district'. The second part of the name was later taken to represent OE *īeg*, 'island', which certainly suits Ely's location on raised land in the Fens. However, it is the 'eels' that gave the name. *Elge* 731, *Elyg* 1086.

Emsworth (town, Hampshire) 'Æmele's enclosure', OE personal name + *worth*, 'enclosure'. The River *Ems* here takes its name from the place. *Emeleswurth* 1224.

Enfield (town, Greater London) 'Eana's open land', OE personal name + *feld*, 'open land' The first part of the name could also represent OE *ēan*, 'lamb', so that the name means 'open land where lambs are reared'. *Enefelde* 1086.

England (country, Great Britain) 'land of the Angles', OE tribal name + *land*, 'land'. The first part of the name represents OE *Engle*, 'Angles', referring to the people who came to Britain from what is now *Angeln*, a district in Schleswig, Germany, south of the border with Denmark. Their own name means '(people of the) angle', alluding to the local topography. *Englaland c* 890.

Ennerdale Water (lake, Cumbria) 'lake in Anundr's valley', OS personal name + *dalr*, 'valley' + English *water*. The river in this valley is the *Ehen*, a name of possibly Celtic origin but unknown meaning. It is represented in the second record, both of which relate to the valley. *Anenderdale c* 1135, *Eghnerdale* 1321.

Epping (town, Essex) '(place of the) people of the lookout', OE *yppe*, 'lookout place' + *-ingas*, 'people of''. The 'lookout' may have been the ancient hill fort known as Ambresbury Banks, south of the town in what is left of Epping Forest. OE *yppe* is related to modern *up*. Cp ◊Uppingham. *Eppinges* 1086.

Epsom (town, Surrey) 'Ebbe's homestead', OE personal name + *hām*, 'homestead'. The personal name may originally have been *Ebbi*. The Domesday Book record has substituted *v* for *b*. *Ebbesham c* 973, *Evesham* 1086.

Epworth (town, Humberside) 'Eoppa's enclosure', OE personal name + *worth*, 'enclosure'. The personal name is found elsewhere, for example for *Epwell*, Oxfordshire. *Epeurde* 1086.

Erith (district, Greater London) 'gravelly landing place', OE *ēar*, 'gravel' + *hȳth*, 'landing place'. The name could denote either a gravelly landing place or a place where gravel was landed. Erith is on the Thames. *Earhyth c* 960, *Erhede* 1086.

Ermine Street (Roman road, England) 'Roman road of Earna's people', OE personal name + *-inga-*, 'of the people of' + *strēt*, 'Roman road'. The same name lies behind that of *Arrington*, Cambridgeshire, and doubtless it originally applied to the stretch of Ermine Street here. The name would then have been extended to the whole road from London to the Humber. It was later transferred to another *Ermine Street*, running from Silchester, Hampshire, to Gloucester. *Earninga stræt* 955.

Esher (town, Surrey) 'district where ash trees grow', OE *æsc*, 'ash tree' + *scearu*, 'district'. The Domesday Book record has *l* for *r*. *Æscæron* 1005, *Aissele* 1086.

Essex (county, England) '(territory of the) East Saxons', OE *ēast* + tribal name. The *Saxons* (OE *Seaxe*) perhaps get their name from the type of knife that was their usual weapon, from a word related to modern English *saw*. *East Seaxe* late 9th century, *Exsessa* 1086.

Eton (town, Berkshire) 'farmstead by the river', OE *ēa*, 'river' + *tūn*, 'farmstead'. The 'river' here is the Thames. *Ettone* 1086.

Everton (district, Liverpool, Merseyside) 'farmstead where wild boars are', OE *eofor*, 'wild boar' + *tūn*, 'farmstead'. The name does not mean that boars were kept on the farm but that wild boars were seen there. *Evretone* 1094.

Evesham (town, Hereford and Worcester) 'Eof's riverside land', OE personal name + *hamm*, 'riverside land'. The town is in a bend of the River Avon. *Eveshomme* 709, *Evesham* 1086.

Ewell (town, Surrey) '(place at the) river source', OE *æwell*, 'river source'. The OE word that gave the name is a compound of *ēa*, 'river', and *wella*, 'source'. The reference is to the stream called the Hogsmill River, which rises here. The Domesday Book record has an added *t*, perhaps because the name was understood as *Atwell*, '(place) at the spring'. *Euuelle* 933, *Etwelle* 1086.

Exeter (city, Devon) 'Roman town on the (River) Exe', Celtic river name + OE *ceaster*, 'Roman town'. The river name means simply 'water', from a Celtic word related to modern Irish *uisce* in this sense. The Roman town here was *Isca Dumnoniorum*, the first word representing the river name, the second meaning 'Dumnonii', the people who gave the name of ◊Devon. *Iska c* 150, *Exanceaster c* 900, *Execestre* 1086.

Exmoor (moor, Somerset/Devon) 'moor by the (River) Exe', Celtic river name + OE *mōr*, 'moor'. The River *Exe* (*see* ◊Exeter) rises on the moor. *Exemora* 1204.

Exmouth (town, Devon) '(place) at the mouth of the Exe', Celtic river name + OE *mūtha*, 'mouth'. *See* ◊Exeter for the meaning of the river name. *Exanmutha c* 1025.

Eye (town, Suffolk) '(place at the) island', OE *ēg*, 'island'. The 'island' here is an area of higher ground by the River Dove among a network of streams. *Eia* 1086.

Eyemouth (town, Borders) '(place at the) mouth of the Eye (Water)', OE river name + *mūtha*, 'mouth'. The river name means simply 'river', from OE *ēa*, 'river'.

Eynsham (town, Oxfordshire) 'Ægen's enclosure', OE personal name + *hamm*, 'enclosure', 'riverside land'. If the name refers to riverside land, the river in question could be either the Thames or the Evenlode. *Egenes homme* 864, *Eglesham* 1086, *Ensham* 1868.

F

Failsworth (town, Greater Manchester) 'fenced enclosure', OE *fĕgels, 'fence' + worth, 'enclosure'. It is not certain what type of 'fence' was involved here. *Fayleswrthe* 1212.

Fairford (town, Gloucestershire) 'fair ford', OE fæger, 'fair' + ford, 'ford'. A 'fair' ford is a clear and clean one, in this case over the River Coln. The opposite name would be *Fulford*, 'foul ford'. *Fagranforda* 862, *Fareforde* 1086.

Fair Isle (island, Shetland) 'island of sheep', OS faar, 'sheep' + ey, 'island'. The name is identical in meaning to that of the *Faroe* Islands, which were also settled by the Scandinavians. *Fároy* 1350.

Fakenham (town, Norfolk) 'Facca's homestead', OE personal name + hām, 'homestead'. The en represents the genitive ending of the personal name. *Fachenham* 1086.

Falkirk (town, Central) 'speckled church', OE fā, 'variegated' + cirice, 'church'. A 'speckled church' is one built from mottled stone. The first record of the name below is Gaelic, the second Latin, the third French, all with the same meaning. *Egglesbreth* 1065, *varia capella* 1166, *vaire chapelle* late 13th century.

Falmouth (town, Cornwall) '(place at the) mouth of the (River) Fal', river name + OE mūtha, 'mouth'. The origin and meaning of the river name is uncertain. The letter f is rare in Celtic languages, which the name might otherwise be. *Falemuth* 1235.

Fareham (town, Hampshire) 'homestead where ferns grow', OE fearn, 'fern' + hām, 'homestead'. The name was originally *Farnham*, but the n has dropped out. *Fearnham* c 970, *Fernham* 1086.

Faringdon (town, Oxfordshire) 'hill where ferns grow', OE fearn, 'fern' + dūn, 'hill'. As early records of the name show, the -ing- was not in the original. *Færndunæ* c 971, *Ferendone* 1086.

Farnborough (town, Hampshire) 'hill where ferns grow', OE *fearn*, 'fern' + *beorg*, 'hill'. The 'hill' here is probably the lowish one that has Farnborough Park at its southern end. *Ferneberga* 1086.

Farne Islands (islands, Northumberland) 'fern islands', OE *fearn*, 'fern'. It is possible the name is of Celtic origin. If so, its meaning is uncertain. *Farne c* 700.

Farnham (town, Surrey) 'riverside land where ferns grow', OE *fearn*, 'fern' + *hamm*, 'river meadow'. The river here is the Wey. *Fernham c* 686, *Ferneham* 1086.

Farnworth (town, Greater Manchester) 'enclosure where ferns grow', OE *fearn*, 'fern' + *worth*, 'enclosure'. The name of *Farnworth*, Cheshire, 20 miles to the southwest, is of identical origin. *Farnewurd* 1185.

Faversham (town, Kent) 'homestead of the smith', OE **fæfer*, 'smith' + *hām*, 'homestead'. Metal workings are believed to have been here since Roman times. The OE word for 'smith' comes from Latin *faber*. *Fefresham* 811, *Faversham* 1086.

Felixstowe (town, Suffolk) 'Filica's place', OE personal name + *stōw*, 'place'. The personal name came to be associated with that of St *Felix*, first bishop of East Anglia. *Filchestou* 1254.

Feltham (district, Greater London) 'homestead where mullein grows', OE *felte*, 'mullein' + *hām*, 'homestead'. 'Mullein' is a plant of the *Verbascum* genus. It is possible that the first part of the name is actually OE *feld*, 'open land', while the second could be *hamm*, 'enclosure'. *Feltham* 969, *Felteham* 1086.

Ferryhill (town, Durham) 'wooded hill', OE *fergen*, 'wooded hill' + *hyll*, 'hill'. The original name, already implying 'hill', was shortened to its first part, and the actual word for 'hill' was explicitly added subsequently. The town is on the end of a ridge. *Feregenne* 10th century, *Ferye on the Hill* 1316.

Fife (region, Scotland) 'Fib's (territory)', personal name. It is not certain who *Fib* was, or even how his name was spelt. *Fib c* 1150, *Fif* 1165.

Filey (town, North Yorkshire) 'five clearings', OE *fíf*, 'five' + *lēah*, 'clearing'. A quite different meaning has also been proposed: 'promontory (shaped like a) sea monster', from OE *fífel*, 'sea monster', and *ēg*, 'island', 'promontory'. If the latter, the reference would be to Filey Rigg, a rocky ridge projecting some distance into the sea here. *Fiuelac* 1086, *Fivelai*, 12th century.

Finchley (district, Greater London) 'clearing where finches are', OE *finc*, 'finch' + *lēah*, 'clearing'. Similar names are found elsewhere, but sometimes the 'finch' may be a personal name, as for *Finchingfield*, Essex, 'open land of Finc's people'. *Finchelee c* 1208.

Fishguard (town, Dyfed) 'fish yard', OS *fiskr*, 'fish' + *garthr*, 'yard'. A 'fish yard' is an enclosure in which fish are caught or are kept after being caught. The Welsh name of the port is *Abergwaun*, '(place at the) mouth of the (River) Gwaun', with the river's name representing Welsh *gwaun*, 'moor', 'meadow'. *Fissigart* 1200.

Flamborough Head (headland, Humberside) 'headland by Flamborough', OE *hēafod*, head + place-name. The headland is named after the village of *Flamborough*, its own name meaning 'Fleinn's stronghold', from an OS personal name and OE *burh*, 'stronghold'. The headland name is first recorded in the 14th century, and the record relates to the village. *Flaneburg* 1086.

Fleet (town, Hampshire) '(place at the) stream', OE *flēot*, 'stream', 'pool'. The reference is to the stream here. The OE word gave the name of the small river after which London's *Fleet* Street is named. *Flete* 1313.

Fleetwood (town, Lancashire) 'Fleetwood's (place)', family name. The town is modern, and takes its name from Sir Peter *Fleetwood*, who laid it out in 1836.

Flint (town, Clwyd) '(place on) hard rock', OE *flint*, 'flint'. The name refers to the hard rock here on which Flint Castle was built. *Le Flynt* 1277.

Folkestone (town, Kent) 'Folca's stone', OE personal name + *stān*, 'stone'. The 'stone' would have been the meeting place of a hundred. *Folcanstan c* 697, *Fulchestan* 1086.

Fordingbridge (town, Hampshire) 'bridge of the people by the ford', OE *ford*, 'ford' + *-inga-*, 'of the people of' + *brycg*, 'bridge'. It may well have been these people who built the first bridge to replace the ford over the Avon here. *Fordingebrige* 1086.

Forest of Dean (forest, Gloucestershire) 'forest of the valley', OE **forst*, 'forest' + *denu*, 'valley'. Many places in and around the wooded region here have *Dean* names, such as *Little Dean*, *Mitcheldean* ('Great Dean') and *West Dean*. *foresta de Dene* 12th century.

Forfar (town, Tayside) 'wood on a ridge', Old Gaelic *fothir*, 'wood' +

fàire, 'ridge'. This is so far only a tentative explanation of the name. *Forfare c* 1200.

Formby (town, Merseyside) 'Forni's farmstead', OS personal name + *bý*, 'farmstead'. The name could also mean 'old farmstead', with the first part representing OS *forn*, 'old'. *Fornebei* 1086.

Forres (town, Grampian) '(place) below the shrubs', Gaelic *fo*, 'below' + *ras*, 'shrub', 'underwood'. The town is in a sheltered location near the mouth of the River Findhorn. *Forais c* 1195.

Forth (river, Central) 'silent one', Celtic word. The name alludes to the river's quiet current. The word that gave it is related to modern Irish *bodhaire*, 'deafness'. *Forthin c* 1200.

Fortrose (town, Highland) '(place) below the promontory', Gaelic *foterros*, 'subsidiary cape'. The Gaelic word that gave the name itself comprises a blend of *foter*, comparative of *fo*, 'below', and *ros*, 'promontory'. *Forterose* 1455.

Fort William (town, Highland) 'William's fort', personal name + *fort*. The town takes its name from the fortress rebuilt here in 1690 and named after *William* III.

Fosse Way (Roman road, England) 'way with a ditch', OE **foss*, 'ditch' + modern *way*. The Roman road runs from Devon to Lincoln and is so called from the ditch it has on either side. The OE word may have come from Latin *fossa* or a similar Celtic word. *strata publica de Fosse* 956.

Foula (island, Shetland) 'bird island', OS *fugl*, 'bird' + *ey*, 'island'. The island is noted for its sea birds.

Foulness (island, Essex) 'bird promontory', OE *fugol*, 'bird' + *næss*, 'promontory'. The island (originally a peninsula) is well known for its wildfowl. *Fughelnesse* 1215.

Fowey (town, Cornwall) '(place by the River) Fowey', Cornish river name. The river name probably derives from an Old Cornish word meaning 'beech tree', related to Latin *fagus*, with the final *-ey* meaning simply 'river'. *Fawe c* 1200.

Fraserburgh (town, Grampian) 'Fraser's town', family name + OE *burh*, 'town'. The town takes its name from Sir Alexander *Fraser*, who in the early 16th century built a harbour here and founded a new town on the site of a place known as *Faithlie*. *The toun and burghe of Faythlie, now callit Fraserburghe* 1597.

Freshwater (village, Isle of Wight) '(place by the river of) fresh water', OE *fersc*, 'fresh' + *wæter*, 'water'. The reference is to the River Yare here, which was probably originally known as the *Freshwater*. See ◊Yarmouth. *Frescewatre* 1086.

Frimley (town, Surrey) 'Fremma's clearing', OE personal name + *lēah*, 'clearing'. There are many *-ley* names in the locality. See ◊Camberley. *Fremle* 1203.

Frinton-on-Sea (town, Essex) 'Fritha's farmstead', OE personal name + *tūn*, 'farmstead'. Another interpretation could be 'protected farmstead', with the first part of the name representing OE **frithen*, 'protected'. The *-on-Sea* suffix is basically commercial, designed to attract visitors to the resort. *Frientuna* 1086.

Frodsham (town, Cheshire) 'Frōd's homestead', OE personal name + *hām*, 'homestead'. The second part of the name could equally be OE *hamm*, here best rendered 'promontory', from the town's location on the banks of the Weaver at its confluence with the Mersey. *Frotesham* 1086.

Frome (town, Somerset) '(place on the River) Frome', Celtic river name. The river name means 'fair', 'brisk', from a word related to modern Welsh *ffraw* in this sense. The reference is to the current. *Froom* 8th century.

Fulham (district, Greater London) 'Fulla's riverside land', OE personal name + *hamm*, 'riverside land'. Fulham is in a bend of the Thames. *Fulanham c* 705, *Fuleham* 1086.

Fylde (district, Lancashire) 'plain', OE *filde*, 'plain'. The OE word is related to *feld*, open land, and so to modern *field*. *Filde* 1246.

G

Gainsborough (town, Lincolnshire) 'Gegn's stronghold', OE personal name + *burh*, 'stronghold'. The personal name, as often, is a short form of a longer name, such as *Gænbeald*. *Gainesburg* 1086.

Galashiels (town, Borders) 'shelters by the Gala (Water)', pre-English river name + Middle English *schele*, 'hut', 'shieling'. The 'shelters' would have been used by shepherds in the summer months here. The meaning of the river name is uncertain. *Galuschel* 1237.

Galloway (district, Dumfries and Galloway) 'stranger Gaels', Gaelic tribal name. The *Gall-Ghóidhil* were the people of mixed Irish and Scandinavian descent who settled here from the 9th century. They were so named by the Scots, who regarded them as foreigners. *Galweya c* 970.

Galston (town, Strathclyde) 'village of the strangers', Gaelic *gall*, 'stranger' + OE *tūn*, 'village'. The name refers to invaders or 'immigrants' of a different background to the native Scots. *Gauston* 1260.

Garforth (town, West Yorkshire) 'Gæra's ford', OE personal name + *ford*, 'ford'. The first part of the name could also represent OE *gāra*, 'triangular piece of land' (modern *gore*). *Gereford* 1086.

Gatehouse of Fleet (town, Dumfries and Galloway) 'gatehouse by (the Water of) Fleet', English *gatehouse* + river name. *Gatehouse* does not mean 'house by a gate' but 'house by a road' (OS *gata*, 'road'). There was originally a single lonely house by the road here. The river name may derive from OE *flēot* or OS *fljot*, both meaning simply 'river'.

Gateshead (town, Tyne and Wear) 'goat's headland', OE *gāt*, 'goat' + *hēafod*, 'headland'. Either goats were kept on the headland here or a goat's head was placed here for some religious reason, perhaps as part of a sacrificial rite. *Gatesheued* 1196.

Gatwick (airport, West Sussex) 'goat farm', OE *gāt*, 'goat' + *wīc*, 'farm'. A 'goat farm' was one that specialized in breeding and rearing goats. *Gatwik* 1241.

Gerrards Cross (town, Buckinghamshire) 'Gerrard's cross', family name + modern *cross*. There was a family named *Jarrard* or *Gerrard* here in the 17th century. The 'cross' could have been a boundary marker or one by a crossroads. *Gerards Cross* 1692.

Gillingham (town, Kent) 'homestead of Gylla's people', OE personal name + *-inga-*, 'of the people of' + *hām*, 'homestead'. Both this town and *Gillingham*, Dorset, have names of identical origin. *Gyllingeham* 10th century, *Gelingeham* 1086.

Glamorgan (county, Wales) 'Morgan's shore', Welsh *glan*, 'shore' + personal name. *Morgan* was a 7th-century prince of Gwent. The original county is now divided into *Mid Glamorgan*, *South Glamorgan* and *West Glamorgan*.

Glasgow (city, Strathclyde) 'green hollow', Celtic words. The 'green hollow' would have been a natural feature here. The words that comprise the name are related to modern Welsh *glas*, 'green', 'greenish grey', and *cau*, 'hollow'. *Glasgu* 1136.

Glastonbury (town, Somerset) 'stronghold of the Glaston people', Celtic place-name + OE *-inga-*, 'of the people of' + *burh*, 'stronghold'. *Glaston* may mean 'place where woad grows', from a word related to modern Welsh *glas*, 'blue'. *Glastingburi* 725, *Glæstingeberia* 1086.

Glenrothes (town, Fife) 'valley of Rothes', English *glen* + aristocratic title. Glenrothes arose as a New Town in 1948 and was give a contrived name, from *glen* and the earls of *Rothes*, who have a historic connection with the locality. There is no obvious glen (valley) here.

Glossop (town, Derbyshire) 'Glott's valley', OE personal name + *hop*, 'valley'. The town is in a narrow valley at the edge of the Peak District. *Glosop* 1086, *Glotsop* 1219.

Gloucester (city, Gloucestershire) 'Roman town (called) Glevum', Celtic place-name + OE *ceaster*, 'Roman town'. *Glevum* probably means 'bright place', from a word related to modern Welsh *gloyw*, 'bright'. The reference is to the river here (the Severn). No doubt the Anglo-Saxons associated the name with OE *glēow*, 'play', 'sport' (modern *glee*). The county name, *Gloucestershire*, is first recorded in the 11th century. *Glowecestre* 1086.

Godalming (town, Surrey) '(settlement of) Godhelm's people', OE personal name + *-ingas*, 'people of'. In the first record below, the *-um* represents the dative plural ending required after *æt*, 'at'. *æt Godelmingum* c 880, *Godelminge* 1086.

Godmanchester (town, Cambridgeshire) 'Godmund's Roman settlement', OE personal name + *ceaster*, 'Roman settlement'. The name of the Roman station here was probably *Durovigutum*, comprising a Celtic word meaning 'fort' followed by what may be a personal name. *Godmundcestre* 1086.

Golders Green (district, Greater London) 'Golder's green', family name + OE *grēne*, 'green'. A family named *Golder* or *Godyere* (modern *Goodyear*) lived by the green here some time before the 17th century. *Golders Greene* 1612.

Goldthorpe (town, South Yorkshire) 'Golda's outlying farmstead', OE personal name + OS *thorp*, 'outlying farmstead'. The OE equivalent name would be *Goldstock*, with OE *stoc*, 'outlying settlement'. *Goldetorp* 1086.

Golspie (town, Highland) 'Gold's farm', OS personal name + *bý*, 'farm'. Further south, in the Danelaw, the name would probably have been *Goldsby*. *Goldespy* 1330.

Goole (town, Humberside) '(place by the) stream', Middle English *goule*, 'stream'. The name relates to the town's location on the River Ouse, with the original 'stream' perhaps being the one that was straightened to form the present Dutch River. Modern *gully* is a related word. *Gulle* 1362.

Gorleston-on-Sea (town, Norfolk) 'Gurl's farmstead', OE personal name + *tūn*, 'farmstead'. The personal name is conjectural. The *-on-sea* suffix is mainly commercial. *Gorlestuna* 1086.

Gosforth (town, Tyne and Wear) 'ford where geese are', OE *gōs*, 'goose' + *ford*, 'ford'. The geese may have been wild or domesticated. If the latter, the ford would have been the one where they were driven over one of the two streams here. *Goseford* 1166.

Gosport (town, Hampshire) 'goose market', OE *gōs*, 'goose' + *port*, 'market town'. The fact that the town is also a port is coincidental to the name. *Goseport* 1250.

Gower Peninsula (peninsula, West Glamorgan) 'crooked peninsula', Welsh *gŵyr*, 'crooked', 'sloping' + English *peninsula*. The peninsula has an irregular coastline.

Gowerton (town, West Glamorgan), 'Gower town'. The name is modern, for the town that developed on the ◊Gower Peninsula in the 19th century.

Grampians (mountains, Scotland). The name is of uncertain origin and meaning. It is possible that 16th-century antiquarians adapted it from *Mons*

Graupius, a name mentioned by Tacitus in the 1st century AD for Bennachie, which is not actually in the Grampians. The former name for the area was *The Mounth*, from Gaelic *monadh*, 'hilly district'.

Grangemouth (town, Central) '(place at the) mouth of the Grange (Burn)', river name + OE *mūtha*, 'mouth'. The river was itself named after the *grange* of Newbattle Abbey here.

Grange-over-Sands (town, Cumbria) '(place at the) outlying farm over the sands', Middle English *grange*, 'outlying farm'. The 'outlying farm' belonged to Cartmel Priory here. The name was originally *Grange*, and the two further words refer to its location across the sands of Morecambe Bay. *Grange* 1491.

Grantchester (village, Cambridgeshire) '(place of the) settlers on the (River) Granta', Celtic river name + OE *sǣte*, 'settlers'. The *-chester* misleadingly suggests a Roman settlement. The river name, which gave the original name of ◊Cambridge, may mean 'fenny one'. Cambridge is only 2 miles away. *Granteseta* 1086.

Grantham (town, Lincolnshire) 'Granta's homestead', OE personal name + *hām*, 'homestead'. It is possible that the first part of the name actually represents OE **grand*, 'gravel', referring to the land by the River Witham on which the town originally arose. *Grantham* 1086.

Grantown-on-Spey (town, Highland) 'Grant's town on (River) Spey', family name + river name. The town arose as a model village laid out on the River Spey in 1765 by James *Grant*. Hence its name. The meaning of the river name, which may be pre-Celtic, is unknown.

Grasmere (lake, Cumbria) 'grassy lake', OE *gres*, 'grass' + *sǣ*, 'lake' + *mere*, 'lake'. The name seems to have evolved from an addition of *-mere*, 'lake', to a word that already meant this (modern *sea*). A 'grassy lake' is either one with good pastureland or one with grass-like vegetation in its waters. *Gressemere* 1245.

Gravesend (town, Kent) '(place at the) end of the grove', OE *grāf*, 'grove' + *ende*, 'end'. The original 'grove' or copse was probably located to the east of the present town, where the Fort Gardens are today. The Domesday Book record of the name has a wrong second part. *Gravesham* 1086, *Grauessend* 1157.

Grays (town, Essex) 'de Grai's (place)', family name. The original name of the town was *Grays Thurrock*, the latter word representing OE *thurruc*,

'bilge', 'place where dirty water collects'. (The reference was to the marshland west of Tilbury.) The first word comes from the name of the Norman
de Grai family, who were here in the 13th century. *Turruc* 1086,
Turrokgreys 1248.

Great Driffield (town, Humberside) 'larger place by dirty open land',
great + OE *drit*, 'dirt' + *feld*, 'open land'. The first part of the main name
may actually be OE *drīf*, 'stubble'. *Great* distinguishes this place from
Little Driffield, a village to the west. *Drifeld* 1086.

Great Malvern *See* ◊Malvern Hills.

Great Ormes Head (peninsula, Gwynedd) 'larger snake(-like) headland',
English *great* + OS *ormr*, 'snake' + *hofuth*, 'headland'. The headland is the
larger of two (the other being *Little Ormes Head*) suggesting the appearance
of a snake. *Ormeshede insula* 15th century.

Great Yarmouth (town, Norfolk) 'larger (place at the) mouth of the
(River) Yare', English *great* + Celtic river name + OE *mūtha*, 'mouth'. The
river name may mean 'babbling one'. The town is *Great* by comparison
with *Little Yarmouth*, to the south. ◊Yarmouth, Isle of Wight, has a name of
different origin. *Gernemwa* 1086.

Greenock (town, Strathclyde) '(place at the) sunny hillock', Gaelic *gri-
anag*, 'sunny hillock'. The terrain here rises from flat land by the Clyde to
higher ground, and this was the original 'sunny hillock'. *Grenok c* 1395.

Greenwich (town, Greater London) 'green port', OE *grēne*, 'green' + *wīc*,
'port'. A 'green port' is a grassy one, in this case by the Thames. *Grenewic*
964, *Grenviz* 1086.

Grimsby (town, Humberside) 'Grímr's farmstead', OS personal name +
bý, 'farmstead'. There are several places in the vicinity presumably named
after the same man, such as *Grimesthorpe*, *Grimsthorpe* and *Grimston*.
Grimesbi 1086.

Guildford (town, Surrey) 'ford by the golden (hill)', OE **gylde*, 'golden'
+ *ford*, 'ford'. The name probably alludes to the ◊Hog's Back, whose earlier
name was the equivalent of *Guildown*, 'golden hill'. The 'ford' would have
been over the Wey to the south of the town, in the district now known as St
Catherine's, where the Pilgrims Way crosses it. *Gyldeforda c* 880,
Gildeford 1086.

Guisborough (town, Cleveland) 'Gígr's stronghold', OS personal name
+ OE *burh*, 'stronghold'. The combination of OS personal name and OE

generic word is not unusual. *Ghigesburg* 1086.

Guiseley (town, West Yorkshire) 'Gīslic's clearing', OE personal name + *lēah*, 'clearing'. The personal name is conjectural. *Gislicleh c* 972, *Gisele* 1086.

Gwent (county, Wales) 'place', pre-Celtic word. The name implies an important location, whether for trading or some other purpose. The same word gave the first part of the name of ◊Winchester.

Gwynedd (county, Wales) '(territory of) Cunedda', Celtic personal name. The name is usually described as representing that of a 5th-century ruler who had a kingdom here in northwest Wales. His son, Ceredig, is said to have given the name of ◊Cardigan. However, it may actually derive from a tribal name.

H

Hackney (town, Greater London) 'Haca's island', OE personal name + *ēg*, 'island'. The 'island' here is the region of dry land among marshes. This is the marshland from which *hackney* horses originally came. *Hakeneia* 1198.

Haddington (town, Lothian) 'farmstead named after Hada', OE personal name + *-ing-*, 'named after' + *tūn*, 'farmstead'. The town is near enough to the English border to have an English name. *Hadynton* 1098.

Hadleigh (town, Essex) 'clearing where heather grows', OE *hǣth*, 'heather' + *lēah*, 'clearing'. The town of *Hadleigh*, Suffolk, has a name of identical origin. The Domesday Book record is corrupt, omitting the first part of the name and with *m* for *h*. *Hǣthlege c* 1000, *Leam* 1086.

Hailsham (town, East Sussex) 'Hægel's homestead', OE personal name + *hām*, 'homestead'. The second part of the name could be OE *hamm*, 'enclosure'. The Domesday Book record of the name has gained an extra *m*. *Hamelesham* 1086, *Helesham* 1189.

Hale (town, Greater Manchester) '(place at the) corner of land', OE *halh*, 'nook'. The 'corner of land' is the bend of the River Bollin in which the town lies. *Hale* 1086.

Halesowen (town, West Midlands) 'corners of land named after Owen', OE *halh*, 'nook' + Welsh personal name. The OE word is represented in the name in a plural form. The personal name is that of the Welsh prince *Owen*, who held the manor here in the early 13th century. *Hala* 1086, *Hales Ouweyn* 1276.

Halesworth (town, Suffolk) 'Hæle's enclosure', OE personal name + *worth*, 'enclosure'. The personal name is conjectural here. *Healesuurda* 1086.

Halifax (town, West Yorkshire) 'area of coarse grass in a corner of land', OE *halh*, 'nook' + **gefeaxe*, 'coarse grass'. The second part of the name is based on OE *feax*, 'hair', as in the surname *Fairfax* ('fair hair'). The grass here must have been 'hairy', or long and tangled. *Halyfax c* 1095.

Halstead (town, Essex) 'place of refuge', OE *hald*, 'protection' + *stede*, 'place'. The town is in a suitable site to afford protection, between a hill and a river (the Colne). *Haltesteda* 1086.

Haltwhistle (town, North Yorkshire) 'junction of two streams at a high place', Old French *haut*, 'high' + OE *twisla*, 'confluence'. The 'high place' here is Castle Hill. The name has come to be popularly associated with quite different modern words. *Hautwisel* 1240.

Hambleton (district, North Yorkshire) '(district of) Hambleton (Hills)', OE hill name. The administrative district takes its name from the *Hambleton* Hills, whose own name derives from a single hill, *Hambleton Hill*, the main word meaning 'crooked hill', from OE **hamel* 'crooked', and *dūn*, 'hill'.

Hamilton (town, Strathclyde) 'farmstead in broken country', OE **hamel*, 'broken country' + *tūn*, 'farmstead'. The name has been popularly associated with the *Hamilton* family, who came here from England. *Hamelton* 1291.

Hammersmith (district, Greater London) '(place with a) hammer smithy', OE *hamor*, 'hammer' + *smiththe*, 'smithy'. A 'hammer smithy' is a forge. The exact site of the original smithy is unknown, but it would have been important to travellers by horse here on a main road out of London. *Hamersmythe* 1294.

Hampshire (county, England) 'district based on Hampton', OE place-name + *scīr*, 'district'. 'Hampton' is ◊Southampton. The 'smoothed' Norman version of the name, as in the Domesday Book record, gave the modern abbreviated name of *Hants*. *Hamtunscir* late 9th century, *Hantescire* 1086.

Hampstead (district, London) 'homestead', OE *hām-stede*, 'homestead'. A 'homestead' could have been anything from a single dwelling, such as a farm, to a small settlement. *Hemstede* 959, *Hamestede* 1086.

Hampton (village, Greater London) 'farmstead in a river bend', OE *hamm*, 'river bend' + *tūn*, 'farmstead'. The 'river bend' here, at the site of Hampton Court Palace, is that of the Thames. *Hamntone* 1086.

Handsworth (district, Sheffield, South Yorkshire) 'Hand's enclosure', OE personal name + *worth*, 'enclosure'. The identically named district of Birmingham has a different personal name, *Hūn*. *Handesuuord* 1086.

Hanley (town, Staffordshire) 'high clearing', OE *hēah*, 'high' and *lēah*, 'clearing'. Hanley is on a hill. The *n* of the name comes from *hēan*, the dative case of *hēah*, used after 'at'. *Henle* 1212.

Hanwell (district, Greater London) 'spring where cocks are', OE *hana* 'cockbird' + *wella*, 'spring'. OE *hana* is the masculine equivalent of *henn*, modern *hen*. *Hanewelle* 959, 1086.

Haringey (borough, Greater London) 'enclosure in the grey wood', OE *hāring*, 'grey wood' + *hæg*, 'enclosure'. The name was revived from the historic records for former *Harringay*. ◊Hornsey is a name of identical origin. It is possible the first part of the name may be the OE personal name *Hæring*. *Haringeie* 1201, *Haringesheye* 1243.

Harlech (town, Gwynedd) 'beautiful rock', Welsh *hardd*, 'beautiful' + *llech*, 'slab', 'smooth rock'. Harlech Castle stands on the original 'beautiful rock'. *Hardelagh c* 1290.

Harlesden (district, Greater London) 'Heoruwulf's farmstead', OE personal name + *tūn*. The personal name could also have been *Herewulf*. The place-name is really *Harlston, cp* ◊Harleston, but ends in *-den* under the influence of nearby *Neasden*. *Herulvestune* 1086.

Harleston (town, Norfolk) 'Heoruwulf's farmstead', OE personal name + *tūn*, 'farmstead'. As for ◊Harlesden, the personal name could also have been *Herewulf*. *Heroluestuna* 1086.

Harlington (district, Greater London) 'estate named after Hygerēd', OE personal name + *-ing-*, 'named after' + *tūn*, 'estate'. The name could have developed into *Hardington*, but the *d* of the personal name has become *l*. *Hygereding tun* 831, *Herdintone* 1086.

Harlow (town, Essex) 'army mound', OE *here*, 'army' + *hlāw*, 'mound'. The 'army mound' would have been both an administrative centre and a meeting place, the latter for the hundred of which Harlow was the centre. The army was probably a Viking one. The site in question was that of the Roman temple in Harlow Old Town. *Herlawe* 1045, *Herlaua* 1086.

Harold Wood (district, Greater London) 'Harold's wood', OE personal name + *wudu*, 'wood'. The personal name is that of King *Harold*, who held the nearby manor of Havering. *Horalds Wood c* 1237.

Harpenden (town, Hertfordshire) '(place in the) valley of the harp', OE *hearpe*, 'harp' + *denu*, 'valley'. The significance of the 'harp' here is uncertain. An alternative meaning would be 'valley of the highway', with the first part from OE *here-pæth*, literally 'army way', referring to a military road. This could have run along Watling Street here. *Herpedene c* 1060.

Harrogate (town, North Yorkshire) '(place at the) road to the cairn', OS *horgr*, 'cairn' + *gata*, 'road'. It was probably not the cairn itself that was significant, but the place to which the road led past it. *Harwegate* 1332.

Harrow (borough, Greater London) 'heathen temple', OE *hearg*, 'heathen shrine'. The Saxon temple here would almost certainly have been where St Mary's Church is today, on the summit of the hill ('Harrow-on-the-Hill'). *Hearge* 825, *Herges* 1086.

Hartlepool (town, Cleveland) '(place at the) pool by the stag peninsula', OE *heorot*, 'stag', 'hart' + *ēg*, 'island' + *pōl*, 'pool'. The 'stag peninsula' would have been one where these animals lived. The 'pool' is Hartlepool Bay. The *-le-* of the name represents the OE word rendered here as 'peninsula' rather than 'island'. *Herterpol c* 1170.

Harwich (town, Essex) 'army camp', OE *here-wīc*, 'army camp'. There was a sizeable Viking camp here in the 9th century. *Herewic* 1248.

Haslemere (town, Surrey) 'pool where hazel trees grow', OE *hæsel*, 'hazel' + *mere*, 'pool'. There is no pool here now. It may have been on a site between the High Street and Derby Road. *Heselmere* 1221.

Haslingden (town, Lancashire) 'valley growing with hazels', OE *hæslen*, 'growing with hazels' + *denu*, 'valley'. The *-ing-* of the name is misleading. The surname *Heseltine* comes from here, or some identically named place. *Heselingedon* 1241.

Hassocks (town, West Sussex) '(field of) clumps of grass', OE *hassuc*, 'clump of grass'. The place arose only in the 19th century, and takes its name from a field here, itself so called for its clumps of coarse grass. The OE word gave modern *hassock*, as a kneeling mat originally made from such grass.

Hastings (town, East Sussex) '(settlement of) Hæsta's people', OE personal name + *-ingas*, 'people of'. The first record below adds OE *ceaster*, 'Roman town'. The name of such a town is unknown. *Hæstingaceaster c* 915, *Hastinges* 1086.

Hatch End (district, Greater London) 'district by the gate', OE *hæcc*, 'gate' + *ende*, 'district'. The 'gate' was probably one into Pinner Park. *Le Hacchehend* 1448.

Hatfield (town, Hertfordshire) 'open land where heather grows', OE *hǣth*, 'heather' + *feld*, 'open land'. The name is a common one. *Hatfield*, South Yorkshire, has a name of identical origin and meaning. *Haethfelth* 731, *Hetfelle* 1086.

Havant (town, Hampshire) 'Hāma's spring', OE personal name + **funta*, 'spring'. The *m* of the personal name has blended with the *f* of *funta*. *Hamanfuntan* 935, *Havehunte* 1086.

Haverfordwest (town, Dyfed) 'western ford where goats cross', OE *west*, 'west' + *hæfer*, 'goat' + *ford*, 'ford'. The place was originally *Haverford*. *West* was then added to distinguish it from ◊Hereford (although that name has a different meaning). The 'goat ford' would have been over the Western Cleddau. *Haverfordia* 1191, *Hareford* 1283.

Haverhill (town, Suffolk) 'hill where oats grow', OS *hafri*, 'oats' + OE *hyll*, 'hill'. The surrounding district is still largely farmland. *Hauerhella* 1086.

Havering (borough, Greater London) '(settlement of) Hæfer's people', OE personal name + *-ingas*, 'people of'. Within the borough is *Havering-atte-Bower*, the last two words meaning 'by the royal residence' (OE *būr*, 'bower'). *Haueringas* 1086, *Hauering atte Bower* 1272.

Hawarden (town, Clwyd) 'high enclosure', OE *hēah*, 'high' + *worthign*, 'enclosure'. The town is on rising ground above the River Dee. *Haordine* 1086.

Hawes (town, North Yorkshire) '(place at the) pass between the hills', OE *hals*, 'neck'. The pass here is a 'neck of land' by the River Ure. *Hawes* 1614.

Haweswater (lake, Cumbria) 'Hafr's lake', OS personal name + OE *wæter*, 'water', 'lake'. The personal name was probably a nickname meaning 'he-goat'. *Havereswater* 1199.

Hawick (town, Borders) 'village (enclosed) by a hedge', OE *haga*, 'hedged enclosure' + *wīc*, 'outlying farm', 'village'. The village may have grown up round a dairy farm here. *Hawic c* 1165.

Haworth (town, West Yorkshire) 'enclosure with a hedge', OE *haga*, 'hedge' + *worth*, 'enclosure'. OE *Haga* also specifically meant 'haw', so that the 'hedge' may have been one of hawthorn. *Hauewrth* 1209.

Haydock (town, Merseyside) 'place where barley grows', Welsh *haidd*, 'barley' + *-og*, adjectival suffix. The town is close enough to Wales to have a Welsh name. *Hedoc* 1169.

Haydon Bridge (town, Northumberland) 'valley of hay with a bridge', OE *hēg*, 'hay' + *denu*, 'valley' + *brycg*, 'bridge'. The 'valley' is that of the South Tyne, and would have been one where hay was made. *Hayden* 1236.

Hayes (district, Greater London) '(land overgrown with) brushwood', OE *hǣs*, 'brushwood'. Both places of this name in Greater London, respectively in Hillingdon and Bromley, have a name of identical origin and meaning. The following records are for the Hillingdon one. *Hæsa* 831, *Hesa* 1086.

Hayfield (town, Derbyshire) 'open land where hay is got', OE *hēg*, 'hay' + *feld*, 'open land'. The Domesday Book record of the name has a misleading d. *Hedfelt* 1086, *Heyfeld* 1285.

Hayle (town, Cornwall) '(place by the River) Hayle', Celtic river name. The river name means 'estuary', and this in fact describes the location of the town. *Heyl* 1265.

Hayling Island (island, Hampshire) 'island of Hægel's people', OE personal name + *-ingas*, 'people of' + Middle English *island*, 'island'. The same personal name lies behind that of ◊Hailsham. *Hailinges island c* 1140.

Hay-on-Wye (town, Powys) 'hedged enclosure on the (River) Wye', OE *hæg*, 'hedged enclosure' + river name. The river name is pre-English and of unknown meaning. The Welsh name of the town is similarly *Y Gelli Gandryll*, 'the broken grove' (Welsh *celli*, 'grove', and *candryll*, 'broken'). When woodland is 'broken' it is fenced off. *Haya* 1144.

Haywards Heath (town, West Sussex) 'heath by the hedged enclosure', OE *hege*, 'hedge' + *worth*, 'enclosure' + *hǣth*, 'heath'. The name was originally *Heyworth*, and *Heath* was added subsequently. The present town developed only in the 19th century, and the first word of the name has become associated with the surname *Hayward*, as if someone so called owned the heath. *Heyworth* 1261, *Haywards Hoth* 1544, *Hayward's Heath* 1868.

Hazel Grove (town, Greater Manchester) 'grove of hazel trees', OE *hæsel*, 'hazel' + *grāf*, 'grove'. There must have been such a grove here at one time. *Hesselgrove* 1690.

Headingley (district, Leeds, West Yorkshire) 'clearing of Heada's people', OE personal name + *-inga-*, 'of the people of' + *lēah*, 'clearing'. The personal name is not the same as that behind ◊Headington. *Hedingeleia* 1086.

Headington (district, Oxford, Oxfordshire) 'Hedena's hill', OE personal name + *dūn*, 'hill'. The final *-ton* of the present name is misleading, since it represents *dūn*, not *tūn*, 'farmstead'. *Hedenandun* 1004, *Hedintone* 1086.

Heanor (town, Derbyshire) '(place at a) high ridge', OE *hēah*, 'high' + **ofer*, 'ridge'. The *n* of the name comes from *hēan*, required after *æt*, 'at', as the dative case of *hēah*. The town is on a hill. *Hainoure* 1086.

Heathfield (town, East Sussex) 'open land where heather grows', OE *hǣth*, 'heather' + *feld*, 'open land'. The name implies that the land was overgrown with heather. *Hadfeld* 12th century.

Heathrow (airport, Greater London), 'row (of houses) by a heath', OE *hǣth*, 'heath' + *rǣw*, 'row'. There must originally have been a row of cottages on Hounslow Heath here. The place was a hamlet until the 20th century. *La Hetherewe c* 1410, *Heath Row* 1822.

Hebburn (town, Tyne and Wear) 'high burial place', *hēah*, 'high' + *byrgen*, 'burial place'. It is not certain where the original burial place or tumulus was. *Heabyrm* 1104.

Hebden Bridge (town, West Yorkshire) '(place by the) bridge in the valley where brambles grow', OE *hēopa*, 'hips', 'brambles' + *denu*, 'valley' + *brycg*, 'bridge'. The 'bridge' is that over the Hebden Water here. *Hebedene* 1086, *Hepdenbryge* 1399.

Hebrides (islands, Scotland). The name is of uncertain origin and meaning. The Roman name for the islands (originally the Inner Hebrides only) was *Ebudae*, and the present form of the name arose as a misreading of *u* as *ri*.

Heckmondwike (town, West Yorkshire) 'Hēahmund's dwelling', OE personal name + *wīc*, 'dwelling'. The 'dwelling' may have originally been a dairy farm. The Domesday Book record has an erroneous *d* (no doubt influenced by the one at the end of the personal name). *Hedmundewic* 1086, *Hecmundewik* 13th century.

Hednesford (town, Staffordshire) 'Heddīn's ford', OE personal name + *ford*, 'ford'. The personal name is probably a diminutive of *Headda*. *Hedenesford* 13th century.

Hedon (town, Humberside) 'hill where heather grows', OE *hǣth*, 'heather' + *dūn*, 'hill'. There is not much of a hill at Hedon, but clearly one was originally distinguished. *Hedon* 12th century.

Helensburgh (town, Strathclyde) 'Helen's town', first name + *burgh*. The town was founded by Sir James Colquhoun in 1776 and he named it after his wife, Lady *Helen* Sutherland.

Helford (village, Cornwall) 'crossing place at the estuary', OE **heyl*, 'estuary' + *ford*, 'ford', 'crossing place'. The village is on the southern side of the River Helford estuary, at a point where there is a ferry across to the northern bank. *Helleford* 1230.

Helmsley (town, North Yorkshire) 'Helm's clearing', OE personal name + *lēah*, 'clearing'. The Domesday Book record is rather wayward. *Elmeslac* 1086, *Helmesley* 12th century.

Helston (town, Cornwall) 'estate by an old court', Cornish **hen-lys*, 'old court' + OE *tūn*, 'estate'. The word meaning 'court' here is also found in the name of the ◊Lizard Peninsula, where the town is actually located. *Henlistone* 1086.

Helvellyn (mountain, Cumbria). The precise meaning of the name is uncertain. It appears to be Celtic in origin, but no record exists earlier than the one given. *Helvillon* 1574.

Hemel Hempstead (town, Hertfordshire) 'homestead in the broken land', OE **hamel*, 'broken land' + *hām-stede*, 'homestead'. 'Broken land' is an irregular terrain with hills and valleys. The present form of the name is a recent reconstruction of the original, which gradually lost the *Hemel* over the centuries, as shown by the following records. *Hamelamestede* 1086, *Hemlamsted* 1339, *Hempsted* 1544, *Hempstead* 1771.

Hemsworth (town, West Yorkshire) 'Hymel's enclosure', OE personal name + *worth*, 'enclosure'. The Domesday Book record of the name seems to have been influenced by OE *hamel*, as for ◊Hemel Hempstead. *Hamelesuurde* 1086, *Hymeleswrde* 12th century.

Hendon (district, London) '(place at the) high hill', OE *hēah*, 'high' + *dūn*, 'hill'. The first part of the name represents OE *hēan*, the dative case of *hēah*, required after *æt*, 'at'. *Heandun c* 975, *Handone* 1086.

Henfield (town, West Sussex) 'stony open land', OE *hān*, 'stone' + *feld*, 'open land'. This is the likely meaning of the name, which is also open to other interpretations. *Hanefeld* 770, *Hamfelde* 1086.

Henley-on-Thames (town, Oxfordshire) 'high wood by the Thames', OE *hēah*, 'high' + *lēah*, 'wood' + river name. 'High' here means 'important' rather than 'elevated'. The suffix differentiates this Henley from others, such as *Henley-in-Arden*, Warwickshire. *Henleiam c* 1140.

Hereford (city, Hereford and Worcester), 'army ford', OE *here*, 'army' + *ford*, 'ford'. An 'army ford' is one where an army can march across a river (here the Wye) without breaking formation. The county name, *Herefordshire*, was first recorded in the 11th century. *Hereford* 958, 1086.

Herne Bay (town, Kent) '(place at the) angle of land', OE *hyrne*, 'angle', 'corner'. The record below relates to the original site, which gave its name to the bay, which then gave the name of the present town, established in 1830. *Hyrnan c* 1100.

Herstmonceux (village, East Sussex) '(place at the) wooded hill of the Monceux family', OE *hyrst*, 'wooded hill' + family name. The *Monceux* family, from *Monceaux* in Normandy, owned the manor here in the 13th century. *Herst* 1086, *Herstmonceus* 1287.

Hertford (town, Hertfordshire) 'ford where harts cross', OE *heorot*, 'hart', 'stag' + *ford*, 'ford'. The town gave the name of nearby *Hertingfordbury*, 'stronghold of the people of Hertford', recorded in the Domesday Book (1086) as *Herefordingeberie*, with *e* instead of *t*. The county name, *Hertfordshire*, is first recorded in the 11th century. *Herutford* 731, *Hertforde* 1086, *Hartford* 1771, *Hertford, or Harford* 1868.

Hertsmere (district, Hertfordshire) 'Hertfordshire boundary'. The name is a modern one for the administrative district formed in 1974. It derives from *Herts*, the abbreviated county name, and *mere*, 'boundary', referring to the boundary between the district and Greater London.

Hessle (town, Humberside) '(place at the) hazel tree', OE *hæsel*, 'hazel'. The form of the name has been influenced by *hesli*, the OS word for 'hazel'. *Hase* 1086, *Hesel* 12th century.

Hetton-le-Hole (town, Tyne and Wear) 'hill where brambles grow by the hollow', OE *hēope*, 'hip', 'bramble' + *dūn*, 'hill' + *hol*, 'hollow'. The second part of the name was added to differentiate this Hetton from others. It implies that the place is not actually on the hill but below it, in a valley. *Heppedun* 1180.

Hever (village, Kent) '(place at the) high bank', OE *hēah*, 'high' + *yfer*, 'bank'. The village lies above Hever Castle, itself above the River Eden. *Heanyfre* 814.

Hexham (town, Northumberland) 'bachelor's homestead', OE *hagustald*, 'warrior' + *hām*, 'enclosure'. OE *hagustald* (modern German *Hagestolz*) literally means 'enclosure occupant', from OE *hæg*, 'hedged enclosure', and *stealdan*, 'to occupy'. The term was used for the younger son of a family who was entitled to have his own holding outside the main village, as here. *Hagustaldes ham* 685.

Heysham (town, Lancashire) 'homestead among the brushwood', OE

*hǣs, 'brushwood' + *hām*, 'homestead'. 'Brushwood' is open land covered with bushes. *Hessam* 1086.

Heywood (town, Greater Manchester) 'high wood', OE *hēah*, 'high' + *wudu*, 'wood'. The terrain here is not noticeably elevated, and the meaning of 'high' might be 'important', 'chief'. *Heghwode* 1246.

Higham Ferrers (town, Northamptonshire) 'high homestead of the Ferrers family', OE *hēah*, 'high' + *hām*, 'homestead' + family name. As elsewhere, 'high' here could mean 'important'. The *Ferrers* family from Normandy were here in the 12th century. *Hecham* 1086, *Heccham Ferrar* 1279.

Highbridge (town, Somerset) '(place by the) high bridge', OE *hēah*, 'high' + *brycg*, 'bridge'. 'High' here is more likely to mean 'chief', 'important', than literally 'elevated'. The river is the Brue. *Highbridge* 1324.

Highgate (district, Greater London) 'high gate', OE *hēah*, 'high' + *geat*, 'gate'. The name refers to the medieval tollgate here on what became the Great North Road, at an elevated site some 400 feet above sea level. *Le Heighgate* 1354.

Highworth (town, Wiltshire) 'high farmstead', OE *heah*, 'high' + *worth*, 'enclosure', 'farmstead'. As shown by early records of the name, the place was originally just *Worth*. *High* was subsequently added to distinguish this 'farmstead' from others. The present town is on an elevated site overlooking three counties (Wiltshire, Berkshire, Gloucestershire). *Wrde* 1086, *Hegworth* 1232.

High Wycombe (town, Buckinghamshire) 'high (place) at the settlements', OE *hēah*, 'high' + *wīc*, 'outlying farm', 'settlement'. The second word of the name represents OE *wīcum*, the dative plural of *wīc* required after *æt*, 'at'. It formerly stood alone, and the first word was added later to differentiate this Wycombe from *West Wycombe*, now part of High Wycombe itself. 'High' probably means 'important' rather than 'elevated'. *Wicumun c* 970.

Hillingdon (district, Greater London) 'Hilda's hill', OE personal name + *dūn*, 'hill'. The misleading *-ing-* represents the genitive case ending of *Hilda*, a man's name. *Hildendune c* 1080.

Hinckley (town, Leicestershire) 'Hȳnca's clearing', OE personal name + *lēah*, 'clearing'. The personal name is male. *Hinchelie* 1086.

Hindhead (town, Surrey) 'hill where hinds are', OE *hind*, 'hind', 'doe' + *hēafod*, 'headland'. The town arose in the early 20th century, and the record below (the earliest found) thus relates to the hill. *Hyndehed* 1571.

Hindley (town, Greater Manchester) 'wood where hinds are', OE *hind*, 'hind', 'doe' + *lēah*, 'wood', 'clearing'. OE *lēah* can mean both 'wood' and 'clearing', but here the former seems right, especially as the town is near Horwich Forest. *Hindele* 1212.

Hitchin (town, Hertfordshire) '(place in the territory of the) Hicce (people)', tribal name. Nothing is known about the *Hicce* except their name, as here. The first record of the name below represents the dative plural of the tribal name. The Domesday Book record of the name was later adopted for that of the river here. *Hiccam c* 945, *Hiz* 1086.

Hoddesdon (town, Hertfordshire) 'Hod's hill', OE personal name + *dūn*, 'hill'. The present town lies to the east of the hill originally so named. *Hodesdone* 1086.

Hog's Back (hill ridge, Surrey) '(ridge shaped like a) hog's back'. The ridge running west of Guildford is first recorded under this name in 1823. Its earlier name was (in modern terms) *Guildown*, probably meaning 'gold-coloured hill', from OE **gylde*, 'golden' + *dūn*. It was this hill that probably gave the name of ◊Guildford. *Geldedon* 1195.

Holbeach (town, Lincolnshire) 'hollow stream', OE *hol*, 'hollow' + *bece*, 'stream'. The name appears to have this meaning, but the description is not really right for the locality. The actual meaning may thus be 'hollow ridge', with the second part of the name representing OE *bæc*, 'ridge', here in the locative form. A 'hollow ridge' would be a slight one. *Holebech* 1086.

Holborn (district, Greater London) 'hollow stream', OE *hol*, 'hollow' + *bruna*, 'stream'. A 'hollow stream' is one flowing in a hollow. The 'hollow' here is a dip in a section of Farringdon Road. The stream, a tributary of the Fleet, was itself actually called the *Holborn*. *Holeburne* 1086.

Holderness (district, Humberside) '(district of the) promontory ruled by a hold', OS *holdr*, 'hold' + *nes*, 'promontory'. A *hold* was a high-ranking yeoman in the Danelaw, the word being related to modern German *Held*, 'hero'. The promontory name was adopted for the modern administrative district. *Heldernesse* 1086.

Holland (district, Lincolnshire) 'district with hill spurs', OE *hōh*, 'hill spur' + *land*, 'district'. The 'hill spurs' here are those by the coast of south-east Lincolnshire, which otherwise is mainly flat. *Hoiland* 1086.

Holloway (district, Greater London) 'hollow road', OE *hol*, 'hollow' +

weg, 'way', 'road'. A 'hollow road' is one running along a hollow as here (now part of the A1) between Highbury and Highgate. *Le Holeweye* 1307.

Holmfirth (town, West Yorkshire) 'woodland by Holme', OE *fyrhth*, 'woodland' + OS place-name. OE *fyrhth* is used of sparse woodland or scrub. The OS place-name means literally 'island', from *holmr*, here applied to raised land in moorland. *Holnefrith* 1274.

Holsworthy (town, Devon) 'Heald's enclosure', OE personal name + *worthig*, 'enclosure'. The personal name means 'bent one'. *Haldeurdi* 1086.

Holt (town, Norfolk) '(place at the) wood', OE *holt*, 'wood'. For a well-disguised form of *holt*, *see* ◊Wormwood Scrubs. *Holt* 1086.

Holyhead (town, Gwynedd) 'holy headland', OE *hālig*, 'holy' + *hēafod*, 'headland'. The town, on Holy Island, Anglesey, has a long history as a Christian centre. The 'headland' is Holyhead Mountain, to the west of the town. The Welsh name of Holyhead is *Caergybi*, 'Cybi's fort', after the saint to whom the town's parish church is dedicated. *Halihefed* 1315.

Holy Island (island, Northumberland) 'holy island', OE *hālig*, 'holy' + *ēg-land*, 'island'. The island, also known as ◊Lindisfarne, has an early association with Christian missionaries. There are other islands of the name in Wales (*see* ◊Holyhead) and Scotland. *Halieland* 1195.

Holywell (town, Clwyd) 'holy well', OE *hālig*, 'holy' + *wella*, 'well'. The name refers to the sacred well or spring of St Winefride, who founded a nunnery here in the 7th century. The Welsh name of the town is *Treffynnon*, 'village of the well'. *Haliwel* 1093.

Honiton (town, Devon) 'Hūna's farmstead', OE personal name + *tūn*, 'farmstead'. The village of *Clyst Honiton*, 16 miles southwest of Honiton, has a name of quite different meaning: 'farmstead on the (River) Clyst belonging to a religious community', with the *Honi-* representing OE *hīwan*, 'religious community' (here Exeter Cathedral). *Honetone* 1086.

Hook (district, Kingston upon Thames, Greater London) '(place by the) hook', OE *hōc*, 'hok'. A *hook* could be either a hook-shaped area of land or a bend in a river or hill. It is not clear which particular kind was involved here. *Hoke* 1227.

Horbury (town, West Yorkshire) 'stronghold on muddy land', OE *horu*, 'dirt', 'filth' + *burh*, 'stronghold'. The town is close to the River Calder. *Horberie* 1086.

Horley (town, Surrey) 'clearing in a horn-shaped area of land', OE **horna*, 'horn-shaped area' + *lēah*, 'clearing'. The 'horn-shaped area' would have been land in between two streams, narrowing at one end. *Horle* 12th century.

Horncastle (town, Lincolnshire) 'Roman settlement on horn of land', OE **horna* 'horn of land' + *ceaster*, 'Roman settlement'. The 'horn of land' is between the rivers Bain and Waring here. The second part of the name, usually *-caster* in such cases, has been corrupted to *-castle*. The Roman settlement was called *Bannovalium*, the first part of which also probably means 'horn' (Gaelic *beinn*, 'peak'). The second part means 'strong' (*cp Luguvalium*, the Roman name of ◊Carlisle). *Hornecastre* 1086.

Hornchurch (town, Greater London) 'church with horns', OE *horn*, 'horn' + *cirice*, 'church'. The reference is to some horn-like embellishment on the church, such as the bull's head fixed to the eastern end of the roof in the 18th century. It is not known what the original adornment was. *Hornechurch* 1233.

Horndean (town, Hampshire) 'valley where dormice are', OE *hearma*, 'dormouse' + *denu*, 'valley'. The first part of the name may be a personal name. *Harmedene* 1199.

Hornsea (town, Humberside) 'lake with a horn-shaped peninsula', OS *horn*, 'horn' + *nes*, 'peninsula' + *sǽr*, 'lake'. The seaside resort takes its name from *Hornsea Mere*, a large lake to the west of the town. The lake has a 'horn' of land projecting into it. *Hornessei* 1086.

Hornsey (district, Greater London) 'enclosure in the grey wood', OE **hāring*, 'grey wood' + *hæg*, 'enclosure'. The first part of the name may be the personal name Hæring. The name is identical in origin to that of ◊Haringey, now the borough in which Hornsey is located. *Haringeie* 1201, *Haringesheye* 1243, *Hornesey* 1564.

Horsham (town, West Sussex) 'homestead where horses are kept', OE *hors*, 'horse' + *hām*, 'homestead'. Horses would have been kept here for breeding. *Horsham* 947.

Horwich (town, Greater Manchester) '(place by the) grey wych elms', OE *hār*, 'grey' + *wice*, 'wych elm'. The name was originally that of a forest here, and the record below refers to this. *Horewic* 1221.

Houghton-le-Spring (town, Tyne and Wear) 'farmstead on a hill spur of the Spring family', OE *hōh*, 'hill spur' + *tūn*, 'farmstead' + family name.

The town is on a spur of land below the hill Warden Law. The last part of the name was added to distinguish this Houghton from others. The *Spring* family were here in the 13th century. *Hoctun, Hoghton Springes c* 1220.

Hounslow (borough, Greater London) 'Hund's mound', OE personal name + *hlāw*, 'mound'. The 'mound' was probably the burial place of the man who bore the personal name (meaning 'hound'). *Honeslaw* 1086, *Hundeslawe* 1217.

Hove (town, East Sussex) '(place by the) hood', OE *hūfe*, 'hood'. The OE word, not evidenced in any other place-name, probably refers either to a hood-shaped hill or to a hood-shaped shelter of some kind. If the latter, it is not clear what this was, but it was almost certainly some natural feature. *La Houue* 1288.

Howden (town, Humberside) 'valley by the headland', OE *hēafod*, 'headland' + *denu*, 'valley'. There is hardly a valley here in the accepted sense, so the reference may be to a valley-like stretch of land. The first part of the name has been influenced by its OS equivalent, *hofuth*. *Heafuddene* 959, *Hovedene* 1086.

Hoxton (district, Greater London) 'Hōc's farmstead', OE personal name + *tūn*, 'farmstead'. The name would originally have been pronounced as if 'Hoaxton'. *Hochestone* 1086.

Hoylake (town, Merseyside) 'lake at the sandbank', OE **hygel*, 'sandbank' + *lacu*, 'lake'. The name refers to a former tidal lake, now silted up, that existed between the mainland and a sandbank known as *Hile* or *Hoyle*. The town developed only from the late 18th century. *Hyle Lake* 1687.

Hucknall (town, Nottinghamshire) 'Hucca's corner of land', OE personal name + *halh*, 'nook'. The *-n-* of the name represents the genitive ending of the personal name. *Hochenale* 1086.

Huddersfield (town, West Yorkshire) 'Hudrǣd's open land', OE personal name + *feld*, 'open land'. It is possible the first part of the name represents OE **hūder*, 'shelter'. *Odresfeld* 1086.

Hugh Town (town, Isles of Scilly) 'town by the spur of land', OE *hōh*, 'spur of land' + modern *town*. The town stands on a spur of land at the foot of a hill. The latter's name was recorded as *Hew Hill* in 1593. *Hugh Town* 17th century.

Hull (city, Humberside) '(place by the River) Hull', river name. The river name may represent either OS *holr*, 'deep one', or come from a Celtic word

meaning 'muddy one'. The town's official name is *Kingston-upon-Hull*, the
first word of which means 'king's estate' (OE *cyning*, 'king', and *tūn*,
'estate'). The reference is to Edward I, who exchanged lands elsewhere for
the port here. *Kyngeston* 1256, *Kyngeston super Hul* 1299.

Humber (river, Humberside). The river name is pre-English and of uncertain origin and meaning. The river gave the name of *Humberside*, the
county formed either side of it in 1974 from the East Riding of Yorkshire
and northern Lincolnshire.

Humberstone (district, Leicester, Leicestershire) '(place by) Hūnbe-
orth's stone', OE personal name + *stān*, 'stone'. The location of the named
stone is not known. It may have been a boundary stone of some kind.
Humerstane 1086.

Hungerford (town, Berkshire) 'hunger ford', OE *hungor*, 'hunger' + *ford*,
'ford'. A 'hunger ford' is one by barren ground. The crossing over the River
Kennet here would have led to land that did not yield well, so that people
went hungry. *Hungreford* 1101.

Hunslet (district, Leeds, West Yorkshire) 'Hūn's stream', OE personal
name + *flēot*, 'stream'. The 'stream' would have flowed into the River Aire
here. *Hunslet* 1086, *Hunesflete* 12th century, *Hunslet, or Hunfleet* 1868.

Hunstanton (town, Norfolk) 'Hūnstān's farmstead', OE personal name
+ *tūn*, 'farmstead'. The name could have been 'smoothed' to *Hunston*, to
match its local pronunciation. *Hunstanestun c* 1035, *Hunestanestuna*
1086.

Huntingdon (town, Cambridgeshire) 'huntsman's hill', OE *hunta*, 'huntsman' + *dūn*, 'hill'. The first part of the name may actually be the OE
personal name *Hunta*. The -*ing*- of the name is misleading, and evolved
from a genitive ending. The county name, *Huntingdonshire*, is first
recorded in the 11th century. *Huntandun* 973, *Huntedun* 1086.

Huntly (town, Grampian) '(Earl of) Huntly's (town)', aristocratic title. The
town was founded in 1769 by Alexander Gordon, 4th Duke of Gordon and
Earl of *Huntly*, and is named after him. His title comes from the lost village
of *Huntly*, Berwickshire (now in Borders).

Hurstpierpoint (town, West Sussex) '(place by the) wooded hill belonging
to de Pierpoint', OE *hyrst*, 'wooded hill' + family name. Robert *de Pierpoint*
owned the manor here from 1086. *Herst* 1086, *Herst Perepunt* 1279.

Huyton (town, Merseyside) 'estate with a landing place', OE *hȳth*, 'landing place' + *tūn*, 'estate'. The landing place would have been on either the River Al or on Ditton Brook here. *Hitune* 1086.

Hyde (town, Greater Manchester) '(estate valued at one) hide', OE *hīd*, 'hide'. A *hide* was the amount of land that could support a single household. Its area varied from one region to another. *Hyde* early 13th century.

Hyndburn (district, Lancashire) '(district of the River) Hyndburn'. The administrative district was formed in 1974 and named after the small river that flows through it.

Hythe (town, Kent) 'landing place', OE *hȳth*, 'landing place'. In names containing this OE word, the reference is usually to a landing stage on a river. This means that at Hythe it would not have been on the coast, but a short distance inland. Its precise location is uncertain. *Hede* 1086.

Ickenham (district, Greater London) 'Ticca's homestead', OE personal name + *hām*, 'homestead'. The name should really be *Tickenham*, but the initial *T* was lost in the 13th century when it was taken to represent *at*, a word frequently found before a place-name. *Ticheham* 1086.

Icknield Way (Roman road, England). The name of this ancient way, which runs from Norfolk to Dorset, is obscure in origin and meaning. Any attempt to link the name with that of the *Iceni* is unwarranted, even though these people had their capital at what is now Caistor St Edmund (Roman name *Venta Icenorum*), Norfolk, in an area where the Icknield Way begins. *Icenhylte* 903.

Ilchester (village, Somerset) 'Roman town on the (River) Gifl', Celtic river name + OE *ceaster*, 'Roman town'. The *Gifl* is the old name of the River *Yeo* here. The village is northwest of ◊Yeovil, on the same river. *Givelcestre* 1086.

Ilford (town, Greater London) 'ford over the (River) Hyle', Celtic river name + OE *ford*, 'ford'. The river name means 'trickling one'. It is now the *Roding*. *Ilefort* 1086.

Ilfracombe (town, Devon) 'valley named after Ælfrēd', OE personal name + *-ing-*, 'named after' + *cumb*, 'valley'. The 'valley' is the one up which the town's steep High Street runs. *Alfreincome* 1086.

Ilkeston (town, Derbyshire) 'Ealāc's hill', OE personal name + *dūn*, 'hill'. The Domesday Book record of the name has added an initial *T* from the preceding word *æt*, 'at'. *Cp* ◊Ickenham, where the opposite has happened. *Tilchestune* 1086, *Elkesdone* early 11th century.

Ilkley (town, West Yorkshire) 'Illica's clearing', OE personal name + *lēah*, 'clearing'. The first part of the name is problematical, and may not even be a personal name. *Hillicleg c* 972, *Illiclei* 1086.

Ilminster (town, Somerset) 'large church on the (River) Isle', Celtic river name + OE *mynster*, 'large church'. The meaning of the river name is uncertain. The 'large church' was the monastery where St Mary's Church now stands. *Illemynister* 995, *Ileminstre* 1086.

Immingham (town, Humberside) 'homestead of Imma's people', OE personal name + *-inga-*, 'of the people of' + *hām*, 'homestead'. The Domesday Book record has *u* as the result of a miscopying. *Imungeham* 1086.

Ince-in-Makerfield (town, Greater Manchester) 'island in Makerfield', Old Welsh **inis*, island + Celtic district name. The 'island' is raised land here. For the origin of the district name, *see* ◊Ashton-in-Makerfield. *Ines* 1202.

Ingatestone (town, Essex) '(manor of the district of) Ing at the stone', OE district name + *æt thǣm*, 'at the' + *stān*, 'stone'. The district name *Ing* means '(place of) the people of the district', from OE **gē*, 'district', and *-ingas*, 'people of'. The 'stone' here was probably a Roman milestone. *Gynges Atteston* 1283.

Innerleithen (town, Borders) '(place at the) mouth of the Leithen', Gaelic *inbhir*, 'mouth' + Celtic river name. The river name may mean something like 'oozing one', from a word related to modern Welsh *llaith*, 'damp'. The first part of the name corresponds to the *Inver-* found elsewhere. *Innerlethan c* 1160.

Inveraray (town, Strathclyde) '(place at the) mouth of the Aray', Gaelic *inbhir*, 'mouth' + Celtic river name. The river name probably means simply 'river', and is thus the same as for ◊Ayr. *Inveraray* mid-18th century.

Invergordon (town, Highland) '(place at a) river mouth (named after) Gordon', Gaelic *inbhir*, 'mouth' + family name. The name is a modern one. The original name of the place here was *Inverbreckie*, 'mouth of the Breckie' ('speckled river'). In about 1760 it was renamed for the landowner here, Sir Alexander *Gordon*, but retained the first part of the original name.

Inverkeithing (town, Fife) '(place at the) mouth of the Keithing (Burn)', Gaelic *inbhir*, 'mouth' + Celtic river name. The river name means 'wooded stream', and is related to the name of ◊Keith. *Hinhirkethy*, mid-11th century.

Inverness (town, Highland) '(place at the) mouth of the (River) Ness', Gaelic *inbhir*, 'mouth' + pre-Celtic river name. The river name probably means simply 'river', from a word related to modern German *nass*, 'wet'. *Invernis* 1300.

Inverurie (town, Grampian) '(place at the) mouth of the (River) Urie', Gaelic *inbhir*, 'mouth' + Celtic river name. The river name may mean 'strong one' or 'holy one', and so be related to that of the *Ure*. *Inverurie* late 12th century.

Iona (island, Strathclyde) '(place of) yew trees', Old Irish *eo*, 'yew tree'. The original name of the island was simply *I* or *Hi*. This was then incorporated into other forms of the name, such as Latin *Ioua insula*, 'island of the (place of) yew trees', recorded *c* 700. The first word of this was read as *Iona*, perhaps by association with the name of the biblical *Jonah*. Hence the present name. St Columba's association with the island caused it to be recorded *c* 1110 as *Hiona-Columcille*, 'Iona of Columba's cell'.

Ipswich (town, Suffolk) 'Gip's harbour', OE personal name + *wīc*, 'landing place', 'harbour'. The town stands at the confluence of the Orwell and the *Gipping*. The latter river takes its name from that of the village of *Gipping* near Newmarket which itself means 'Gip's people', referring to the same man called *Gip*. *Gipeswic c* 975, 1086.

Irlam (town, Greater Manchester) 'homestead on the (River) Irwell', OE river name + *hām*, 'homestead'. The river name means 'winding stream', from OE *irre*, 'winding', and *wella*, 'stream'. The second part of the name may be OE *hamm*, 'riverside enclosure'. *Urwelham c* 1190.

Ironbridge (town, Shropshire) '(place by the) iron bridge'. The name is a modern one, from the *iron bridge* that spans the Severn here. It was the first cast-iron bridge in the world, built in 1778.

Irthlingborough (town, Northamptonshire) 'fortified manor of the ploughmen', OE *yrthling*, 'ploughman' + *burh*, 'fortified manor'. It is possible the first part of the name represents an OE personal name. The name has survived the 'smoothing' (and corruption) seen in the Domesday Book record. *Yrtlingaburg* 780, *Erdinburne* 1086.

Irvine (town, Strathclyde) '(place by the River Irvine', Celtic river name. The river name perhaps means 'green river', from words related to modern Welsh *ir*, 'fresh', 'green', and *afon*, 'river' (*cp* ◊Avon).

Isis (river, Oxfordshire). The name is an alternative for the Thames above Oxford. *See* ◊Thames for the origin.

Islay (island, Strathclyde) 'swelling island', Celtic word. The original form of the name lacked the *s*, which was inserted by association with English *island*. The latter part of the name appears to have been influenced by OS *ey*, 'island'. *Ilea c* 690, *Ile* 800, *Islay, or Ilay* 1868.

Isleworth (district, Greater London) 'Gīslhere's enclosure', OE personal name + *worth*, 'enclosure'. Isleworth is on the Thames, and the first part of the name may have been influenced by *isle*. *Gistelesworde* 1086.

Islington (borough, Greater London) 'Gīsla's hill', OE personal name + *dūn*, 'hill'. The *-ington* of the name is misleading, since the *-ing-* represents the *-n* of a genitive case ending, and the *-ton* is really *-don*. *Gislandune* c 1000, *Iseldone* 1086.

Islwyn (district, Gwent) '(district of the mountain called Mynydd) Islwyn', Welsh mountain name. The name was devised for the administrative district formed here in 1974. The mountain name means 'under the bushes' (Welsh *is*, 'under', and *llwyn*, 'bush'). The district name also commemorates the bardic name of the poet William Thomas, born near the mountain in 1832.

Itchen (district, Hampshire) '(district of the River) Itchen', river name. The river name is an ancient, pre-Celtic one of unknown origin and meaning. It was adopted for the administrative district formed here in 1974.

Iver (village, Buckinghamshire) '(place by the) slope', OE *yfer*, 'slope'. The name probably refers to the low spur of land here overlooking marshy ground. The *-am* of the Domesday Book record represents a Latin ending. *Evreham* 1086.

Ivybridge (town, Devon) 'ivy bridge', OE *īfig*, 'ivy' + *brycg*, 'bridge'. An 'ivy bridge' is one covered in this climbing plant. The bridge is over the River Erme. *Ivebrugge* 1292.

J

Jarrow (town, Tyne and Wear) '(settlement of the) fen people', OE tribal name. The name alludes to the *Gyrwe*, who once lived here. Their name derives from OE *gyr*, 'fen', 'marsh'. *Gyruum c* 730.

Jedburgh (town, Borders) 'enclosure by the (River) Ged', Celtic river name + OE *worth*, 'enclosure'. The river name means 'winding one' from a word related to modern Welsh *gwden*, 'withe'. The *-burgh* of the name is misleading. *Gedwearde* 800.

Johnstone (town, Strathclyde) 'John's settlement', OE personal name + *tūn*, 'village'. It is not known who the *John* was who gave the name. *Jonestone* 1292.

Jura (island, Strathclyde) 'Doirad's island', Celtic personal name + Gaelic *eilean*, 'island'. The final *-a* of the name may have been influenced by ON *ey*, 'island'. *Doirad Eilinn* 678.

K

Kearsley (town, Greater Manchester) 'clearing where cress grows', OE *cærse*, 'cress' + *lēah*, 'clearing'. The 'clearing' was probably more a meadow than an area cleared of trees. *Cherselawe* 1187, *Kersleie c* 1220.

Keele (village, Staffordshire) 'cow hill', OE *cū*, 'cow' + *hyll*, 'hill'. A 'cow hill' is one where cows graze. The reference may be to the hill on which Keele Hall now stands. The first part of the name represents OE *cȳ*, the genitive singular of *cū*. *Kiel* 1169.

Keighley (town, West Yorkshire) 'Cyhha's clearing', OE personal name + *lēah*, 'clearing'. The modern name is pronounced 'Keethley' in a rare attempt to preserve the sound of OE *h*, which in the personal name would have been something like the *ch* in German *ich*. *Chichelai* 1086.

Keith (town, Grampian) '(place by the) wood', Celtic word. The word that gave the name is related to modern Welsh *coed*, 'wood'. The man's name *Keith* comes from this place, originally as a family name. *Ket* 1203.

Kelso (town, Borders) 'chalk hill spur', OE *cal*, 'chalk' + *hōh*, 'hill spur'. The 'hill spur' here is the low broad one to the north of the town. *Calkou* 1126.

Kelty (town, Fife) '(place by the) woods', Gaelic *coilltean*, 'woods'. The Gaelic word that gave the name is the plural of *coille*, 'wood'. *Quilte* mid-13th century.

Kendal (town, Cumbria) 'village with a church in Kendal', OS *kirkju-bý*, 'village with a church' + district name. The original name of the place was *Kirkby Kendal*, the first word being the name of the village, the second that of the district in which it was located. Only the latter has survived. It means 'valley of the (River) Kent', from a Celtic river name of uncertain meaning and OS *dalr*, 'valley'. *Cherchebi* 1086, *Kircabikendala c* 1095, *Kendale* 1452.

Kenilworth (town, Warwickshire) 'Cynehild's enclosure', OE personal name + *worth*, 'enclosure'. The personal name is that of a woman. The

Domesday Book record has dropped its second part. *Chinewrde* 1086, *Chenildeworda* early 12th century.

Kennet (district, Wiltshire) '(district of the River) Kennet', Celtic river name. The river name, of uncertain origin and meaning, was adopted for the administrative district set up here in 1974.

Kennington (district, Greater London) 'farmstead named after Cēna', OE personal name + *-ing-*, 'named after' + *tūn*, 'farmstead'. *Kennington*, Oxfordshire, has a name of identical origin, but *Kennington*, Kent, means 'royal manor'. *Chenintune* 1086.

Kensal Green (district, Greater London) 'village green by the king's wood', OE *cyning*, 'king' + *holt*, 'wood' + *grēne*, 'green'. The second word was added later to the original name, and OE *holt* has all but disappeared. *Kingisholte* 1253, *Kynsale Green* 1550.

Kensington (borough, Greater London) 'estate named after Cynesige', OE personal name + *-ing-*, 'named after' + *tūn*, 'estate'. It is a coincidence that the royal borough has a name that (in modern terms) suggests *king*. *Chenesitun* 1086.

Kent (county, England) 'coastal district', Celtic word. This is the traditional explanation of the name, from a word related to modern Welsh *cant*, 'edge', 'rim', alluding to the coast. But the actual meaning may be 'land of the hosts', ie armies, from a word related to modern Welsh *cant*, 'hundred'. *Cantium* 51 BC.

Kentish Town (district, Greater London) 'estate held by Kentish', Middle English family name + OE *tūn*, 'estate'. The surname means 'man from Kent'. *Kentisston* 1208.

Kesteven (district, Lincolnshire) 'meeting place in the wood', Celtic word + OS *stefna*, 'meeting place'. The name is an unusual combination of Celtic and Scandinavian, the Celtic word being related to modern Welsh *coed*, 'wood'. The mixture of languages shows that the 'meeting place in the wood', wherever it was, must have been used by the Danes as well as earlier by the Britons. *Ceoftefne c* 1000, *Chetsteven* 1086.

Keston (district, Greater London) 'Cyssi's stone', OE personal name + *stān*, 'stone'. The 'stone' was a boundary marker here. *Cysse stan* 973, *Chestan* 1086.

Keswick (town, Cumbria) 'cheese farm', OE *cēse*, 'cheese' + *wīc*, 'farm'. A 'cheese farm' is a dairy farm that specializes in making cheese. The initial *K* of the name is due to Scandinavian influence. The name has its exact southern counterpart in ◊Chiswick. *Kesewick c* 1240.

Kettering (town, Northamptonshire) '(settlement of) Cytra's people', OE personal name + *-ingas*, 'people of'. The personal name is problematical, but it could be as stated. *Cytringan* 956, *Cateringe* 1086.

Kew (district, Greater London) 'spur of land by a landing place', Middle English *key*, 'quay', 'landing place' + OE *hōh*, 'spur of land'. The first part of the name could equally represent OE *cǣg*, 'key', denoting a key-shaped area of land. Kew is on the Thames. *Cayho* 1327.

Keymer (town, West Sussex) '(place by the) cow pond', OE *cū*, 'cow' + *mere*, 'pond'. The name probably referred to one of the streams of the River Adur here, where cows must have had a regular watering place. *Chemere* 1086.

Keynsham (town, Avon) 'Cǣgin's riverside land', OE personal name + *hamm*, 'riverside land'. The river in question is the Avon. *Cægineshamme c* 1000, *Cainesham* 1086.

Kidderminster (town, Hereford and Worcester) 'Cydela's monastery', OE personal name + *mynster*, 'monastery'. The monastery was founded here in the 8th century on the site now occupied by All Saints Church. *Chideminstre* 1086, *Kedeleministre* 1154.

Kidsgrove (town, Staffordshire) 'Cyda's grove', OE personal name + *grāf*, 'grove'. No early forms of the name are known, so the interpretation is open to some conjecture.

Kidwelly (town, Dyfed) '(place of) Cadwal', Welsh personal name. The final *-y* of the name represents the Welsh ending, *-i*, that denotes the territory of the named person. The Welsh form of the name is *Cydweli*. *Cetgueli* 10th century.

Kielder Forest (forest, Northumberland) 'forest by Kielder Water', Celtic river name + modern English *forest*. Kielder Water is a reservoir that takes its name from the *Kielder* Burn, a river whose own name probably means 'rapid stream', from words related to modern Welsh *caled*, 'harsh', and *dŵr*, 'water'. *Keilder* 1326.

Kilbirnie (town, Strathclyde) '(St) Brendan's church', Celtic saint's name + Gaelic *cill*, 'church'. It is not clear whether the saint was the famous St Brendan who was a friend of St Columba. *Kilbyrny* 1413.

Kilburn (district, Greater London) '(place by the) cows' stream', OE *cū*, 'cow' + *burna*, 'stream'. There is some doubt about the first part of the name. In the record, it may represent OE *cūna*, the genitive plural of *cū*. There is no stream here now. *Cuneburna c* 1130.

Kilmacolm (town, Strathclyde) '(St) Columba's church', Celtic saint's name + Gaelic *cill*, 'church'. The saint's name appears here in a form literally meaning 'my Colm', with Gaelic *mo*, 'my', added to the name to express a personal dedication to him, as a sort of affectionate 'possession'.

Kilmarnock (town, Strathclyde) '(St) Ernan's church', Celtic saint's name + Gaelic *cill*, 'church'. As for ◊Kilmacolm, the saint's name appears in an affectionate 'possessive' form, effectively translating as 'my little Ernan', from Gaelic *mo*, 'my', and the diminutive suffix *-oc*. Ernan was a 6th-century saint and disciple of St Columba. *Kelmernoke* 1299.

Kilwinning (town, Strathclyde) '(St) Vinin's church', Celtic saint's name + Gaelic *cill*, 'church'. The saint's name is that of an Irish monk who is said to have founded a monastery here in the early 8th century on the site of the present Kilwinning Abbey. *Killvinin c* 1160.

Kimbolton (village, Cambridgeshire) 'Cynebald's farmstead', OE personal name + *tūn*, 'farmstead'. The village so named in Hereford and Worcester has an identical origin and meaning. *Chenebaltone* 1086.

Kincardine (district, Grampian) 'head of the grove', Gaelic *ceann*, 'head' + Pictish word. The name occurs in various parts of Scotland, with *Kincardine*-on-Forth a town in Fife. The historic county of *Kincardineshire* took its name from *Kincardine* Castle. The second part of the name represents a Pictish word related to modern Welsh *cardden*, 'thicket'.

Kinghorn (town, Fife) 'head of the marsh', Gaelic *ceann*, 'head' + *gronn*, 'marsh'. The name appears to have been influenced by English *king*. *Kingorn c* 1140, *Kyngor* 1150.

Kingsbridge (town, Devon) 'king's bridge', OE *cyning*, 'king' + *brycg*, 'bridge'. It is not known which king owned the bridge here over the Kingsbridge Estuary. *Cinges bricge* 962.

Kingsbury (district, Greater London) 'king's manor', OE *cyning*, 'king' + *burh*, 'manor'. The manor was granted by Edward the Confessor to Westminster Abbey. *Kynges Byrig* 1044 *Chingesberie* 1086.

King's Langley (village, Hertfordshire) 'long wood of the king', OE *cyning*, 'king' + *lang*, 'long' + *lēah*, 'wood', 'clearing'. The village evolved from a manor house granted to the king in the 12th century. The first word distinguishes this Langley from ◊Abbots Langley. *Langelai* 1086, *Kyngeslangeley* 1436.

King's Lynn (town, Norfolk) 'king's (manor in) Lynn', modern English *king's* + Celtic place-name. The second word of the name, used alone until the 16th century, means 'pool', from a Celtic word related to modern Welsh *llyn*. The 'pool' would have been the mouth of the Ouse, where the town now stands. The 'king' was Henry VIII, who acquired the manor from the Bishop of Norwich. *Lena* 1086, *Lynna c* 1105, *Lynn-Regis* 1771.

Kingsteignton (town, Devon) 'king's farmstead on the (River) Teign', OE *cyning*, 'king' + Celtic river name + OE *tūn*, 'farmstead'. The name was originally *Teignton*, and *king* was added after the manor was held by the king in the 11th century. For the meaning of the river name, *see* ◊Teignmouth. *Teintona* 1086, *Kingestentone* 1274.

Kingston upon Hull *see* ◊Hull.

Kingston upon Thames (town, Greater London) 'king's estate on the Thames', OE *cyning*, 'king' + *tūn*, 'estate' + Celtic river name. The original estate here was held by the king in the 9th century. The name was simply *Kingston* for years, and the added words came later to distinguish this Kingston from the many others. *See* ◊Thames for the meaning of the river name. *Cyninges tun* 838, *Chingestune* 1086, *Kyngeston super Tamisiam* 1321.

Kingswear (town, Devon) 'king's weir', OE *cyning*, 'king' + *wer*, 'weir'. The weir here was on the River Dart. The king at the time of the record was Henry II. *Kingeswere* 12th century.

Kingswood (town, Avon) 'king's wood', OE *cyning*, 'king' + *wudu*, 'wood'. The king at the time of the record was Henry III, but the royal ownership may be of earlier date. *Kingeswode* 1231.

Kington (town, Hereford and Worcester) 'royal manor', OE *cyning*, 'king' + *tūn*, 'manor'. The king at the time of the record was William the Conqueror, but the original royal owner was almost certainly one before him. *Chingtune* 1086.

Kingussie (town, Highland) 'head of the pinewood', Gaelic *ceann*, 'head' + *giuthseach*, 'pinewood'. The pines are still much in evidence here in Strathspey. *Kinguscy c* 1210.

Kinlochleven (town, Highland) 'head of Loch Leven', Gaelic *ceann* + Celtic loch name. For the name of the loch, *see* ◊Leven.

Kinross (town, Tayside) 'head of the promontory', Gaelic *ceann*, 'head' + *ros*, 'promontory'. The 'promontory' is the one that juts into Loch Leven here. *Kynros c* 1144.

Kinver (town, Staffordshire) '(place by the) hill', Celtic word. The first part of the name is of obscure origin and meaning. The second part is related to modern Welsh *bre*, 'hill', here as *fre* in its mutated form. *Cynibre* 736.

Kirkby (town, Merseyside) 'village with a church', OS *kirkju-bý*. The compound OS word represents *kirkja*, 'church', and *bý*, 'village'. *Cherchebi* 1086.

Kirkby in Ashfield (town, Nottinghamshire) 'village with a church in Ashfield', OS *kirkju-bý*, 'village with a church' + OE district name. The district name means 'open land with ash trees', from OE *æsc*, 'ash tree', and *feld*, 'open land'. *Chircebi* 1086, *Kirkeby in Esfeld* 1216.

Kirkby Lonsdale (town, Cumbria) 'village with a church in Lonsdale', OS *kirkju-bý*, 'village with a church' + district name. The district name means 'valley of the (River) Lune', from a Celtic river name (*see* ◊Lancaster) and OS *dalr*, 'valley'. *Cherchebi* 1086, *Kircabi Lauenesdale* 1090.

Kirkbymoorside (town, North Yorkshire) 'village with a church at the head of the moor', OS *kirkju-bý*, 'village with a church' + OE *mōr*, 'moor' + *hēafod*, 'head'. The *-side* of the name is misleading. The main street of the town climbs steeply to the moors. *Chircebi* 1086, *Kirkeby Moresheved c* 1170.

Kirkby Stephen (town, Cumbria) 'Stephen's village with a church', personal name + OS *kirkju-bý*, 'village with a church'. The personal name may be either that of the saint to whom the church was dedicated or that of an early owner. *Cherkaby Stephan c* 1094.

Kirkcaldy (town, Fife), 'fort of the hard hill', Celtic words. The words that comprise the name are related to modern Welsh *caer*, 'fort', and *caled din*, 'hard hill'. The 'fort' was probably on the site of the present 15th-century Ravenscraig Castle. *Kircalethyn* 12th century.

Kirkconnel (town, Dumfries and Galloway) '(St) Congal's church', OS *kirkja*, 'church' + Celtic saint's name. It is likely that the Scandinavian word for 'church' replaced an original Gaelic *cill*. *Kyrkconwelle* 1347.

Kirkcudbright (town, Dumfries and Galloway) '(St) Cuthbert's church', OS *kirkja*, 'church' + OE saint's name. As for ◊Kirkconnel, OS *kirkja* probably replaced Gaelic *cill*. St Cuthbert (originally *Cūthbeorht*) was a

7th-century Northumbrian monk who made many missionary journeys in Galloway. *Kircuthbright* 1286.

Kirkham (town, Lancashire) 'village with a church', OS *kirkja*, 'church' + OE *hām*, 'village'. The OS word replaced an original OE *cirice*, 'church'. The Domesday Book record of the name has omitted the *r*. *Chicheham* 1086.

Kirkintilloch (town, Strathclyde) 'fort at the head of the hillock', Celtic word + Gaelic *ceann*, 'head' + *tulach*, 'hillock'. The first part of the name is related to modern Welsh *caer*, 'fort'. The name as a whole refers to a Roman fort on the Antonine Wall here. *Kirkintulach c* 1200.

Kirklees (district, West Yorkshire) 'wood belonging to a church', OS *kirkja*, 'church' + OE *lēah*, 'wood'. The name of the modern administrative district directly derives from that of *Kirklees* Hall, a Jacobean mansion built on the site of a Cistercian nunnery (the 'church'). The OS first part of the name probably replaced an earlier OE *cirice*, 'church'. *Kyrkelegh* 1246.

Kirkwall (town, Orkney) 'church by the bay', OS *kirkja*, 'church' + *vágr*, 'bay'. The 'bay' is the Bay of Kirkwall, to the north of the town. The 'church' is the 12th-century cathedral of St Magnus. The present form of the name appears to have been influenced by English *wall*. *Kirkiuvagr c* 1225, *Kyrkvaw* 1364.

Kirriemuir (town, Tayside) 'great quarter', Gaelic *ceathramh*, 'quarter' + *mōr*, 'great'. A 'quarter' was a measure of land considered large enough to support a single household. *Kerimor* 1250.

Kirton in Lindsey (town, Humberside) 'village with a church in Lindsey', OS *kirkja*, 'church' + OE *tūn*, 'village' + Celtic district name. OS *kirkja* probably replaced an original OE *cirice*, 'church'. For the district name, *see* ◊Lindsey. *Chirchetone* 1086.

Knaresborough (town, North Yorkshire) 'Cēnheard's stronghold', OE personal name + *burh*, 'stronghold'. It is possible the first part of the name represents OE *cnearr*, 'rugged rock', referring to the rock on which Knaresborough Castle stands, as the site of the original fort. *Chenaresburg* 1086.

Knebworth (town, Hertfordshire) 'Cnebba's enclosure', OE personal name + *worth*, 'enclosure'. The Domesday Book record has *p* for *b*. *Chenepeworde* 1086, *Knebbewrth* 1220.

Knighton (town, Powys) 'knights' village', OE *cniht*, 'knight' + *tūn*, 'village'. 'Knights' here means servants or personal followers of a baron or lord. The Welsh name of the town is different: *Trefyclo*, 'farm by the dyke', from *tref*, 'farm', *y*, 'the', and *clawdd*, 'dyke', this being Offa's Dyke nearby. *Chenistone* 1086, *Cnicheton* 1193.

Knightsbridge (district, Greater London) 'knights' bridge', OE *cniht*, 'knight' + *brycg*, 'bridge'. As for ◊Knighton, the 'knights' would have been the servants of a baron or lord. The 'bridge' here, over the River Westbourne, would have been one where these young men gathered. *Cnihtebricge c* 1050.

Knottingley (town, West Yorkshire) 'clearing of Cnotta's people', OE personal name + *-inga-*, 'of the people of' + *lēah*, 'clearing'. The personal name here is conjectural. *Notingeleia* 1086.

Knowle (district, Bristol, Avon) '(place at the) hill top', OE *cnoll*, 'hill top', 'hillock'. It is not certain which particular 'hill top' is intended here. There are several places of the name in Somerset and Devon. *Canole* 1086.

Knowsley (district, Merseyside) 'Cēnwulf's clearing', OE personal name + *lēah*, 'clearing'. The personal name could equally be *Cynewulf*. The administrative district takes its name from the village of *Knowsley*, near Liverpool. *Chenulueslei* 1086.

Knutsford (town, Cheshire) 'Knútr's ford', OS personal name + OE *ford*, 'ford'. The personal name has traditionally been associated with King *Cnut* (Canute). It is uncertain where the 'ford' was, as the town is not on a river. *Cunetesford* 1086.

Kyle of Lochalsh (town, Highland) '(place by the) strait of Loch Alsh', Gaelic *caol*, 'narrow' + Celtic loch name. The name of the loch may mean 'foaming one' (Gaelic *aillsach*).

Kyles of Bute (strait, Strathclyde) 'strait of Bute', Gaelic *caol*, 'narrow' + island name. The island of *Bute* has a Gaelic name apparently meaning 'fire' (*bocht*), presumably referring to signal fires. An English plural *s* has been added to the Gaelic word for 'strait'.

L

Lambeth (borough, Greater London) 'landing place for lambs', OE *lamb*, 'lamb' + *hȳth*, 'landing place'. Lambeth is on the south bank of the Thames. *Lamhytha* 1088.

Lambourn (town, Berkshire) 'stream where lambs are washed', OE *lamb*, 'lamb' + *burna*, 'stream'. The town takes its name from the stream here. *Lambburnan c* 880, *Lamborne* 1086.

Lammermuir (region, Borders) 'lambs' moor', OE *lamb*, 'lamb' + *mōr*, 'moor'. The first part of the name represents OE *lambra*, the genitive plural of *lamb*. The record refers to Lammermuir Hills, the highest point of the region. *Lombormore* 800.

Lampeter (town, Dyfed) '(St) Peter's church', Welsh *llan*, 'church' + *Pedr*, 'Peter'. The Welsh name of the town is *Llanbedr Pont Steffan*, '(St) Peter's church at Stephen's bridge', the latter words from *pont*, 'bridge', and *Steffan*, 'Stephen'. Stephen would have been the man appointed to look after the bridge. *Lanpeter* 1284, *Lampeter Pount Steune* 1301.

Lanark (town, Strathclyde) '(place by the) glade', Celtic word. The word that gave the name is related to modern Welsh *llannerch*, 'glade'. *Lannarc* 1188.

Lancashire (county, England) 'county of Lancaster', place-name + OE *scīr*, 'district'. The county takes its name from ◊Lancaster, as the record demonstrates. *Lancastreshire* 14th century.

Lancaster (city, Lancashire) 'Roman fort on the (River) Lune', Celtic river name + OE *cæster*, 'Roman fort'. The river name probably means 'healthy', 'pure'. The name of the Roman fort here is unknown, although it was almost certainly based on the river name. *Loncastre* 1086.

Lanchester (town, Durham) 'long Roman fort', OE *lang*, 'long' + *ceaster*, 'Roman fort'. The name of the Roman fort here was *Longovicium*, a Celtic-based name probably meaning 'place of the ship fighters', with the first part corresponding to modern Welsh *llong*, 'ship'. The *Lan-* of the present name may thus be a reduced form of this. *Langecestr* 1196.

Lancing (town, West Sussex) '(settlement of) Wlanc's people', OE personal name + *-ingas*, 'people of'. There are several similar names ending in *-ing* here, implying that this people's territory must have been quite small. *Lancinges* 1086.

Land's End (peninsula, Cornwall), 'end of the (main)land'. The peninsula is the most westerly point in mainland England. *See also* ◊Penwith. *Londeseynde* 1337.

Langbaurgh (district, Cleveland) 'long hill', OE *lang*, 'long' + *beorg*, 'hill'. The administrative district formed here in 1974 took its name from *Langbaurgh* Ridge.

Langdale Pikes (peaks, Cumbria) 'pointed hills by the long valley', OE *lang*, 'long' + OS *dalr*, 'valley' + OE *pīk*, 'pike'. In the valley name, OS *dalr* has replaced OE *denu*, 'valley'.

Langport (town, Somerset) 'long market place', OE *lang*, 'long' + *port*, 'market place'. The reference is to Bow Street, the long straight street that climbs through the town, off which the weekly market is still held. *Longport* 10th century, *Lanport* 1086.

Largs (town, Strathclyde) '(place by a) slope', Gaelic *learg*, 'slope'. The town is sheltered by lofty hills. An English plural *s* has been added to the Gaelic word. *Larghes c* 140.

Lauder (town, Borders) '(place by the) Leader (Water)', Celtic river name. The river name may mean 'wash', implying a current that 'washes' the soil or land. *Louueder* 1208.

Launceston (town, Cornwall) 'estate by (St) Stephen's church', Cornish **lann*, 'church' + saint's name + OE *tūn*, 'estate'. The reference is to the former village of *St Stephens*, north of the town. In the Domesday Book record, *c* has been written for *t*. *Lanscavetone* 1086, *Lanstavaton c* 1125, *Lanson* 1478.

Laurencekirk (town, Grampian), '(St) Laurence's church', saint's name + OS *kirkja*, 'church'. The saint's name is that of St Laurence of Canterbury, to whom the church is dedicated.

Lavenham (town, Suffolk) 'Lāfa's homestead', OE personal name + *hām*, 'homestead'. The *-n* of the name represents the genitive ending of the personal name. *Lauanham c* 995, *Lauenham* 1086.

Leamington (town, Warwickshire) 'farmstead on the (River) Leam', Celtic river name + OE *tūn*, 'farmstead'. The river name means either 'elm river' or 'marshy river'. *Cp* ◊Lymington, ◊Lympne. The town is now normally known as *Leamington Spa*, and formally since 1838 as *Royal Leamington Spa*. *Lamintone* 1086.

Leatherhead (town, Surrey) '(place by the) grey ford', Celtic words. The words that gave the name are related to modern Welsh *llwyd*, 'grey', and *rhyd*, 'ford'. The 'grey ford' would have been over the Mole here. *Leodridan c* 880, *Leret* 1086.

Lechlade (village, Gloucestershire) '(place at the) crossing near the (River) Leach', OE river name + *gelād*, 'river crossing'. The 'crossing' would have been over the Thames here. The river name means 'boggy stream', from OE **læc* or **lece* in this sense. The Leach joins the Thames half a mile away. *Lecelade* 1086.

Ledbury (town, Hereford and Worcester) 'fortified place on the (River) Leadon', Celtic river name + OE *burh*, 'fortified place'. The river name means 'broad stream'. *Liedeberge* 1086.

Leeds (city, West Yorkshire) '(settlement of the) people living by the fast flowing river', Celtic river name. The name refers to the River Aire, which formerly must have been called something like *Lāt*. The people were the *Ladenses*. *Loidis* 731, *Ledes* 1086.

Leek (town, Staffordshire) '(place by the) brook', OS *lækr*, 'brook'. The reference is to the stream that flows through the town as a tributary of the River Churnet. *Lec* 1086.

Leicester (city, Leicestershire) 'Roman town of the Ligore (people)', tribal name + OE *ceaster*, 'Roman town'. The origin and meaning of the tribal name are uncertain. The name of the Roman town was *Ratae Coritanorum*, 'fortifications of the Coritani'. Again, the origin of the tribal name is unknown. The county name, *Leicestershire*, is first recorded in the 11th century. *Ligera ceaster* early 10th century, *Ledecestre* 1086.

Leigh (town, Greater Manchester) '(place at the) clearing', OE *lēah*, 'clearing'. A more precise rendering of the OE word here would be 'meadow', as Leigh stands on an area of low marshland. *Legh* 1276.

Leighton Buzzard (town, Bedfordshire) 'leek farm of the Busard family', OE *lēac*, 'leek' + *tūn*, 'farm' + family name. The *Busard* family were here in the 13th century. *Lestone* 1086, *Letton Busard* 1254.

Leiston (town, Suffolk) 'farmstead by a fire', OE *lēg*, 'fire' + *tūn*, 'farmstead'. The 'fire' would have been a beacon or signal fire. The site of the town near the coast is suitable for this. *Leistuna* 1086.

Lennoxtown (town, Strathclyde) 'town of the Lennox family', family name + *town*. The *Lennox* family took their name from the ancient territory of *Lennox*, its own name meaning '(place of) elm trees', from Gaelic *leamhanach*, 'abounding in elms' (from *leamh*, 'elm').

Leominster (town, Hereford and Worcester) 'church in Leon', Celtic district name + OE *mynster*, 'church'. The district name means '(place) at the streams', from a word related to modern Welsh *llieni*, 'streams'. It relates to a triangle of land between the rivers Arrow and Lugg here. *Leomynster* 10th century, *Leominstre* 1086.

Lerwick (town, Shetland) '(place by) bay of mud', OS *leirr*, 'mud' + *vík*, 'bay'. The bay in question is Bressay Sound, on the east coast of Mainland. *Lerwick* 1625.

Leslie (town, Fife) 'holly enclosure', Celtic words. The words that gave the name are related to modern Welsh *llys*, 'court', and *celyn*, 'holly'. *Lesslyn c* 1180.

Letchworth (town, Hertfordshire) 'enclosure that can be locked', OE **lycce*, 'locked place' + *worth*, 'enclosure'. The unrecorded OE word that gave the first part of the name is based on *loc*, the source of modern *lock*. *Leceworde* 1086.

Leven (town, Fife) '(place by the River) Leven', Gaelic river name. The river name means 'elm river', from Gaelic *leamhain*, 'elm'. *Cp* ◊Leamington and ◊Lennoxtown. *Levin c* 1535.

Levenshulme (district, Manchester, Greater Manchester) 'Lēofwine's island', OE personal name + OS *holmr*, 'island'. The 'island' would have been raised ground in marshland here. *Lewyneshulm* 1246.

Lewes (town, East Sussex) 'burial mounds', OE *lǣw*, 'burial mound'. The OE word has here added a plural *s*. *Lǣwes c* 959, *Lewes* 1086.

Lewis (island, Western Isles) 'marshy place', Gaelic *leoig*, 'ditch', 'marsh'. Much of the island is a vast expanse of peat and moss, with many lochs and streams. *Leodur c* 1100.

Lewisham (town, Greater London) 'Lēofsa's homestead', OE personal name + *hām*, 'homestead'. The personal name is conjectural. *Levesham* 1086.

Leyburn (town, North Yorkshire) 'sheltered place by a stream', OE **hlēg*, 'shelter' + *burna*, 'stream'. The first part of the name is of conjectural interpretation. *Leborne* 1086.

Leyland (town, Lancashire) '(place of) untilled land', OE **lǣge*, 'fallow', 'untilled' + *land*, 'land', 'ground'. Presumably much of the land by the River Lostock here was used for grazing rather than growing crops. *Lailand* 1086.

Leyton (town, Greater London) 'farmstead on the (River) Lea', Celtic river name + OE *tūn*, 'farmstead'. The river name may mean 'bright river'. ◊Luton is on the same river, so has a name of identical origin. *Lugetune c* 1050, *Leintune* 1086.

Lichfield (city, Staffordshire) 'open land by Letocetum', Celtic placename + OE *feld*, 'open land'. *Letocetum* was the name of the Roman station at what is now the village of Wall, 2 miles southwest of Lichfield. Its name means 'grey wood', from words related to modern Welsh *llwyd*, 'grey', and *coed*, 'wood'. *Licitfelda* 710.

Lincoln (city, Lincolnshire) 'Roman colony by the pool', Celtic word + Latin *colonia*, 'colony'. The 'pool' was the marshland and pools of the River Witham, part of which survives today in Brayford Pool. The 'colony' was one for retired legionaries. The word that gave the first part of the name is related to modern Welsh *llyn*, 'lake'. The county name, *Lincolnshire*, is first recorded in the 11th century. *Lindon c* 150, *Lindum colonia* late 7th century, *Lincolia* 1086.

Lindisfarne (island, Northumberland) 'island of the travellers from Lindsey', Celtic district name + OE *fara*, 'traveller' + *ēg*, 'island'. The 'travellers from Lindsey' were probably those making a regular religious pilgrimage to this island. *Cp* its other name, ◊Holy Island. *See also* ◊Lindsey. *Lindisfarnae c* 700.

Lindsey (district, Lincolnshire) '(district of) Lincoln'. The district is in the north of the county, and takes its name from an old name of ◊Lincoln there. *See also* ◊Lindisfarne. *Lindissi c* 730, *Lindesi* 1086.

Lingfield (village, Surrey) 'open land of the dwellers in the clearing', OE *lēah*, 'clearing' + *-inga-*, 'of the people of' + *feld*, 'open land'. The initial *L-* of the name is all that remains of OE *lēah*. *Leangafelda* 9th century.

Linlithgow (town, Lothian) '(place by) Linlithgow (Loch)', Celtic lake name. The name of the loch means 'lake in a damp hollow', from words corresponding to modern Welsh *llyn*, 'lake', *llaith*, 'moist', and *cau*, 'hollow'. *Linlidcu c* 1138.

Liphook (village, Hampshire) 'angle of land by the deer leap', OE *hlīep*, 'leap' + *hōc*, 'hook', 'angle of land'. It is not certain where exactly the 'deer leap' would have been. *Leophok* 1364.

Liskeard (town, Cornwall) 'Kerwyd's court', Cornish **lys*, 'court' + personal name. The second part of the name is more likely to be a personal name than Cornish *carow*, 'stag', as has been suggested. *Lys Cerruyt c* 1010, *Liscarret* 1086.

Liss (village, Hampshire) '(place by the) court', Celtic word. The 'court' would have been the chief house in the district. The word that gave the name is related to the first part of ◊Liskeard and ◊Lizard, as well as to modern Welsh *llys*, 'court'. *Lis* 1086.

Littleborough (town, Greater Manchester) 'little fort', OE *lȳtel*, 'little' + *bur*, 'fort'. No record for this name has been found earlier than the one below. *Littlebrough* 1577.

Littlehampton (town, West Sussex) 'little home farm', OE *lȳtel*, 'little' + *hām-tūn*, 'home farm'. The name was originally *Hampton*. *Little* was added subsequently to distinguish this Hampton from the one at ◊Southampton, which was also originally *Hampton* (but not a 'home farm'). *Hantone* 1086, *Lyttelhampton* 1482.

Littleover (district, Derby, Derbyshire) 'little (place by the) ridge', OE *lȳtel*, 'little' + **ofer*, 'ridge'. The district lies to southwest of the city on a slope, and this is the 'ridge'. The first part of the name distinguishes it from nearby ◊Mickleover. The first word of the Domesday Book record is Latin for 'little'. *Parva Ufre* 1086.

Liverpool (city, Merseyside) 'pool with muddy water', OE *lifer*, 'clotted' + *pōl*, 'pool'. The name literally means 'livered pool', *ie*, one that is muddy or clotted with weeds. The reference is to *The Pool*, a creek of the Mersey that has now been filled in. *Liuerpul c* 1190.

Liversedge (town, West Yorkshire) 'Lēofhere's edge', OE personal name + *ecg*, 'edge', 'ridge'. The name refers to the long low ridge where the town lies, above the River Calder. *Livresec* 1086.

Livingston (town, Lothian) 'Leving's farmstead', OE personal name + *tūn*, 'farmstead'. The personal name derives from OE *lēofing*, 'dear one', 'darling'. *Uilla Leuing* mid-12th century, *Leiggestun* late 12th century.

Lizard, The (peninsula, Cornwall) 'court on a height', Cornish **lys*, 'court' + **ardh*, 'height'. The 'court' was a local administrative centre here in medieval times. Its location was probably at or near the present village of *Lizard* at the southern end of the peninsula. *Lisart* 1086.

Llanberis (town, Gwynedd) 'church of (St) Peris', Welsh *llan*, 'church' + saint's name. St Peris is said to have arrived in Wales as a missionary from Rome in the 6th century.

Llandaff (district, Cardiff, South Glamorgan) 'church on the (River) Taff', Welsh *llan*, 'church' + Celtic river name. The river name probably means simply 'water', from the same root word that gave the name of the ◊Thames. *Lanntaf c* 1150, *Landaph* 1191.

Llandeilo (town, Dyfed) 'church of (St) Teilo', Welsh *llan*, 'church' + saint's name. St Teilo, also known as St Elidius, was a 6th-century saint and bishop influential in South Wales. The second word of the record means 'great', to distinguish this Llandeilo from others. *Lanteliau Mawr* 1130.

Llandovery (town, Dyfed) 'church by the stream', Welsh *llan*, 'church' + *am dŵfr*, 'by the stream'. The town is a mile from the confluence of the Bran and the Towy. Its name is an English form of the Welsh original, *Llanymddyfri*, shortened to *Llanddyfri*. *Llanamdewri* 12th century.

Llandrindod Wells (town, Powys) 'Trinity church by the wells', Welsh *llan*, 'church' + *trindod*, 'Trinity' + English *wells*. The 'wells' are the natural springs here that were first exploited in the 18th century. The earlier name of the place was *Llanddwy*, 'God's church', from *llan*, 'church', and *Duw*, 'God', and this is represented by the first record. *Lando* 1291, *Llandyndodd* 1535, *Llandrindodd c* 1555.

Llandudno (town, Gwynedd) 'church of (St) Tudno', Welsh *llan*, 'church' + saint's name. Little is known about St Tudno, who may have been active here in the 6th century.

Llandyssul (town, Dyfed) 'church of (St) Tysul', Welsh *llan*, 'church' + saint's name. As often, little is known about this particular saint, who may have been here in the 6th century.

Llanelli (town, Dyfed) 'church of (St) Elli', Welsh *llan*, 'church' + saint's name. St Elli, a woman saint, is said to have been the daughter of the legendary prince Brychan, who gave the name of ◊Brecon. *Lan Elli c* 1173.

Llanfair Caereinion (town, Powys) 'church of (St) Mary by fort of Einion', Welsh *llan*, 'church' + saint's name + *caer*, 'fort' + Celtic river name. *Llanfair*, 'St Mary's church', is found so commonly in Wales that a distinguishing addition is usually needed. *Fair* is the mutated form of *Mair*, 'Mary'.

Llanfairfechan (town, Gwynedd) 'little church of (St) Mary', Welsh *llan*, 'church' + saint's name + *bychan*, 'little'. The addition of 'little' distinguishes this 'St Mary's church' from the larger one at Conwy.

Llanfairpwllgwyngyllgogerychwyrndrobwllllandysiliogogogoch (village, Gwynedd). The artificial name for this Anglesey village was devised by a local tailor in the 19th century. The meaning is 'church of (St) Mary near the pool of the white hazel near the fierce whirlpool and church of (St) Tysilio by the cave'.

Llanfyllin (town, Powys) 'church of (St) Myllin', Welsh *llan*, 'church' + saint's name. Almost nothing is known about this saint. *Llanvelig* 1254.

Llangefni (town, Gwynedd) 'church by the (River) Cefni', Welsh *llan*, 'church' + Celtic river name. The river name may mean 'stream from the ridge', from Welsh *cefn*, 'back', 'ridge'. *Llangevni* 1254.

Llangollen (town, Clwyd) 'church of (St) Collen', Welsh *llan*, 'church' + saint's name. St Collen is said to have been a former Roman army soldier who came to Britain in the 7th century to become Abbot of Glastonbury. *Lancollien* 1234.

Llanidloes (town, Powys) 'church of (St) Idloes', Welsh *llan*, 'church' + saint's name. The saint is said to have been active here in the 7th century. *Lanidloes* 1254

Llanrwst (town, Gwynedd) 'church of (St) Grwst', Welsh *llan*, 'church' + saint's name. Little is known about the saint. *Lhannruste* 1254.

Llantwit Major (town, South Glamorgan) 'greater church of (St) Illtyd', Welsh *llan*, 'church' + saint's name + Latin *major*, 'greater'. The named saint founded a monastery here in the 6th century. The place is 'greater' compared to *Llantwit Fardre* ('by the steward's house'), Mid Glamorgan, and *Llantwit-juxta-Neath'* ('near Neath'), West Glamorgan. This last is also *Llantwit Minor*, 'lesser Llantwit'.

Lleyn Peninsula (peninsula, Gwynedd). The name is of uncertain origin and meaning. It may be a Celtic tribal name, referring to the people known to the Romans as the *Lagenii*. Their own name may come from that of *Leinster*, Ireland, from where they perhaps emigrated.

Loanhead (town, Lothian) 'head of the loan'. *Loan* is a northern dialect word corresponding to English *lane*. The original 'loan' here may have been the one that ran up from the North Esk river. *Loneheid* 1618.

Lochaber (district, Highland) 'lake at the confluence', Gaelic *loch*, 'lake' + Celtic *aber*, 'river mouth', 'confluence'. There is no actual loch of the name here now, and the original lake must have dried up.

Lochgelly (town, Fife) '(place by) Loch Gelly', Gaelic lake name. The name of the loch represents Gaelic *geal*, 'bright', 'shining'. *Lochgellie* 1606.

Lochgilphead (town, Strathclyde) '(place at the) head of Loch Gilp', Gaelic lake name + English *head*. The loch derives its name from Gaelic *gilb*, 'chisel', alluding to its shape. *Lochgilpshead* 1650.

Lochinvar (loch, Dumfries and Galloway) 'lake on the height', Gaelic *loch*, 'lake' + *an bharra*, 'on the height'. The loch is located among hills.

Lochinver (town, Highland) '(place by) Loch Inver', Gaelic lake name. The name of the loch represents Gaelic *inbhir*, 'river mouth'. The loch itself is open to the sea and stands at the mouth of the river of the same name.

Lochmaben (town, Dumfries and Galloway). The name is of uncertain origin and meaning. The town is surrounded by several lochs, but none of them is called *Maben*, which itself may be a personal name, or perhaps that of a pagan god.

Lochnagar (mountain, Grampian) '(mountain by) Lochnagar', Gaelic lake name. The small loch here has a name representing Gaelic *loch na gaire*, 'lake of the outcrop'.

Lockerbie (town, Dumfries and Galloway) 'Locard's farmstead', OS personal name + *bý*, 'farmstead'. Scandinavian names are not unusual in this part of Scotland. *Lokardebi* 1306.

Loddon (town, Norfolk) '(place by the River) Loddon', Celtic river name. The river name, perhaps meaning 'muddy stream', is an old name for what is now the River *Chet* (from the nearby village of *Chedgrave*). *Lodne* 1043, *Lotna* 1086.

Lomond, Loch (loch, Central/Strathclyde) '(loch by) Ben Lomond', Celtic mountain name. The name of the mountain means 'beacon hill', from a word related to Gaelic *laom*, 'blaze'.

London (city, Greater London). The name is obscure in origin and meaning. It was long thought to derive from *Londinos*, a Celtic personal name perhaps meaning 'bold one'. *Londinium c* 115.

Long, Loch (loch, Strathclyde), 'lake of the ships', Gaelic *loch*, 'lake' + *long*, 'ship'. The loch would have been a safe anchorage for ships that had sailed up the Clyde.

Long Eaton (town, Derbyshire) 'long estate on dry land in marshland', OE *lang*, 'long' + *ēg*, 'island' + *tūn*, 'estate'. The name was originally *Eaton*, with *Long* added later for differentiation from other places of the same name. The estate extended further than that at *Little Eaton*, north of Derby. *Aitune* 1086, *Long Eyton* 1288.

Long Melford (town, Suffolk) 'long ford by a mill', OE *lang*, 'long' + *myln*, 'mill' + *ford*, 'ford'. A 'long ford' is one that runs for some distance from one bank of the river (here the Ouse) to the other, as distinct from one that is 'broad', or wide. *Melaforda* 1086.

Long Mynd, The (hills, Shropshire), OE *lang*, 'long' + Welsh *mynydd*, 'mountain'. The name refers to the central ridge of the range of hills. The name is half English, half Welsh, as befits the location. *Longameneda* 12th century.

Longridge (town, Lancashire) 'long ridge', OE *lang*, 'long' + *hrycg*, 'ridge'. The town takes its name from nearby *Longridge* Fell. *Langrig* 1246.

Longtown (town, Cumbria) 'long farmstead', OE *lang*, 'long' + *tūn*, 'estate'. The town extends alongside the River Esk. *Longeton* 1267.

Looe (town, Cornwall) '(place by the) pool', Cornish **logh*, 'pool', 'inlet'. The name is properly that of the river here, which divides the town into East and West Looe. *Loo c* 1220.

Lossiemouth (town, Grampian) '(place at the) mouth of the (River) Lossie', Gaelic river name + English *mouth*. The river name means 'rich in plants', from a word related to Welsh *llysiau*, 'herbs'.

Lostwithiel (town, Cornwall) 'tail end of the woodland', Cornish *lost*, 'tail' + *gwyth*, 'trees'. The name refers to the original location of the place at the 'tail' end of a district of many trees known as *Withiel*. The final *-iel* is probably an adjectival suffix. *Lostwetell* 1194.

Lothian (region, Scotland). The meaning of the name is uncertain. It may be a tribal name, perhaps related to one *Leudonus*, although nothing is known about him. *Loonia c* 970, *Lodoneo* 1098, *Louthion c* 1200.

Loughborough (town, Leicestershire) 'Luhhede's fortified place', OE personal name + *burh*, 'fortified place'. The Domesday Book record of the name has *n* instead of *u*. *Lucteburne* 1086.

Loughton (town, Essex) 'estate named after Luca', OE personal name + -*ing*-, 'named after' + *tūn*, 'estate'. The -*ing*- of the name has disappeared. It has survived for the Wiltshire village of *Luckington*, which has the same meaning. *Lochetuna* 1086.

Louth (town, Lincolnshire) '(place by the River) Lud', OE river name. The river name means 'loud one', from OE *hlūde, 'loud'. *Cp* ◊Ludlow. *Lude* 1086.

Lowestoft (town, Suffolk) 'Hlothvér's homestead', OS personal name + *toft*, homestead'. One of the Viking -*toft* names typically found in the East Midlands and East Anglia. *Lothu Wistoft* 1086.

Lowther Hills (hills, Strathclyde/Dumfries and Galloway). The origin of the name is obscure. The range as a whole takes the name of two of its highest mountains, *Green Lowther* and *Lowther Hill*.

Ludgershall (town, Wiltshire) 'corner of land with a trapping spear', OE *lūte-gār, 'trapping spear' + *halh*, 'nook'. A 'trapping spear' is a spear set to impale wild animals, and a 'corner of land' would obviously be a good place to set such a trap. Here, it was probably one of the valleys that run into the flat-topped hill on which the town stands. The Domesday Book record is corrupt. *Lutegaresheale* 1015, *Litlegarsele* 1086.

Ludlow (town, Shropshire) 'hill by a noisy torrent', OE *hlūde, 'loud stream' + *hlāw*, 'hill'. The town is on a hill above the River Teme, which here has a fast current. *Ludelaue* 1138.

Lulworth (village, Dorset) 'Lulla's enclosure', OE personal name + *worth*, 'enclosure'. There are actually two separate villages here, *East Lulworth* and *West Lulworth*. *Lulvorde* 1086.

Lundy (island, Devon) 'puffin island', OS *lundi*, 'puffin' + *ey*, 'island'. The island has long been noted for its puffins, although few remain today. *Insula de Lundeia* 1189.

Luton (town, Bedfordshire) 'farmstead on the (River) Lea', Celtic river name + OE *tūn*, 'farmstead'. The river name probably means 'bright', 'light'. ◊Leyton is on the same river, so has a name of identical origin. It is not clear why the name devolved into the present different forms. *Lygetun* 792, *Loitone* 1086.

Lutterworth (town, Leicestershire) 'enclosure on the (River) Hlutre', OE river name + *worth*, 'enclosure'. The river here now is the *Swift*, but its earlier name may have been *Hlūtre*, meaning 'clear one', from OE *hlūttor*, 'clear', 'clean'. *Lutresurde* 1086.

Luxulyan (village, Cornwall) 'chapel of (St) Sulian', Cornish **log*, 'chapel' + saint's name. The saint's name is that of the abbot who founded a monastery here in the 6th century. He probably came from Brittany. *Luxulian* 1282.

Lydd (town, Kent) '(place at the) slopes', OE *hlid*, 'slope'. The name would have derived from the OE phrase *æt thāra hlidum*, 'at the slopes'. The town arose on a slight slope above the marsh here. *Cp* ◊Lytham St Annes. *Hlidum* 774, *Hlide c* 1100.

Lydney (town, Gloucestershire) 'Lida's island', OE personal name + *ēg*, 'island'. The town is located between two streams, and this is the 'island'. The personal name means 'sailor'. *Lideneg c* 853, *Ledenei* 1086.

Lyme Regis (town, Dorset) '(place by the River) Lim honoured by the king', Celtic river name + Latin *regis*, 'of the king'. The river name means simply 'stream'. The place acquired its royal suffix in the late 13th century, when Edward I declared it a free borough. *Lim* 774, *Lime* 1086, *Lyme Regis* 1285.

Lymington (town, Hampshire) 'farmstead on the (River) Limen', Celtic river name + OE *tūn*, 'farmstead'. The river here now has the same name as the town. Originally its name must have been something like *Limen*, meaning 'elm river' or possibly 'marshy river'. *Cp* ◊Leamington, ◊Lympne. *Lentune* 1086, *Limington* 1186.

Lymm (town, Cheshire) '(place by the River) Lymm', OE river name. The town stands on a stream that flows north to the Mersey. Its original name represents OE *hlimme*, 'noisy stream'. *Lime* 1086.

Lympne (village, Kent) '(place by the River) Limen', Celtic river name. The *Limen* is a former name of the East Rother here. The meaning is probably 'elm river' or 'marshy river'. *Cp* ◊Leamington, ◊Lymington. *Lemanis* 4th century.

Lyndhurst (town, Hampshire) 'wooded hill where lime trees grow', OE *lind*, 'lime tree' + *hyrst*, 'wooded hill'. The name is appropriate for the so called 'capital of the New Forest'. *Linhest* 1086.

Lynmouth (town, Devon) '(place at the) mouth of the (River) Lyn', OE river name + *mūtha*, 'mouth'. The river name represents OE *hlynn*, 'torrent'. ◊Lynton stands on the same river. *Lymmouth* 1330.

Lynton (town, Devon) 'farmstead on the (River) Lyn', OE river name + *tūn*, 'farmstead'. For the origin of the river name, *see* ◊Lynmouth. *Lintone* 1086.

Lytham St Annes (town, Lancashire) '(place at the) slopes with St Anne's church', OE *hlith*, 'slope' + saint's name. The first word of the name derives from the OE phrase *æt thāra hlithum*, 'at the slopes', in which *hlith* has a dative plural ending. *Cp* ◊Lydd. The second word was added in 1922 when Lytham merged with neighbouring *St Anne's-on-Sea*, named from its parish church (built 1872). *Lidun* 1086.

M

Mablethorpe (town, Lincolnshire) 'Malbert's outlying farmstead', Old German personal name + OS *thorp*, 'outlying farmstead'. The personal name has probably been influenced by English *Mabel*. *Malbertorp* 1086.

Macclesfield (town, Cheshire) 'Maccel's open land', OE personal name + *feld*, 'open land'. The 'open land' would have been part of the former forest here in the Peak District. *Maclesfeld* 1086.

Macduff (town, Grampian) '(town of) Duff's son', family name. The town takes its name from James *Duff*, 2nd Earl of Fife, who rebuilt the settlement here in the late 18th century. He himself named it after his father, the 1st Earl, William *Duff*, with *Mac-* meaning 'son of'. James Duff also claimed to be descended from the semi-mythical *Macduff* of Shakespeare's *Macbeth*. *Cp* ◊Dufftown.

Machynlleth (town, Powys) 'Cynllaith's plain', Celtic word + personal name. The *Ma-* of the name means 'plain' and probably refers to the tract of open land on the left bank of the River Dovey here. It is not known who *Cynllaith* was. *Machenleyd* 1254.

Maentwrog (village, Gwynedd) '(place by St) Twrog's stone', Welsh *maen*, 'stone' + saint's name. The personal name is that of a 6th-century saint. The 'stone' is a plain round block, about four feet high, at the south-west corner of St Twrog's church.

Maesteg (town, Mid Glamorgan) 'fair field', Welsh *maes*, 'field' + *teg*, 'fair'. The town arose only in the 19th century and took its name from the original field site here.

Maghull (town, Merseyside) 'corner of land where mayweed grows', OE *mægthe*, 'mayweed' + *halh*, 'nook'. There is no obvious 'corner of land' here, and the name may have been influenced by OE *hyll*, 'hill', which actually suits the topography better. *Magele* 1086, *Maghal* 1219.

Maidenhead (town, Berkshire) 'landing place of the maidens', OE *mæg-den*, 'maiden' + *hȳth*, 'landing place'. The name does not necessarily imply that young women landed from the Thames here, but that there was a landing place where they regularly gathered. The *-head* of the name is misleading. *Maidenhee* 1202, *Maydenhith* 1262.

Maidstone (town, Kent) 'stone of the maidens', OE *mægden*, 'maiden' + *stān*, 'stone'. The name implies a stone where young women and girls regularly gathered. Cp ◊Maidenhead. *Mægthan stan* late 10th century, *Meddestane* 1086.

Mainland (island, Shetland) 'main land', OS *megin*, 'main' + *land*, 'land'. The island is the largest and most important in the group. *Mainland*, Orkney, has a name of identical origin.

Maldon (town, Essex) 'hill with a cross', OE *mǣl*, 'cross' + *dūn*, 'hill'. The town stands in a commanding position and it is likely the Anglo-Saxons erected a cross or crucifix here, perhaps on the site now occupied by All Saints Church. *Mældune* early 10th century, *Malduna* 1086.

Mallaig (town, Highland) 'bay of gulls', OS *már*, 'gull' + *vík*, 'bay'. The second part of the name actually represents OS-Gaelic *aig*, 'bay'.

Malmesbury (town, Wiltshire) 'Maeldub's stronghold', Old Irish personal name + OE *burh*, 'stronghold'. The *m* in the name comes from that of Bishop *Aldhelm*, who built a chapel on the site of the monastery founded by *Maeldub* ('black chief') in the 7th century. *Maldumesburg* 685, *Malmesberie* 1086.

Malpas (town, Cheshire) 'difficult passage', Old French *mal*, 'bad' + *pas*, 'pass'. The town is not actually in a 'difficult passage' but above one, on a hill. The name exists elsewhere. *Malpas c* 1125.

Maltby (town, South Yorkshire) 'Malti's farmstead', OS personal name + *bý*, 'farmstead'. The first part of the name could equally represent OS *malt*, 'malt', so that the meaning is 'farm where malt is made'. *Maltebi* 1086.

Malton (town, North Yorkshire) 'middle farmstead', OS *methal*, 'middle' + OE *tūn*, 'farmstead'. The first part of the name could also represent OE *mæthal*, 'assembly', so that the meaning is 'farmstead where an assembly is held'. *Maltune* 1086.

Malvern Hills (hills, Hereford and Worcester) 'bare hills', Celtic words + English *hills*. The name represents words related to modern Welsh *moel*, 'bare', and *bryn*, 'hill'. The hills gave the names of the town of *Great Malvern*, villages of *Little Malvern* and *West Malvern*, and district of *Great*

Malvern known as *Malvern Link*. This last word represents OE *hlinc*, 'ledge'. *Mælfern c* 1030, *Malferna* 1086.

Manchester (city, Greater Manchester) 'Roman fort of Mamucium', Celtic place-name + OE *ceaster*, 'Roman fort'. The first part of the name is a shortened form of the original Celtic name, probably meaning 'breast-shaped hill', from a word related to Latin *mamma*, 'breast', 'mother'. The Roman fort was built on a round hill at the confluence of the rivers Irwell and Medlock. *Mamucio* 4th century, *Mamecestre* 1086.

Mangotsfield (town, Avon) 'Mangod's open land', Old German personal name + OE *feld*, 'open land'. Many names ending in -*field* have a personal name for their first part, as here. *Manegodesfelle* 1086.

Manningtree (town, Essex) 'Manna's tree', OE personal name + *trēow*, 'tree'. The tree could have been one where people met, or a cross erected by the named man. But the name could also mean simply '(place of) many trees', the first part representing OE *manig*, 'many'. *Manitre* 1248.

Mansfield (town, Nottinghamshire) 'open land by the (River) Maun', Celtic river name + OE *feld*, 'open land'. The river gets its name from a hill 4 miles to the southwest of the town. Its own name means 'breast-shaped hill', as for ◊Manchester. *Mamesfelde* 1086.

Mansfield Woodhouse (town, Nottinghamshire) 'woodland settlement near Mansfield', place-name + OE *wudu*, 'wood' + *hūs*, 'house'. The name implies that a new settlement was established here by people from ◊Mansfield, immediately to the south. *Wodehuse* 1230, *Mamesfeud Wodehus* 1280.

Marazion (town, Cornwall) 'little market', Cornish *marghas*, 'market' + *byghan*, 'little'. The market here would have been 'little' by comparison with the one at Penzance, 3 miles away. *Marghasbigan c* 1265.

March (town, Cambridgeshire) '(place at the) boundary', OE *mearc*, 'boundary'. It is not certain what the boundary actually marked, and the town has never been on a county boundary. It may have been the western boundary of the district of Ely. *Merche* 1086.

Margate (town, Kent) 'gate leading to the sea', OE *mere*, 'sea' + *geat*, 'gate'. The 'gate' would have been a gap in the cliffs here, leading to the sea or a particular sea pool. *Meregate* 1254.

Market Bosworth (town, Leicestershire) 'Bōsa's enclosure with a market', Middle English *market* + OE personal name + *worth*, 'enclosure'. The first word of the name was added in the 16th century, referring to the important market here. The word also distinguishes this place from the village of *Husbands Bosworth*, 20 miles west. *Boseworde* 1086.

Market Deeping (town, Lincolnshire) 'deep place with a market', Middle English *market* + OE **dēoping*, 'deep place'. The town arose on low-lying land by the River Witham among fens and marshes, now drained. It is actually formed by the combined villages of Market Deeping and *Deeping St James*, with *Deeping St Nicholas* some distance to the east and *West Deeping* to the west. *Estdepinge* 1086, *West Depinge* 1086.

Market Drayton (town, Shropshire) 'farmstead at a dragging place with a market', Middle English *market* + OE *dræg*, 'drag' + *tūn,* 'farmstead'. A 'dragging place' is a slope or 'slide' where boats can be dragged out of a river or timber from a forest. The first word distinguishes this Drayton from others and denotes its important market. *Draitune* 1086.

Market Harborough (town, Leicestershire) '(place by a) hill where oats are grown with a market', Middle English *market* + OS *hafri*, 'oats' + *berg*, 'hill'. The main name could also derive from OE **hæfera* and *beorg*, in the same sense. The first part could alternatively be OS *hafr* or OE *hæfer*, 'goat'. *Haverbergam* 1153, *Mercat Heburgh* 1312.

Market Rasen (town, Lincolnshire) '(place at a) plank bridge with a market', Middle English *market* + OE *ræsn*, 'plank'. The 'plank bridge' would have been over the stream that runs through the town. *Market* not only denotes the commercial activity but distinguishes the place from the villages of *Middle Rasen* and *West Rasen*, both to the west. *Resne* 1086.

Market Weighton (town, Humberside) 'farmstead by a historic settlement where willows grow with a market', modern *market* + OE *wīc*, 'historic settlement' + *tūn*, 'farmstead'. The name has OE *wīc* in its use to refer to a historic Romano-British settlement. The first word of the name was added only in the 19th century, although there has long been a market here. *Wicstun* 1086, *Market-Weighton* 1828.

Markinch (town, Fife) 'meadow where horses are kept', Gaelic *marc*, 'horse' + *innis*, 'island', 'riverside meadow'. The town is by the River Leven. *Marchinke* 1055.

Markyate (village, Hertfordshire) 'gate at the boundary', OE *mearc*, 'boundary' + *geat*, 'gate'. The village is near the border with Bedfordshire, and the 'gate' would have probably been through the former forest here. *Markyate* 12th century.

Marlborough (town, Wiltshire) 'Mærla's hill', OE personal name + *beorg*, 'hill'. The first part of the name could also be OE *meargealla*, 'gentian'. This plant may have grown here and been used for medicinal purposes. *Merleberge* 1086.

Marlow (town, Buckinghamshire) '(place on) land remaining after a pool has been drained', OE *mere*, 'pool' + *lāf*, 'remains', 'leavings'. The pool would have linked with the Thames here. *Merelafan* 1015, *Merlaue* 1086.

Marple (town, Greater Manchester) 'boundary stream', OE *gemǣre*, 'boundary' + *pyll*, 'pool', 'stream'. The name refers to the River Goyt here, which was the former county boundary between Cheshire and Derbyshire. *Merpille* early 13th century.

Marsden (town, West Yorkshire) 'boundary valley', OE *mercels*, 'boundary' + *denu*, 'valley'. The town is in a deep valley on the River Colne. The boundary would have been that between Yorkshire and Lancashire, 2 miles to the southwest. *Marchesden* 12th century.

Marske-by-the-Sea (town, Cleveland) '(place at the) marsh by the sea', OE *mersc*, 'marsh' + modern *by the sea*. The name refers to the marshy terrain here, by the coast. The spelling of the name with *sk* is the result of Scandinavian influence. The suffix is a 19th-century addition. *Mersc* 1086.

Martock (town, Somerset) 'outlying farmstead by a pool', OE *mere*, 'pool' + *stoc*, 'outlying farmstead'. The *s* of the second OE word is missing through Norman influence. *Mertoch* 1086.

Marylebone (district, London) '(place by St) Mary's stream', saint's name + OE *burna*, 'stream'. The stream here was originally the *Tyburn*. Its name was changed to *Maryburn* in the 15th century, from the dedication of the church. The middle *-le-* is a later addition, perhaps by association with the church of St *Mary-le-Bow*. *Maryburne* 1453, *Tyborne otherwise called Maryborne* 1490.

Maryport (town, Cumbria) 'Mary's port', personal name + modern *port*. The town was founded as a coal *port* in the 18th century by Humphrey Senhouse, who named it after his wife *Mary*. *Mary-port* 1762.

Masham (town, North Yorkshire) 'Mæssa's homestead', OE personal name + *hām*, 'homestead'. As often, the personal name is in a conjectural form. *Massan* 1086.

Matlock (town, Derbyshire) 'oak tree where meetings are held', OE *mæthel*, 'assembly' + *āc*, 'oak tree'. The reference is apparently to the meeting place of a hundred, although there is no record of Matlock being such a meeting place. The Domesday Book record is somewhat corrupt. *Meslach* 1086.

May, Isle of (island, Fife) 'gull island', OS *már*, 'gull' + *ey*, 'island'. The island is a noted seabird colony. *Mai* 1143.

Maybole (town, Strathclyde) 'plain of danger', Gaelic *magh*, 'plain' + *baoghail*, 'danger'. Presumably the open terrain here afforded little protection to those crossing it. *Mayboill* 1275.

Mayfair (district, Greater London) '(place of the) May fair'. An annual May fair was held here, on the site of the modern Brook Street, until it was suppressed in the early 18th century.

Medina (district, Isle of Wight) 'middle one', OE river name. The administrative district takes its name from the river here, which rises near the south coast and flows north, almost dividing the island in two. *Medine* 1196.

Medway (river, East Sussex/Kent). The ancient river name is of uncertain origin and meaning. Its base is the name *Wey*, as for ◊Weybridge, to which has perhaps been added a Celtic or OE word meaning 'mead' (OE *medu*), referring to the colour or sweetness of the water. *Medeuuæge* 8th century.

Meirionnydd (district, Gwynedd). The administrative district has the Welsh form of the name of ◊Merioneth.

Melbourne (town, Derbyshire) 'mill stream', OE *myln*, 'mill' + *burna*, 'stream'. The stream in question would have been the Carr Brook, flowing north through the town to the Trent. *Mileburne* 1086.

Melksham (town, Wiltshire) 'homestead where milk is produced', OE *meoluc*, 'milk' + *hām*, 'homestead'. The second part of the name could equally represent OE *hamm*, 'riverside land'. The town is on the Avon. *Melchesham* 1086.

Melrose (town, Borders) 'bare moor', Celtic words. The name comprises words related to modern Welsh *moel*, 'bare', and *rhos*, 'moor'. *Mailros c* 700.

Meltham (town, West Yorkshire) 'homestead where smelting is done', OE **smelt*, 'smelting' + *hām*, 'homestead'. The initial *s* of the OE word would have been lost through Norman influence. *Meltham* 1086.

Melton Mowbray (town, Leicestershire) 'middle farmstead of the de Moubray family', OE *middel*, 'middle' + *tūn*, 'farmstead' + family name. The first part of the name has been influenced by OS *methal*, 'middle'. The *de Moubray* family, from *Montbray*, Normandy, were here in the 12th century. *Medeltone* 1086, *Melton Moubray* 1284.

Menai Bridge (town, Gwynedd) '(place by the) Menai (Strait) bridge', Celtic river name + modern English *bridge*. The *Menai* Strait has a name probably meaning 'moving', referring to its swift current, from a word related to modern Welsh *men*, 'carriage', 'cart'. The bridge across it from Anglesey to the mainland was built in 1826, and the town arose soon after. The record below refers to the strait. *Mene* 11th century.

Mendip Hills (hills, Somerset) 'hills with valleys', Celtic word + OE *hop*, 'valley'. The first part of the name is related to modern Welsh *mynydd*, 'mountain'. The second is either OE *hop*, 'valley', or *yppe*, 'upland'. *Menedepe* 1185.

Menstrie (town, Central) 'settlement on the plain', Celtic words. The words that make up the name are related to modern Welsh *maes*, 'plain', and *tref*, 'settlement'. *Mestryn* 1261.

Merioneth (historic county, Wales) '(district of) Meirion', Welsh personal name. The named man was the son (or grandson) of the 5th century *Cunedda*, who perhaps gave the name of *Gwynedd*. The old name is preserved in the modern district of *Meirionnydd*. *See also* ◊Portmeirion.

Mersey (river, Greater Manchester/Merseyside) 'boundary river', OE *gemǣre*, 'boundary' + *ēa*, 'river'. The river formed the old county boundary between Cheshire and Lancashire, and before that, between the Anglo-Saxon kingdoms of Mercia and Northumbria. The historic link was broken in 1974 when the new county of *Merseyside* was formed. *Mærse* 1002.

Merthyr Tydfil (town, Mid Glamorgan) '(St) Tydfil's burial place', Welsh *merthyr*, 'martyr' + saint's name. *Tydfil* was a woman saint, said to be the daughter of *Brychan*, who gave the name of ◊Brecon. According to tradition, she was murdered by pagans in the 5th century and buried here. *Merthir* 1254, *Merthyr Tutuil*, 13th century.

Merton (borough, Greater London) 'farmstead by a pool', OE *mere*, 'pool' + *tūn*, 'farmstead'. The 'pool' would have been in the River Wandle here. *Mertone* 967, *Meretone* 1086.

Mevagissey (town, Cornwall) '(church of St) Meva and (St) Issey', Cornish saint's name + *hag*, 'and' + saint's name. Nothing is known about either saint, except that they were both men. *Meffagesy c* 1400.

Mexborough (town, South Yorkshire) 'Mēoc's stronghold', OE personal name + *burh*, 'stronghold'. The personal name could also be a Scandinavian one, *Mjúkr*. *Mechesburg* 1086.

Mickleover (district, Derby, Derbyshire) '(place at the) big ridge', OE *micel*, 'big' + **ofer*, 'ridge'. The first part of the name contrasts this place with ◊Littleover. The first word of the third record is Latin for 'big'. *Vfre* 1011, *Ufre* 1086, *Magna Oufra c* 1100.

Middlesbrough (town, Cleveland) 'middlemost stronghold', OE *midlest*, 'middlemost' + *burh*, 'stronghold'. It is not certain where the places were of which Middlesbrough was the 'middlemost'. Durham and Whitby have been suggested, although these do not have 'stronghold' names. *Midelesburc c* 1165.

Middlesex (historic county, England) '(territory of the) Middle Saxons', OE *middel*, 'middle' + *Saxe*, 'Saxon'. The 'Middle Saxons' (their tribal name) were those between the East Saxons of ◊Essex and the West Saxons of ◊Wessex. The original territory was much larger than the county. *Middelseaxan* 704, *Midelsexe* 1086.

Middleton (town, Greater Manchester) 'middle estate', OE *middel*, 'middle' + *tūn*, 'farmstead'. The name is common, and this particular 'middle estate' was probably so called from its location between Manchester and Rochdale. *Middelton* 1194.

Middlewich (town, Cheshire) 'middlemost saltworks', OE *midlest*, 'middlemost' + *wīc*, 'specialized building', 'saltworks'. The town derives its name from its location roughly midway between ◊Northwich and ◊Nantwich. The second Domesday Book record has transposed the *dl*. *Wich, Mildestuich* 1086.

Midhurst (town, West Sussex) 'place between wooded hills', OE *mid*, 'amid' + *hyrst*, 'wooded hill'. The town is situated between high woodland to the north and the woods of the South Downs to the south. *Middeherst* 1186.

Midlothian (district, Lothian) 'middle Lothian', OE *midd*, 'middle' + district name. The name is that of the historic county in which Edinburgh is located, and was formerly an alternative name for the city itself. *See also* ◊Lothian.

Midsomer Norton (town, Avon) 'northern farmstead of the midsummer (festival)', OE *midsumer*, 'midsummer' + *north*, 'northern' + *tūn*, 'farmstead'. The name refers to the festival of St John the Baptist, patron saint of the town's parish church, which was held on Midsummer Day (24 June). *Midsomeres Norton* 1248.

Milborne Port (town, Somerset) 'market town by the mill stream', OE *myln*, 'mill' + *burna*, 'stream' + *port*, 'market town'. The present name arose after the town had been declared a borough (in 1225). *Meleburne* 1086, *Milleburnport* 1249.

Mildenhall (village, Suffolk) 'middle corner of land', OE *middel*, 'middle' + *halh*, 'nook', 'corner of land'. The 'corner of land' would probably have been a recess or indentation in a hill. It is possible the first part of the name may be as for ◊Mildenhall, Wiltshire. *Mildenhale c* 1050.

Mildenhall (village, Wiltshire) 'Milda's corner of land', OE personal name + *halh*, 'nook', 'corner of land'. The 'corner of land' would have been a recess in Mildenhall Hill here. *Mildanhald* 803, *Mildenhalle* 1086.

Milford Haven (town, Dyfed) 'port of the sandy inlet', OS *melr*, 'sand' + *fjorthr*, 'inlet' + English *haven*, 'port'. The name properly applies to the harbour here. The town's Welsh name is *Aberdaugleddau*, 'mouth of the two Cleddau (rivers)', from *aber*, 'mouth', *dau*, 'two', and the name of the Eastern and Western *Cleddau*. *de Milverdico portu c* 1191, *Mellferth* 1207.

Milford on Sea (town, Hampshire) 'ford by a mill on the sea', OE *myln*, 'mill' + *ford*, 'ford' + modern English *on sea*. The suffix was added in the early 20th century. *Melleford* 1086.

Millom (town, Cumbria) '(place at the) mills', OE *myln*, 'mill'. The form of the name derives from OE *mylnum*, the dative plural of *myln*, required after *æt*, 'at'. The 'mills' may have been on or near the hill where Millom Castle now stands. *Millum c* 1180.

Millport (town, Strathclyde) 'port with a mill', modern English *mill* + *port*. The 'mill' was the grain mill that formerly stood over the harbour. The town developed only in the early 19th century.

Milngavie (town, Strathclyde) '(place with a) windmill', Gaelic *muileann gaoithe*, 'windmill'. The exact location of the former windmill is uncertain.

Milton Keynes (town, Buckinghamshire) 'middle farmstead of the de Cahaignes family', OE *middel*, 'middle' + *tūn*, 'farmstead' + family name. The *de Cahagnes* family, from *Cahagnes*, Normandy, were here in the 12th century. The name thus long predates the New Town designated in 1967. *Middeltone* 1086, *Middeltone Kaynes* 1227.

Milverton (town, Somerset) 'farmstead by the mill at the ford', OE *myln*, 'mill' + *ford*, 'ford' + *tūn*, 'farmstead'. The 'ford' part of the name has lost its *d*, as it was not stressed when the name was spoken. *Milferton* 11th century, *Milvertone* 1086.

Minch, The (strait, Highland/Western Isles) '(strait by the) great headland', OS *megin*, 'great' + *nes*, 'headland'. The 'great headland' could have been either Cape Wrath, at the northern end of the strait, or the Butt of Lewis, at the southern end, or even both.

Minehead (town, Somerset) 'hill of the headland', Celtic word + OE *hēafod*, 'headland'. The name was originally that of the hill here. The *Mine-* is probably from a word related to modern Welsh *mynydd*, 'mountain'. *Mynheafdon* 1046, *Maneheve* 1086.

Minster Lovell (village, Oxfordshire) '(place with the) monastery held by the Luvel family', OE *mynster*, 'monastery', 'large church' + family name. The *Luvel* family held the manor here in the 13th century. *Minstre* 1086, *Ministre Lovel* 1279.

Mirfield (town, West Yorkshire) 'pleasant open land', OE *myrge*, 'pleasant' + *feld*, 'open land'. The name could equally be understood as 'open land where festivities are held'. The *Mir-* of the name is related to modern *merry*. *Mirefeld* 1086.

Mitcham (district, Greater London) 'large village', OE *micel*, 'large' + *hām*, 'village'. Mitcham may have been regarded as 'large' by comparison with nearby Streatham. *Michelham* 1086.

Moel Hebog (mountain, Gwynedd) 'bare hill of the hawk', Welsh *moel*, 'bare' + *hebog*, 'hawk'. The name alludes to the mountain's appearance, not the actual bird. It has a toothed escarpment, like a hawk's talon.

Moffat (town, Dumfries and Galloway) '(place in the) long plain', Gaelic *magh*, 'plain' + *fada*, 'long'. The 'long plain' is the valley of the River Annan. The first part of the name represents *mo*, the locative form of Gaelic *magh*.

Mold (town, Clwyd) 'high hill', Old French *mont*, 'hill' + *hault*, 'high'. The 'high' hill in question is Bailey Hill, northwest of the town. The Welsh name of the town is *Yr Wyddgrug*, 'the burial mound'. *Montem Altum* 1278, *Moald* 1284.

Monklands (district, Strathclyde) 'lands of the monks'. The administrative district takes its name from the former parishes of Old and New *Monkland*, themselves named for the monks of Newbattle Abbey, granted lands here in the 12th century.

Monmouth (town, Gwent) '(place at the) mouth of the (River) Monnow', Celtic river name + OE *mūtha*, 'mouth'. The river name means 'fast flowing'. The Welsh name of the town is *Trefynwy*, 'homestead on the (River) Mynwy', the latter being the same river name. *Munwi Mutha* 11th century, *Monenmvde* 1086, *Munemuda* 1190.

Montacute (village, Somerset) '(place by the) pointed hill', Old French *mont*, 'hill' + *aigu*, 'pointed'. The reference is to the hill now called *Flamdon Hill*, for which the Normans transferred their own name from France. The OE name for the place was the equivalent of *Bishopston*, 'bishop's estate', from *biscop*, 'bishop', and *tūn*, 'estate'. *Biscopestone*, *Montagud* 1086.

Montgomery (town, Powys) '(place of) Montgomery', family name. The Norman family name is that of Roger *de Montgomery*, who built a castle here below what is now Castle Hill. The town's Welsh name is *Trefaldwyn*, 'Baldwin's homestead', after *Baldwin* de Boller, the Norman who retook the first castle after its capture by the Welsh. *Montgomeri* 1086, *Trefaldwyn* 1440.

Montrose (town, Tayside) 'moor of the promontory', Gaelic *moine*, 'moor' + *ros*, 'promontory'. The town is on a low promontory at the entrance to Montrose Basin. *Munros c* 1178.

Moray (district, Grampian) 'sea settlement', Celtic words. The present administrative district took its name from the historic county which in turn took the name of the ancient province. The name comes from words related to modern Welsh *môr*, 'sea', and *tref*, 'town'. The province gave the name of the *Moray Firth*. *Moreb c* 970, *Morauia* 1124.

Morden (district, Greater London) 'hill in marshland', OE *mór*, 'marshland' + *dūn*, 'hill'. There is hardly a hill here in the modern sense, but the ground rises betwen Beverley Brook and the River Wandle. *Mordune* 969, *Mordone* 1086.

Morecambe (town, Lancashire) 'curved inlet', Celtic words. The present name is a revival of the ancient one for the bay here, as recorded below, from words related to modern Welsh *môr*, 'sea', and *cam*, 'crooked', 'curving'. The original name of the resort was *Poulton-le-Sands* (*see* ◊Poulton-le-Fylde). The present name was adopted in the 19th century. *Morikambe c* 150.

Moretonhampstead (town, Devon) 'homestead by the farmstead in moorland', OE *mōr*, 'moor' + *tūn*, 'farmstead' + *hām-stēde*, 'homestead'.

The name was originally *Morton*. The addition could perhaps be a family name, but otherwise is that of a nearby place that itself was originally *Hampstead*. *Mortone* 1086, *Morton Hampsted* 1493.

Moreton-in-Marsh (town, Gloucestershire) 'farmstead in moorland in marsh with moorhens', OE *mōr*, 'moor' + *tūn*, 'farmstead' + *henn*, 'hen' + *mersc*, 'marsh'. The 'hen' element has dropped from the name, which was originally just *Morton*. *Mortun* 714, *Mortune* 1086, *Morton in Hennemersh* 1253.

Morley (town, West Yorkshire) 'clearing by a moor', OE *mōr*, 'moor' + *lēah*, 'clearing'. The region must have been heavily wooded here at one time, as testified by the many names ending in *-ley*. *Moreleia* 1086.

Morpeth (town, Northumberland) 'murder path', OE *morth*, 'murder' + *pæth*, 'path'. The name implies that a memorable murder had taken place here at some time. The 'path' would be the road (the former Great North Road, now the A1) that crosses the River Wansbeck. *Morthpath c* 1200.

Mortlake (district, Greater London) 'Morta's stream', OE personal name + *lacu*, 'stream'. The first part of the name could also derive from OE **mort*, 'young salmon'. The 'stream' is not the Thames but probably Beverley Brook. *Mortelage* 1086.

Moseley (district, Wolverhampton, West Midlands) 'Moll's clearing', OE personal name + *lēah*, 'clearing'. *Moll* is a man's name. *Moleslei* 1086.

Mossley (town, Greater Manchester) 'clearing by a swamp', OE *mos*, 'swamp', 'bog' + *lēah*, 'clearing'. The first part of the name could represent *mosi*, the Scandinavian equivalent. The River Tame here would contribute to the marshy state of the terrain. *Moselegh* 1319.

Motherwell (town, Strathclyde) 'mother's well'. 'Mother' here means 'Mother of God', otherwise the Virgin Mary. A former well dedicated to her has its site marked by a plaque in Ladywell Road. *Matervelle c* 1250, *Moydirwal* 1265.

Mountain Ash (town, Mid Glamorgan) '(settlement by the) Mountain Ash (inn)'. The town grew up here in the 19th century. Its Welsh name is *Aberpennar*, 'mouth of the Pennardd', referring to a stream that joins the River Cynon here.

Mousehole (village, Cornwall) '(place by the) mousehole', OE *mūs*, 'mouse' + *hol*, 'hole'. The name was originally that of a large cave here, like a large mousehole. *Musehole* 1284.

Mow Cop (hill, Cheshire/Staffordshire) 'heap hill', OE *mūga*, 'heap' + *hyll*, 'hill' + *copp*, 'hilltop'. The reference is probably to a former cairn here, presumably marking the county boundary. The first two OE words have blended, and the third was added later. *Mowel c* 1270, *Mowle-coppe* 1621, *Mole-Cop* 1868.

Much Wenlock (town, Shropshire) 'great white monastery', OE *mycel*, 'great' + Celtic words. The main name derives from words related to modern Welsh *gwyn*, 'white', and *loc*, 'lock', 'enclosed place', 'monastery'. The name passed to the nearby hill ridge *Wenlock Edge. Wynloca c* 1000, *Wenloch* 1086.

Muck (island, Highland) '(island of) pigs', Gaelic *muc*, 'pig'. No doubt pigs were pastured on the island at one time. The first part of the name recorded below represents Gaelic *eilean*, 'island'. *Helantmok* 1370.

Muckle Flugga (island, Shetland) '(island of) great precipices', OS *mikill*, 'great' + *flugi*, 'precipice'. The description is appropriate for the island.

Muirkirk (town, Strathclyde) 'moorland church', OS *mór*, 'moor' + *kirkja*, 'church'. The town is on the River Ayr by the tract of moorland known as Airds Moss ('marsh of the heights').

Mull (island, Strathclyde) '(island of the) headland', OS *múli*, 'snout', 'headland'. It is possible the name derives from Gaelic *muileach*, 'dear one', implying that the island is favourable in some way. *Malaia c* 150.

Mullion (village, Cornwall) '(church of St) Melanus', saint's name. The name is said to be that of the 4th-century bishop to whom the parish church here is dedicated. *Sanctus Melanus* 1262.

Mull of Kintyre (cape, Strathclyde) 'cape of the end of the land', Gaelic *maol*, 'bald' + *ceann*, 'head', 'end' + *tire*, 'land'. The peninsula name is essentially the same as that of ◊Land's End. English *mull* could also represent OS *múli*, literally 'snout'. *Cp* ◊Mull.

Musselburgh (town, Lothian) 'mussel town', OE *musele*, 'mussel' + *burh*, 'town'. The town, on the Firth of Forth, has long been famous for its mussels. *Muselburge c* 1100.

Muswell Hill (district, Greater London) 'mossy spring by a hill', OE *mēos*, 'moss' + *wella*, 'spring' + modern *hill*. The original spring here is said to have been dedicated to St Mary and to have had medicinal properties. The second word of the name was added only in the 17th century. *Mosewella c* 1155, *Muswell* 1535, *Muswell Hill* 1610.

N

Nailsea (town, Avon) 'Nægl's island', OE personal name + *ēg*, 'island'. The 'island' is the raised terrain on which the town stands east of Nailsea Moor. *Nailsi* 1196.

Nailsworth (town, Gloucestershire) 'Nægl's enclosure', OE personal name + *worth*, 'enclosure'. The personal name is the same as that for ◊Nailsea. *Nailleswurd* 1196.

Nairn (town, Highland) '(place by the River) Nairn', Celtic river name. The river name probably means something like 'penetrating one'. The original *Inver-* of the name, denoting a location at a river mouth, has disappeared. *Inuernaren c* 195, *Narne* 1382.

Nantwich (town, Cheshire) 'well-known saltworks', Middle English *named*, 'renowned' + OE *wīc*, 'special building', 'saltworks'. The saltworks here must have become better known than those at ◊Middlewich and ◊Northwich. *Wich* 1086, *Nametwihc* 1194.

Narberth (town, Dyfed) '(place) by the hedge', Welsh *yn*, 'in' + *yr*, 'the' + *perth*, 'hedge'. The *n* of *yn* begins the present name. Its Welsh equivalent is *Arberth*. *Nethebert* 1220.

Naseby (village, Northamptonshire) 'Hnæf's stronghold', OE personal name + *burh*, 'stronghold'. The name was originally the equivalent of *Nasebury*, as shown by the Domesday Book record. When the Danes arrived in the 12th century, they replaced OE *burh* by OS *bý*, 'village'. *Navesberie* 1086.

Nayland (town, Suffolk) '(place) at the island', Middle English *atten*, 'at the' + OE *ēg-land*, 'island'. The 'island' is land in a bend of the River Stour. The initial *N-* comes from the final letter of *atten*. *Cp* ◊Neyland and ◊Stoke-by-Nayland. *Eilanda* 1086, *Neiland* 1227.

Naze, The (headland, Essex) 'headland', OE *næss*, 'promontory'. The record shows that an earlier name was 'Eadwulf's headland'. *Eadulfes næsse* 1052.

Neasden (district, Greater London) 'nose-shaped hill', OE **neosu*, 'nose-shaped' + *dūn*, 'hill'. It is difficult to say which was the original 'nose-shaped hill' here. *Neosdune c* 1000.

Neath (town, West Glamorgan) '(place by the River) Neath', Celtic river name. The river name may mean 'shining one'. The Welsh name of the town is *Castell-nedd*, referring to the Roman fort here, called *Nidum*, also from the river.

Needham Market (town, Suffolk) 'needy homestead with a market', OE *nēd*, 'need', 'poverty' + *hām*, 'homestead' + Middle English *market*, 'market'. The name is an oxymoron, since the first word implies poverty, and the second fertility. The original impoverished settlement clearly grew and prospered. The second word was added in the 16th century. *Nedham* 13th century, *Nedeham Markett* 1511.

Nelson (town, Lancashire) '(place by the Lord) Nelson (Inn)'. The town arose in the 19th century with the growth of the textile industry, taking its name from an inn here. Its own name refers to Nelson's victory at the Battle of Trafalgar (1805).

Ness, Loch (loch, Highland) '(loch of the River) Ness', pre-Celtic river name. The river name probably means simply 'river', 'stream'. It also gave the name of ◊Inverness.

Neston (town, Cheshire) 'farmstead on the promontory', OE *næss*, 'promontory' + *tūn*, 'farmstead'. The town is on the Wirral peninsula, which perhaps was itself at one time called simply *Ness*, so that the town's name would mean 'farmstead on Ness'. *Nestone* 1086.

Newark (town, Nottinghamshire) 'new building', OE *nīwe*, 'new' + *weorc*, 'work', 'building'. The name refers to new building by some existing buildings, such as fortifications. The 'old building' here was almost certainly the Roman fort of *Margidunum*, at what is now Castle Hill, East Bridgford. This is some 10 miles from Newark, and the fort was linked to it by the Fosse Way. *Niweweorce c* 1080, *Neuuerche* 1086.

Newbiggin-by-the-Sea (town, Northumberland) 'new building by the sea', OE *nīwe*, 'new' + Middle English *bigging*, 'building' + modern *by the sea*. The name refers to new building carried out near existing buildings. *Niwebiginga* 1187.

New Brighton (district, Wallasey, Merseyside). The resort developed in the first half of the 19th century and saw itself as a northern rival to ◊Brighton.

Newburgh (town, Fife) 'new town', OE *nīwe*, 'new' + *burh*, 'town'. Despite its name, the town is old, dating from at least the 12th century. But it would originally have been 'new' by comparison with an even older place. *Niwanbyrig* 1130, *Novus burgus* 1266.

Newburn (district, Newcastle upon Tyne, Tyne and Wear) 'new stream', OE *nīwe*, 'new' + *burna*, 'stream,' A 'new stream' is one that has changed its course. *Neuburna* 1121.

Newbury (town, Berkshire) 'new borough', OE *nīwe*, 'new' + *burh*, 'borough'. The town developed from an earlier settlement here called *Ulvritun*, 'estate of Wulf's people'. *Neuberie c* 1080, *Neweburgh* 1431.

Newcastle Emlyn (town, Dyfed) 'new castle in Emlyn', OE *nīwe*, 'new' + *castel*, 'castle' + Welsh district name. *Emlyn* means 'round the valley', from Welsh *am glyn*. The castle was 'new' here in the 13th century by comparison with the one at Cilgerran, 8 miles away. *Novum Castrum de Emlyn c* 1240.

Newcastle-under-Lyme (town, Staffordshire) 'new castle near Lyme', OE *nīwe*, 'new' + *castel* + Celtic district name. The district name means 'region of elm trees', from a word related to modern Welsh *llwyf*, 'elm'. *Cp* ◊Leamington. *Novum castellum subtus Lymam* 1173.

Newcastle upon Tyne (city, Tyne and Wear) 'new castle on the (River) Tyne', OE *nīwe*, 'new' + *castel*, 'castle' + pre-Celtic river name. The castle was 'new' here in the 11th century, when it was built on the site of the old Roman fort of *Pons Aelii*. For the river name, *see* ◊Tynemouth. *Novem Castellum* 1130.

New Forest (forest, Hampshire) 'new forest', OE *nīwe*, 'new' + **forst*, 'forest'. There was already a forest here when a 'new' one was created as a hunting preserve by William the Conqueror in the 11th century. *Nova Foresta* 1086.

New Galloway (town, Dumfries and Galloway) 'new (town named after) Galloway'. The town arose in 1629 when its royal charter was granted by Charles I to Sir John Gordon, who had family ties in ◊Galloway. It was not in that county itself, but in Kirkcudbrightshire. *The New Town of Galloway* 1682.

Newham (borough, Greater London) 'new (place called) Ham'. The borough was created in 1965 as an amalgamation of *East Ham* and ◊West Ham, in which *Ham* represents OE *hamm*, 'riverside land' (here by the Thames).

Newhaven (town, East Sussex) 'new harbour', OE *nīwe*, 'new' + *hæfen*, 'harbour'. The town arose in the mid-16th century when a 'new harbour' was built at the mouth of the River Ouse. *Newehaven* 1587.

Newington (district, Greater London) 'new farmstead', OE *nīwe*, 'new' + *tūn*, 'farmstead'. The *-ing-* of the name is misleading, and represents the dative ending of *nīwe*. *Neuton c* 1200, *Niwentone* 13th century.

Newlyn (village, Cornwall) 'pool for a fleet of boats', Cornish *lu*, 'army', 'fleet of boats' + *lyn*, 'pool'. The name implies a safe or spacious harbour. The first part of the name has been influenced by English *new*. *Nulyn* 1279, *Lulyn* 1290.

New Malden (district, Greater London) 'new Malden', modern English *new* + OE place-name. The district arose as a northern expansion of *Malden* in the 19th century. The basic name has the same meaning as that of ◊Maldon, *ie* 'hill with a cross'. It is not clear which hill is referred to, but it could be the small one on which the parish church of St John the Baptist now stands. *Meldone* 1086.

Newmarket (town, Suffolk) '(town with a) new market', OE *nīwe*, 'new' + Middle English *market*, 'market'. The name denotes an established place that has acquired the right to hold a market. *Novum Forum* 1200, *la Newmarket* 1418.

Newnham (district, Cambridge, Cambridgeshire) 'new homestead', OE *nīwe*, 'new' + *hām*, 'homestead'. The second part of the name could equally represent OE *hamm*, 'enclosure'. The name is a fairly common one. *Newham* 1195.

Newport (town, Gwent) 'new market town', OE *nīwe*, 'new' + *port*, 'market town'. This town and other of the same name, such as *Newport*, Isle of Wight, have a name of identical origin and meaning. Many of them are also 'ports' in the modern sense. *Novus Burgus* 1138.

Newport-on-Tay (town, Fife) 'new port on the Tay'. The town arose as a 'new port' in medieval times.

Newport Pagnell (town, Buckinghamshire) 'new market town of the Paynel family', OE *nīwe*, 'new' + *port*, 'market town' + family name. The *Paynel* family were here in the 12th century. *Neuport* 1086, *Neuport Paynelle* 1220.

Newquay (town, Cornwall) '(town with a) new quay'. The 'new quay' was built here in the 15th century to enable ships to shelter under its wall, which the earlier harbour lacked. *Newe Kaye* 1602.

New Romney (town, Kent) 'new (place in) Romney (Marsh)'. The town is 'new' by contrast with the nearby village now known as *Old Romney*, 2 miles west. The latter's name was recorded as *Old Rumney* in 1575. For the main name, *see* ◊Romney Marsh. *Romenel* 1086.

Newton Abbot (town, Devon) 'new estate of the abbot', OE *nīwe*, 'new' + *tūn*, 'estate' + *abbod*, 'abbot'. The common name *Newton* is frequently followed by a distinguishing word, as here. This 'new estate' was given to the *abbot* of Torre Abbey in the 12th century. *Nyweton c* 1200, *Nyweton Abbatis* 1270.

Newton Aycliffe (town, Durham) 'new town near Aycliffe'. The name is a modern adoption of the traditional *Newton* for the 'New Town' designated in 1947 and named after the nearby village of *Aycliffe* ('oak wood').

Newton Ferrers (town, Devon) 'new farmstead of the de Ferers family', OE *nīwe*, 'new' + *tūn*, 'farmstead' + family name. The 'new farmstead' here was held by the Norman *de Ferers* family in the 13th century. *Niwetone* 1086, *Neweton Ferers* 1303.

Newtongrange (town, Lothian) 'new estate with a grange', OE *nīwe*, 'new' + *tūn*, 'estate' + Old French *grange*, 'granary'. The name was apparently given for distinction from *Prestongrange*, both estates being granges of the abbots of Newbattle Abbey. A *grange* in this sense was not simply a granary but the place where an abbey's rates and tithes were paid.

Newton-le-Willows (town, Merseyside) 'new farmstead among the willows', OE *nīwe*, 'new' + *tūn*, 'farmstead' + modern *willows*. The town's original name was *Newton-in-Makerfield* (*see* ◊Ashton-in-Makerfield). The present name was adopted in the 19th century. *Neweton* 1086, *Neuton Macreffeld* 1257, *Newton-in-Mackerfield* 1868, *Newton-in-Makerfield (otherwise Newton-le-Willows)* 1897.

Newton Stewart (town, Dumfries and Galloway) 'Stewart's new town'. The town is named after William *Stewart*, son of the 2nd Earl of Galloway, who laid it out in the 17th century.

Newtown (town, Powys) 'new town', OE *nīwe*, 'new' + *tūn*, 'estate'. The 'New Town' designated here in 1967 was already a 'new town' (or new estate) in medieval times. It is thus the only one of Britain's New Towns to have been already so designated. *Newentone* 13th century.

New Tredegar (town, Mid Glamorgan) 'new (town named after Lord) Tredegar'. The town was founded in the mid-19th century and named after

Lord *Tredegar*, who took his title from the family seat at *Tredegar* Park, near Newport, Gwent. It was regarded as 'new' by comparison with ◊Tredegar.

Neyland (town, Dyfed) '(place) at the island', Middle English *atten*, 'at the' + OE *ēg-land*, 'island'. The 'island' is the virtual peninsula on which the town stands. The initial *N-* represents the final letter of *atten*, exactly as for ◊Nayland. For some years in the 19th and early 20th centuries Neyland was known as *New Milford*, as a rival to ◊Milford Haven. *Nailand* 1596, *New Milford, or Neyland* 1868.

Norbiton (district, Greater London) 'northern outlying farm', OE *north*, 'north' + *bere-tūn*, 'grange', 'outlying farm'. The place is the geographical counterpart of ◊Surbiton, and both granges belonged to the royal manor of Kingston. *Norberton* 1205.

Norfolk (county, England) '(territory of the) northern people (of the East Angles)', OE *north*, 'north' + *folc*, 'folk', 'people'. The territory is the geographical counterpart of ◊Suffolk. Both names evolved without a territorial *-land*, as for ◊Northumberland or ◊Westmorland. *Nordfolc* 1086.

Normanton (town, West Yorkshire) 'farmstead of the Northmen', OE *Northman*, 'Northman' + *tūn*, 'farmstead'. The 'Northmen' were the Norwegian Vikings. The OE components of the name show that it was given by the Anglo-Saxons, not the Vikings themselves. *Normantone* 1086.

Northallerton (town, North Yorkshire) 'northern farmstead of Ælfhere', Middle English *north*, 'north' + OE personal name + *tūn*, 'farmstead'. The place was originally *Allerton*. *North* was then added to distinguish it from another Allerton of the same name (but not necessarily the same origin, *see* ◊Allerton). *Aluretune* 1086, *North Alverton* 1293.

Northam (town, Devon) 'northern enclosure', OE *north*, 'north' + *hamm*, 'enclosure'. The 'enclosure' here would have been the promontory on which the town was located. It is not clear where any corresponding 'southern enclosure' would have been. *Northam* 1086.

Northampton (town, Northamptonshire) 'northern homestead', OE *north*, 'north' + *hām-tūn*, 'homestead'. The original name of the place was *Hampton*. *North* was then added to distinguish it from ◊Southampton (although that name has a different origin and meaning). The county name, *Northamptonshire*, is first recorded in the 11th century. *Hamtun* early 10th century, *Northantone* 1086.

Northfleet (town, Kent) 'northern (place at the) stream', OE *north*, 'north' + *flēot*, 'stream'. *North* was added to the original name to distinguish this stream from the one at what is now the village of *Southfleet*, southwest of Gravesend. *Flyote* 10th century, *Norfluet* 1086.

Northiam (village, East Sussex) 'northern promontory of hay', OE *north*, 'north' + *hīg*, 'hay' + *hamm*, 'promontory'. The village is 'north' by comparison with *Higham*, 'high meadow', just south of it. This suggests that the first part of its name could also be OE *hēah*, 'high'. The *north* was a later addition either way. *Hiham* 1086, *Nordhyam c* 1200.

Northolt (district, Greater London) 'northern nooks of land', OE *north*, 'north' + *halh*, 'nook'. The place is 'north' by contrast with ◊Southall, although the OE word meaning 'nook' has developed differently for each name. The *-um* in the first record is the dative plural ending of *halh*, required after *æt*, 'at'. *æt northhealum* 960, *Northala* 1086.

North Shields (town, Tyne and Wear) 'northern sheds', Middle English *north*, 'north' + *schele*, 'shed', 'shieling'. The 'sheds' were fishermen's huts on the north bank of the Tyne estuary here. They were later designated *North* to be distinguished from those at ◊South Shields, over the river. *Chelis* 1268, *Nortscheles* 1275.

Northumberland (county, England) 'land of the Northhymbre', OE tribal name + *land*, 'land'. The *Northhymbre* or Northumbrians were the 'north Humber' people, *ie* those who lived north of the River Humber. Their territory and kingdom was much larger than the present county, whose southern border is far north of the Humber. (The county was diminished further in 1974, when the new county of Tyne and Wear took some of the southeastern part.) *Norhumberland* 1130.

North Walsham (town, Norfolk) 'northern homestead of Walh', OE *north*, 'north' + personal name + *hām*, 'homestead'. The place was originally *Walsham*. *North* was then added to distinguish it from what is now the village of *South Walsham*, 12 miles southeast of it. *Northwalsham* 1044, *Walsam* 1086.

Northwich (town, Cheshire) 'northern saltworks', OE *north*, 'north' + *wīc*, 'special place', 'saltworks'. The town is 'north' by contrast with ◊Nantwich, with ◊Middlewich lying between them. *Wich*, *Norwich* 1086.

Northwood (district, Greater London) 'northern wood', OE *north*, 'north' + *wudu*, 'wood'. The 'northern wood' is north of Ruislip. *Cp* ◊Norwood. *Northwode* 1435.

Norwich (town, Norfolk) 'northern port', OE *north*, 'north' + *wīc*, 'port'. The 'northern port' was long thought to be so named by relation to Ipswich, to the south, but recent research suggests that the original 'northern port' was simply a settlement on the River Wensum that was north of others across the river. The settlements then merged to form the present town, which took the name 'northern port' because this particular settlement was the most important. *Nordvico c* 900, *Noruic* 1086.

Norwood (district, Greater London) 'northern wood', OE *north*, 'north' + *wudu* 'wood'. The 'northern wood' was to the north of Croydon, and was not entirely cut down until the 19th century. *Cp* ◊Northwood. *Norwude* 1176.

Nottingham (town, Nottinghamshire) 'homestead of Snot's people', OE personal name + *-inga-*, 'of the people of' + *hām*, 'homestead'. The initial *S-* of the personal name was dropped under Norman influence. It has survived in *Sneinton*, 'farmstead of Snot's people', now an eastern district of Nottingham, named for the same man. The county name, *Nottinghamshire*, is first recorded in the 11th century. *Snotengaham* late 9th century, *Snotingeham* 1086.

Notting Hill (district, Greater London) 'hill at the place named after Cnotta', OE personal name + *-ing*, 'named after' + *hyll*, 'hill'. It has also been suggested that *Notting* is a family name deriving from *Knotting*, Bedfordshire. The meaning would then be 'hill at the place of the Notting family'. *Knottynghull* 1356.

Nuneaton (town, Warwickshire) 'farmstead by a river with a nunnery', OE *nunne*, 'nun' + *ēa*, 'river' + *tūn*, 'farmstead'. The original name was *Eaton* (*cp* ◊Eton). *Nun-* was added when a Benedictine nunnery was founded here in the 12th century. *Etone* 1086, *Nonne Eton* 1247.

Nunney (village, Somerset) 'Nunna's island', OE personal name + *ēg*, 'island'. The 'island' is the land by the River Frome here. The first part of the name could also represent OE *nunne*, 'nun', referring to a local nunnery. The Domesday Book record has an added *n*. *Nuni* 954, *Nonin* 1086.

O

Oadby (town, Leicestershire) 'Authi's farmstead', OS personal name + *bý*, 'farmstead'. The Scandinavian name is characteristic of this region of England. The Domesday Book record has an added *l*. *Oldebi* 1086, *Outheby* 1199.

Oakham (town, Leicestershire) 'Occa's homestead', OE personal name + *hām*, 'homestead'. The second part of the name could equally be OE *hamm*, 'riverside land', and the town is on a tongue of land between two streams. *Ocham* 1067, *Ocheham* 1086.

Oban (town, Strathclyde) 'little bay', Gaelic *òban*, 'little bay'. The Gaelic word that gave the name is a diminutive of *òb*, 'bay'. The town's full Gaelic name is *An t-òban Latharnach*, 'the little bay of Lorn', *Lorn* being the name of the territory here by the west coast.

Ochill Hills (hills, Central/Tayside) 'high ones', Celtic word + English *hills*. The name comes from a word related to modern Welsh *uchel*, 'high'.

Offa's Dyke (earthwork, Wales/England). The lengthy earthwork was built by King *Offa* in the 8th century to mark the boundary between Anglo-Saxon and Welsh territory. Offa is said to have been buried at *Offley*, 'Offa's clearing', Hertfordshire.

Okehampton (town, Devon) 'farmstead on the (River) Okement', Celtic river name + OE *tūn*, 'farmstead'. The river name probably means 'swift one', from a root word ultimately related to English *acute*. The *-hampton* of the name is thus misleading. *Ocmundtun c* 970, *Ochenemitona* 1086.

Oldbury (district, Warley, West Midlands) 'old fortification', OE *ald*, 'old' + *burh*, 'fortification'. It is uncertain to which precise 'old fortification' here the name refers. *Aldeberia* 1174.

Oldham (town, Greater Manchester) 'old promontory', OE *ald*, 'old' + OS *holmr*, 'island', 'promontory'. The 'promontory' is the spur at the western edge of Saddleworth Moor on which the town is situated. It was perhaps called 'old' because it had long been the site of a settlement. The *-ham* is thus misleading. *Aldholm* 1226.

Olney (town, Buckinghamshire) 'Olla's island', OE personal name + *ēg*, 'island'. The 'island' is the land in a bend of the River Ouse here. *Ollanege* 979, *Olnei* 1086.

Orford (village, Suffolk) 'ford by the shore', OE *ōra*, 'shore' + *ford*, 'ford'. The 'shore' is that of the east coast nearby. The 'ford' would have been over the River *Ore* here, which takes its name from that of the village. *Oreford* 1164.

Orkney (islands, Scotland). The precise meaning of the name is uncertain. It may mean 'whale island', from a word related to Latin *orca*, Irish *orc* or English *orc*. The final *-ey* is OS *ey*, 'island'. *Orkas* 330 BC, *Orkaneia* 970.

Ormskirk (town, Lancashire) 'Ormr's church', OS personal name + *kirkja*, 'church'. The named man was not necessarily the founder of the place or the builder of the church. *Ormeschirche c* 1190.

Oronsay (island, Strathclyde) '(St) Oran's island', saint's name + OS *ey*, 'island'. There are more than one island of the name. St *Oran*, a disciple of Columba, is said to have founded a monastery in the 6th century on the one off Colonsay, Inner Hebrides. *Orvansay* 1549.

Orpington (town, Greater London) 'estate named after Orped', OE personal name + *-ing-*, 'named after' + *tūn*, 'estate'. The second part of the personal name (meaning 'strenuous') has disappeared. *Orpedington* 1032, *Orpintun* 1086.

Orwell (river, Suffolk) 'stream', Celtic river name + OE *wella*, 'stream'. The OE word was added to the original Celtic (or pre-Celtic) word, meaning 'river', 'stream', when this was no longer understood. The name thus says 'stream' twice. *Arewan* 11th century, *Orewell* 1341.

Ossett (town, West Yorkshire) 'Osla's fold', OE personal name + *set*, 'fold'. The name could equally mean 'fold where blackbirds gather', with the first part from OE *ōsle*, 'blackbird' (modern *ouzel*). *Osleset* 1086.

Oswaldtwistle (town, Lancashire) 'Oswald's river junction', OE personal name + *twisla*, 'confluence' 'river junction'. Two streams meet at Oswaldtwistle. It is not known who the named man was, despite attempts to identify him with King Oswald of Northumbria. *Cp* ◊Oswestry. *Oswaldestwisel* 1246.

 Oswestry (town, Shropshire) 'Oswald's tree', OE personal name + *trēow*, 'tree'. The name has been traditionally linked with St Oswald, 7th-century king of Northumbria, but no connection has been definitely proved. *Osewaldstreu c* 1190.

Otley (town, West Yorkshire) 'Otta's clearing', OE personal name + *lēah*, 'clearing'. There was formerly an extensive woodland here. *Ottanlege c* 972, *Otelai* 1086.

Ottery St Mary (town, Devon) 'St Mary's (place by the River) Ottery', OE river name + saint's name. The river name means 'otter stream', from OE *oter*, 'otter', and *ēa*, 'stream'. The rest of the name, from the dedication of the town's church, distinguishes it from *Upottery* ('up the Otter') to the north and *Venn Ottery* ('fenland village on the Otter') to the southwest. *Otri* 1086, *Otery Sancte Marie* 1242.

Oulton (district, Lowestoft, Suffolk) 'Áli's farmstead', OS personal name + OE *tūn*, 'farmstead'. The first part of the name could equally be OE *ald*, 'old'. *Aleton* 1203.

Oundle (town, Northamptonshire) '(settlement of the) Undalas', OE tribal name. The tribal name probably means 'non-sharing people', from OE *un-*, 'not', and *dāl*, 'share' (modern *dole*). The implication is that the territory was given to these people after the land had been divided up and otherwise apportioned elsewhere. *Undolum c* 710, *Undele* 1086.

Ouse (river, England), 'water', Celtic river name. There are many rivers of the name, and almost all have a name meaning 'water', from a Celtic or pre-Celtic word related to Greek *hydro-* in English words and to the Gaelic word *uisge* that gave English *whisky*. The one exception is the Sussex *Ouse*, which got its name from ◊Lewes.

Oxford (city, Oxfordshire) 'ford used by oxen', OE *oxa*, 'ox' + *ford*, 'ford'. The records of the name below contain *oxna*, the genitive plural of *oxa*. The location of the actual ford over the Thames was perhaps just below Folly Bridge. *Oxnaforda* 10th century, *Oxeneford* 1086.

Oxshott (village, Surrey) 'Ocga's projecting piece of land', OE personal name + *scēat*, 'projecting piece of land'. Early records of the name show that the first part is not OE *oxa*, 'ox'. *Okesseta* 1179.

Oxted (town, Surrey) 'place where oak trees grow', OE *āc*, 'oak' + *stede*, 'place'. The record of the name shows that the reference is to oaks, not oxen. *Acstede* 1086.

P

Paddington (district, Greater London) 'estate named after Padda', OE personal name + -ing-, 'named after' + tūn, 'estate'. As often, the identity of the named man is unknown. *Padington c* 1050.

Paddock Wood (town, Kent) 'small enclosure by a wood', OE *pearroc*, 'paddock' + modern *wood*. Modern English *paddock* has a more specific meaning ('enclosure for horses') than the sense here. The *rr* of the original word is now *dd*. *Parrok* 1279, *Parrocks* 1782, *Paddock-Wood* 1868.

Padstow (town, Cornwall) '(St) Petroc's church', saint's name + OE *stōw*, 'holy place', 'church'. The second part of the saint's name has disappeared. *Sancte Petroces stow* 11th century, *Padristowe* 1351, *Padestou* 1361.

Pagham (village, West Sussex) 'Pæcga's homestead', OE personal name + hām, 'homestead'. The location of Pagham by the coast suggests that the second part of the name could equally represent OE *hamm*, 'promontory'. *Pecganham* 680, *Pageham* 1086.

Paignton (town, Devon) 'estate named after Pæga', OE personal name + -ing-, 'named after' + tūn, 'estate'. Until the mid-19th century the form of the name was regularly *Paington*, and the present spelling seems to have been introduced by the Great Western Railway, perhaps to match the name of ◊Teignmouth, 12 miles up the coast. *Peintone* 1086.

Painswick (town, Gloucestershire) 'dairy farm of Pain (Fitzjohn)', family name + OE *wīc*, 'dairy farm. The manor here was held by *Pain* Fitzjohn in the early 12th century. *Wiche* 1086, *Painswike* 1237.

Paisley (town, Strathclyde) '(place with a) church', Celtic word. The word that gave the name is of Irish origin and related to Latin *basilica*, 'church'. A name of identical origin is that of the Welsh village of *Bassaleg*, Gwent. *Passeleth* 1157, *Paisleth* 1158.

Pangbourne (town, Berkshire) 'stream of Pæga's people', OE personal name + -inga-, 'of the people of' + burna, 'stream'. The town is on the

River *Pang*, which takes its name from it. *Pegingaburnan* 844, *Pangeborne* 1086.

Par (town, Cornwall) '(place by the) cove', Cornish *porth*, 'cove', 'harbour'. *Porth* is found for various coastal places in Cornwall, among them ◊Perranporth and (though disguised) ◊Polperro. *Le Pare* 1573.

Partick (district, Glasgow, Strathclyde) 'bushy place', Celtic word. The word that gave this name, represented by modern Welsh *perth*, 'bush', is also found behind ◊Narberth and ◊Perth. *Perdeyc c* 1136.

Peacehaven (town, East Sussex) 'haven of peace'. The name is a modern one, chosen in 1917 to denote not only a 'peaceful haven', or safe harbour, but to express a desire for peace to end World War I.

Peak District (district, Derbyshire/Staffordshire/Cheshire) 'district of the peak', OE **pēac*, 'peak' + modern *district*. The name does not refer to a particular peak. The first record of the name below means 'land of the peak dwellers', from OE *sǣte*, 'dwellers', and *land*, 'land'. *Pecsǣtna lond* 7th century, *Pec* 1086.

Peckham (district, Greater London) 'homestead by a peak', OE **pēac*, 'peak' + *hām*, 'homestead'. There is hardly a 'peak' in the modern sense here, but historic Peckham is on higher ground west of the area now known as Telegraph Hill. *Pecheham* 1086.

Peebles (town, Borders) 'shelters', Celtic word. The Celtic word that gave the name, with an English plural *s* added, is related to modern Welsh *pabell*, 'tent', plural *pebyll*. The 'shelters' would have been shielings (temporary huts) for shepherds. *Cp* ◊Galashiels. *Pebles c* 1125.

Pembroke (town, Dyfed) '(place at the) end of the land', Celtic words. The words that gave the name have their modern equivalent in Welsh *pen*, 'head', 'end', and *bro*, 'region', 'land'. Hence *Penfro*, the town's Welsh name. The name is essentially the same as that of ◊Land's End and *Finistère* (Latin, *finis terrae*, 'end of the land') in western Brittany. *Pennbro c* 1150, *Pembroch* 1191.

Penarth (town, South Glamorgan) '(place on) Penarth (Head)', Welsh hill name. The name of the promontory on which the town is situated means 'headland of the hill', from Welsh *pen*, 'head', and *garth*, 'hill'.

Pendlebury (town, Greater Manchester) 'manor by (the hill called) Penn', Celtic hill name + OE *hyll*, 'hill' + *burh*, 'manor'. The original hill name no longer exists, but OE *hyll* must have been added to it when the meaning of the Celtic word (modern Welsh *pen*) was no longer understood. *Cp* ◊Pendle Hill. *Penelbiri* 1202.

Pendle Hill (hill, Lancashire) 'hill of the hill called Penn', Celtic hill name + OE *hyll*, 'hill' + modern *hill*. OE *hyll* was added to the original Celtic hill name (related to modern Welsh *pen*, 'hill') when it was no longer understood. That gave *Pendle*, to which modern *hill* was then added in turn. The complete name thus says 'hill' three times. *Pennehille* 1296.

Penge (district, Greater London) '(place at the) end of the wood', Celtic words. The name represents two Celtic words with modern equivalents in Welsh *pen*, 'end', and *coed*, 'wood'. But since the first word can also mean 'head', the meaning could equally be 'chief wood'. *Penceat* 1067.

Penicuik (town, Lothian) '(place by) cuckoo hill', Celtic hill name. The hill that gave the name of the town derives its own name from words related to modern Welsh *pen*, 'hill', and *cog*, 'cuckoo'. *Penikok* 1250.

Penistone (town, South Yorkshire) 'farmstead by Penning', Celtic hill name + OE *tūn*, 'farmstead'. The hill name, which no longer exists, derives from a word related to modern Welsh *pen*, 'hill', plus OE *-ing*. The town occupies a lofty site. *Pengestone* 1086, *Peningeston* 1199.

Penmaenmawr (town, Gwynedd) '(place by) Penmaen Mawr', Welsh mountain name. The name of the nearby mountain means 'great stony head', from Welsh *pen*, 'head', *maen*, 'stone', and *mawr*, 'big'.

Pennines (mountains, England) 'hills'. The name is not recorded before the 18th century. It is probably based on a Celtic word related to modern Welsh *pen*, 'hill', but may have been artificially devised from the name of the *Apennines* in Italy.

Penrhyndeudraeth (town, Gwynedd) 'promontory with two beaches', Welsh *penrhyn*, 'promontory' + *dau*, 'two' + *traeth*, 'beach'. The 'promontory' is the ridge of land on which the town stands at the confluence of two rivers as they flow through Traeth Bach ('little beach') to create an estuary, part of which is Traeth Mawr ('big beach'). These are the 'two beaches'. *Penrryn Devdraeth* 1457.

Penrith (town, Cumbria) 'ford by the hill', Celtic words. The name comprises Celtic words related to modern Welsh *pen*, 'hill', and *rhyd*, 'ford'. The first word can also mean 'head', so the meaning could equally be 'chief ford'. The hill would be Penrith Beacon, east of the town. The ford was probably by Brougham Castle, 2 miles south. *Penrith c* 1100.

Penryn (town, Cornwall) 'promontory', Cornish *penn rynn*, 'head land'. The town is on a small promontory at the head of the River Penrhyn, named after it. *Penryn* 1236.

Penshurst (village, Kent) 'Pefen's wooded hill', OE personal name + *hyrst*, 'wooded hill'. The same personal name is found for ◊Pevensey. *Pensherst* 1072.

Pentland Firth (strait, Highland/Orkney) 'land of the Picts', tribal name + OS *land*, 'land' + *fjorthr*, 'firth', 'strait'. *Pentland*, or 'Pictland', was the name used by the Vikings generally for northern Scotland. *Pettaland fjorthr* c 1085.

Pentland Hills (hills, Strathclyde/Borders/Lothian) 'hills of the land of Penn', Celtic hill name + OE *land*, 'land' + modern *hills*. The first part of the name represents a Celtic word meaning 'hill' related to modern Welsh *pen*. The overall name thus means 'hills of the land of hills'. *Cp* ◊Pendle Hill.

Penwith (district, Cornwall) 'end district', Cornish **penwyth*, 'far end'. The name was originally the Cornish name of ◊Land's End, and essentially has the same meaning. *Penwid* 1186.

Penzance (town, Cornwall) 'holy headland', Cornish *penn*, 'headland' + *sans*, 'holy', 'saintly'. The name alludes to the old chapel of St Mary, which stood on the headland here, and which is represented today by St Mary's parish church. *Pensans* 1284.

Perivale (district, Greater London) 'valley of pear trees', Middle English *perie*, 'pear tree' + *vale*, 'valley'. This name replaced the earlier one of *Little Greenford*. *Greneforde Parva* 1254, *Pyryvale* 1508.

Perranporth (town, Cornwall) '(St) Piran's cove', saint's name + Cornish *porth*, 'cove', 'harbour'. St *Piran* was a 5th-century monk who came from Ireland or Wales to settle in Cornwall. *St Perins creeke* 1577, *Perran Porth* 1810.

Perry Barr (district, Birmingham, West Midlands) '(place by the) pear trees near (Great) Barr', OE *pirige*, 'pear tree' + Celtic hill name. The place is close to *Great Barr*, the second word of which means 'hill' (*cp* ◊Barry). *Pirio* 1086.

Pershore (town, Hereford and Worcester) 'slope where osiers grow', OE **persc*, 'osier' + *ōra*, 'slope', 'bank'. The name probably alludes to land between the River Avon and a slight hill to the west of the town, where osiers would have grown, their twigs being used to make baskets. *Perscoran* 972, *Persore* 1086.

Perth (town, Tayside) '(place by a) thicket', Pictish word. The name comes from a word related to modern Welsh *perth* in the same sense. *Pert c* 1128.

Peterborough (city, Cambridgeshire) '(St) Peter's town', saint's name + OE *burh*, 'town'. The site here was originally called *Medeshampstead*, 'homestead by the whirlpool'. The present name comes from the dedication of the 12th-century abbey. *Medeshamstedi c* 750, *Burg* 1086, *Petreburgh* 1333.

Peterhead (town, Grampian) '(St) Peter's headland', saint's name + OE *hēafod*, 'headland'. The original name of the site here was *Inverugie*, 'mouth of the (Rive) Ugie'. The present name comes from the dedication of the 12th-century church. *Petyrheid* 1544.

Peterlee (town, Durham) '(place named after) Peter Lee'. The New Town was designated in 1948 and named in memory of *Peter Lee*, a popular local miner and trades union leader, who died in 1935.

Petersfield (town, Hampshire) '(settlement on) open land by (St) Peter's (church)', saint's name + OE *feld*, 'open land'. The medieval 'new town', which arose after the Conquest, took the name of the existing church. *Peteresfeld* 1182.

Petworth (town, West Sussex) 'Pēota's enclosure', OE personal name + *worth*, 'enclosure'. It is not clear where exactly the 'enclosure' would have been. *Peteorde* 1086.

Pevensey (village, East Sussex) '(place by) Pefen's river', OE personal name + *ēa*, 'river'. The same personal name lies behind ◊Penshurst. *Pefenesea* 947, *Pevenesel* 1086.

Pewsey (town, Wiltshire) 'Pefe's island', OE personal name + *ēg*, 'island'. The 'island' would be the raised land here by the River Avon. *Pefesigge c* 880, *Pevesie* 1086.

Pickering (town, North Yorkshire) '(settlement of) Pīcer's people', OE personal name + *-ingas*, 'people of'. It is possible the name may be a tribal one based on OE *pīc*, 'pointed hill', referring to the North Yorks Moors nearby. *Picheringa* 1086.

Piddletrenthide (village, Dorset) '(estate on the River) Piddle (assessed at) thirty hides', OE river name + Old French *trente*, 'thirty' + OE *hīd*, 'hide'. A 'hide' was the amount of land needed for one family to live on. The river name means 'marshy one', from OE **pidele*, 'marsh', 'fen'. *Cp* ◊Puddletown. *Uppidelen* 966, *Pidrie* 1086, *Pidele Trentehydes* 1212.

Pilgrims Way (trackway, Hampshire/Surrey/Kent), 'pilgrims' way'. The ancient trackway follows the southern slope of the South Downs and was probably used by medieval pilgrims journeying to Canterbury. The name is not recorded before the 18th century. *Pilgrim Road* 1778.

Pinner (district, Greater London) '(place by a) peg-shaped ridge', OE *pinn*, 'peg' + *ōra*, 'ridge', 'bank'. The name refers to the 'pin-shaped' or humped ridge that crosses Pinner Park. The River *Pin* here gets its name from the place. *Pinnora* 1232.

Pitlochry (town, Tayside) 'portion of the stones', Pictish word + Gaelic *cloichreach*, 'stony place'. The first part of the name represents a conjectural Pictish word corresponding to modern Welsh *peth*, 'part'. (It may relate to the name of the *Picts* themselves, so that they are the 'portion people', 'people who hold a piece of land'.) The 'stones' may have been stepping stones, as a crossing place on the River Tummel here.

Pittenweem (town, Fife) 'portion of the cave', Pictish word + Gaelic *na h-uamha*, 'of the cave'. For the first part of the name, *see* ◊Pitlochry. Pittenweem is a port. *Petnaweme c* 1150.

Plaistow (district, Greater London) 'place for playing', OE *plega*, 'play' + *stōw*, 'place'. The name denotes an open space where people gathered for sport and recreation. The record relates to Plaistow, Bromley, although the name is found elsewhere. *Playstowe* 1414.

Plumstead (district, Greater London) 'place where plum trees grow', OE *plūme*, 'plum tree' + *stede*, 'place'. The name is found elsewhere, notably in Norfolk. *Plumstede* 961, *Plumestede* 1086.

Plymouth (city, Devon) '(place at the) mouth of the (River) Plym', OE river name + *mūtha*, 'mouth'. The river takes its name from nearby *Plympton*, whose own name means 'farmstead with plum trees', from OE *plūme*, 'plum tree', and *tūn*, 'farmstead'. Plymouth's original name was *Sutton*, 'southern village', with its manor held by the priory of Plympton. *Plymmue* 1230, *Sutton Prior vulgariter Plymmouth c* 1450.

Plympton (district, Plymouth, Devon). For the origin of this name, *see* ◊Plymouth.

Plynlimon (mountain, Dyfed) 'five beacons', Welsh *pum*, 'five' + *llumon*, 'chimney'. This is the traditional explanation of the name, referring to the mountain's five distinct summits, on one or more of which a beacon could have been lit in medieval times.

Pocklington (town, Humberside) 'estate named after Pocela', OE personal name + *-ing-*, 'named after' + *tūn*, 'estate'. The personal name is conjectural, as is often the case. *Poclinton* 1086.

Polperro (town, Cornwall) 'Pyra's harbour', Cornish *porth*, 'harbour' + personal name. The second part of the name may be a river name, referring to the small stream here. *Portpira* 1303.

Polruan (village, Cornwall) 'Ruveun's harbour', Cornish *porth*, 'harbour' + personal name. The personal name is said to be that of a 6th-century monk from Glastonbury. *Porthruan* 1284.

Pontardawe (town, West Glamorgan) 'bridge over the (River) Tawe', Welsh *pont*, 'bridge', *ar*, 'over' + Celtic river name. The river name may mean 'strong stream' or 'silent stream'. It is of the same origin as the name of the *Tay* (*see* ◊Tayside).

Pontardulais (town, West Glamorgan) 'bridge over the (River) Dulais', Welsh *pont*, 'bridge' + *ar*, 'over' + Celtic river name. The river name means 'black water'. *Cp* ◊Dawlish.

Pontefract (town, West Yorkshire) '(place by the) broken bridge', Latin *pons*, 'bridge' + *fractus*, 'broken'. The 'broken bridge' was probably over the Wash Dike, where Bubwith Bridge is now. The crossing here would have been an important one, giving access to the Great North Road. The record represents the Latin ablative (locative) form of the name, *ponte fracto*, 'at the broken bridge'. *Pontefracto* 1090.

Ponteland (town, Northumberland) 'river land by the (River) Pont', Celtic river name + OE *ēa-land*, 'river land'. 'River land' here means land that is well watered, hence cultivated land. The river name means 'valley', from a word related to modern Welsh *pant* in this sense. *Punteland* 1203.

Pontycymer (town, West Glamorgan) 'bridge at the confluence', Welsh *pont*, 'bridge' + *y*, 'the' + *cymer*, 'confluence'. The town is at a location where two streams meet.

Pontypool (town, Gwent) 'bridge by the pool', Welsh *pont*, 'bridge' + English *pool*. The 'pool' was probably the River Llwyd ('grey one') on which the town stands. *Pont y Poole* 1617.

Pontypridd (town, Mid Glamorgan) 'bridge by the earthen house', Welsh *pont*, 'bridge' + *y*, 'the' + *tŷ*, 'house' + *pridd*, 'earth'. The Welsh word *tŷ* later disappeared from the name, as its two letters were already present in *pont* and *y*. The town was known as *Newbridge* for some time after its famous single span bridge was built over the River Taff in 1755. *Pont y Ty Pridd c*1700, *Newbridge* 1868, *Pontypridd (formerly Newbridge)* 1897.

Poole (town, Dorset) '(place at the) pool', OE *pōl* 'pool'. The 'pool' here is the harbour. *Pole* 1183.

Pooley Bridge (village, Cumbria) '(place by a) mound by a pool with a bridge', OE *pōl*, 'pool' + OS *haugr*, 'mound' + modern English *bridge*. The 'pool' would be the lower end of Ullswater, and the 'mound' the ancient camp site on the nearby hill known as Bowerbank. The 'bridge' is over the River Eamont, which leaves Ullswater here. *Pulhoue* 1252, *Pooley-Bridge* 1793.

Poplar (district, Greater London) '(place at the) poplar tree', Middle English *popler*, 'poplar'. The record of the name is dated earlier than the first record of the word (1382) in the *Oxford English Dictionary. Popler* 1327.

Porlock (town, Somerset) 'enclosure by the harbour', OE *port*, 'harbour' + *loca*, 'locked place', 'enclosure'. The town is at the foot of a steep hill not far from the coast. *Portloca* 10th century, *Portloc* 1086.

Portchester (town, Hampshire) 'Roman fort by the harbour', OE *port*, 'harbour' + *ceaster*, 'Roman fort'. The town is on the north shore of Portsmouth Harbour. The Roman fort here was called *Portus Adaoni*, 'fort of the height', the second word being Celtic in origin. The 'height' is Portsdown. *Porteceaster c* 960, *Portcestre* 1086, *Porchester, or Portchester* 1897.

Port Dinorwic (town, Gwynedd) 'port of Dinorwic', Welsh *porth*, 'port' + place-name. The town was formerly the *port* for the slate quarries at the village of *Dinorwic*, and takes its name from the latter. The village name comes from the *Ordovices*, an ancient tribe here, whose own name is Celtic in origin and probably means 'hammer fighters', from a word related to modern Welsh *gordd*, 'hammer'.

Port Ellen (town, Strathclyde) 'port of Ellen(or)'. The town, the chief port of Islay, is named after Lady *Ellenor* Campbell, wife of the Gaelic scholar W.F. Campbell, who planned the settlement in 1821. Her mother, Lady *Charlotte* Campbell, gave the name of the village of *Port Charlotte*, in southwest Islay.

Port Glasgow (town, Strathclyde) 'port of Glasgow'. The town arose in the 1660s with the aim of being the main port and harbour for ◊Glasgow, 17 miles away.

Porth (town, Mid Glamorgan) 'gateway', Welsh *porth*, 'gateway'. The 'gateway' is the confluence of the Rhondda and Little Rhondda rivers here, which give access to places further south in the Rhondda Valley. The Welsh word that gave the name is the masculine noun *porth*, 'gateway', as distinct from the feminine noun *porth*, 'port'.

Porthcawl (town, Mid Glamorgan) 'habour of sea kale', Welsh *porth*, 'harbour' + *cawl*, 'kale'. Doubtless this plant, cultivated for its edible shoots, grew here at one time. *Portcall* 1632.

Porthleven (town, Cornwall) 'smooth harbour', Cornish *porth*, 'cove', 'harbour' + *leven*, 'smooth'. It is possible the second part of the name may have been the name of the stream here – the name would mean 'harbour on the Leven'. The reference would be to a smooth current. *Port-levan c* 1605.

Porthmadog (town, Gwynedd) 'port of Madocks', Welsh *porth*, 'harbour' + surname. The town takes its name from the MP W.A. *Madocks* (1772-1828), who in 1821 built a harbour here for the shipping of local slate.

Portishead (town, Avon) 'headland by the harbour', OE *port*, 'harbour' + *hēafod*, 'headland'. The 'headland' is the ridge of hills that run along the Severn estuary here. The Domesday Book record of the name has omitted the final *d* of the OE word for 'headland'. *Portesheve* 1086, *Portesheved* 1200.

Portland, Isle of (peninsula, Dorset) 'island of the estate by the harbour', OE *port*, 'harbour' + *land*, 'estate' + modern *isle*. The 'harbour' is Portland Harbour, between the Isle of Portland and Weymouth. *Isle* is strictly speaking a misnomer for a peninsula. *Port* 9th century, *Portlande* 862, *Porland* 1086.

Portmeirion (town, Gwynedd) 'port of Meirion(nydd)'. The resort was planned in the 1920s. Its name relates to its coastal location and its situation in ◊Meirionnydd, as the Welsh name of the historic county of *Merioneth*.

Portpatrick (town, Dumfries and Galloway) '(St) Patrick's harbour'. The town (or rather its harbour) took its name from the dedication of a chapel here.

Portree (town, Highland) 'harbour by the slope', Gaelic *port*, 'harbour' + *ruighe*, 'slope'. The name is popularly interpreted as 'royal harbour', Gaelic *port righe*, referring to the visit of James V to Skye in 1540. *Portri* 1549.

Portsea Island (island, Hampshire) 'harbour island', OE *port*, 'harbour' + *ēg*, 'island' + modern *island*. The 'island' is the land on which most of

◊Portsmouth lies, and the 'harbour' is Portsmouth Harbour. The second word was added when 'island' in the first word was no longer understood. *Portesig* 982, *Porteseia c* 1125.

Port Seton (town, Lothian) 'port of the Seton family'. The *Seton* family had a castle here in the 16th century. The present town is formed by Port Seton jointly with Cockenzie.

Portslade-by-Sea (town, East Sussex) 'crossing place near the harbour', OE *port*, 'harbour' + *gelād*, 'crossing place'. The name implies that at one time there may have been sea inlets here which needed to be crossed by means of special causeways. The suffix is a recent addition. *Porteslage* 1086.

Portsmouth (city, Hampshire) '(place at the) mouth of the harbour', OE *port*, 'harbour' + *mūtha*, 'mouth'. The town is named for its own harbour, which in Roman times was called simply *Portus*. *Portesmuthan* late 9th century.

Port Talbot (town, West Glamorgan) 'port of the Talbot family'. The town arose in 1836 when docks were built here, and took its name from the *Talbot* family of nearby Margam Abbey, who sponsored the enterprise.

Port William (town, Dumfries and Galloway), 'William's port'. The town was founded in about 1770 by Sir *William* Maxwell of Monreith, and is named after him.

Potterne (village, Wiltshire) 'building where pots are made', OE *pott*, 'pot' + *ærn*, 'building'. The local clayey soil would have suitable for making earthenware pottery. *Poterne* 1086.

Potters Bar (town, Hertfordshire) 'gate of the Potter family', Middle English surname + *barre*, 'gate'. The 'gate' was almost certainly one that led into Enfield Chase. *Potterys Barre* 1509.

Potton (town, Bedfordshire) 'farmstead where pots are made', OE *pott*, 'pot' + *tūn*, 'farmstead'. *Cp* the name of ◊Potterne. *Pottun c* 960, *Potone* 1086.

Poulton-le-Fylde (town, Lancashire) 'farmstead by a pool in (the district of) The Fylde', OE *pōl*, 'pool' + *tūn*, 'farmstead' + district name. The district name means 'the plain', from OE *feld*, 'open land'. It was added to the main name to distinguish this Poulton from *Poulton-le-Sands*, the former name of ◊Morecambe. *Poltun* 1086.

Powys (county, Wales) 'provincial (district)', Latin *pagus*, 'province'. The name, that of a former kingdom here, implies that the inhabitants were 'country folk', living on open land that was not protected in the same way as the regions to the north and south, where hills and valleys provided shelter.

Poynton (town, Cheshire) 'estate named after Pofa', OE personal name + *-ing-*, 'named after' + *tūn*, 'estate'. The original *-ing-* of the name is represented by the middle *n*. *Povinton* 1249.

Prescot (town, Merseyside) 'priests' cottage', OE *prēost*, 'priest' + *cot*, 'cottage'. The name may indicate an endowment for the church at nearby Eccleston. *Prestecota* 1178.

Preseli (district, Dyfed) '(district by Mynydd) Preseli', Welsh mountain name. The name of the hill ridge here may be based on Welsh *prys*, 'wood', 'grove', or some dialect form of this. (*Mynydd* means 'mountain'.)

Prestatyn (town, Clwyd) 'priests' village', OE *prēost*, 'priest' + *tūn*, 'village'. The name is a Welsh-influenced form of the English name ◊Preston. *Prestetone* 1086.

Presteigne (town, Powys) 'priests' household', OE *prēost*, 'priest' + *hǣmed*, 'household', 'society'. The exact sense of the name is uncertain, but it generally denoted a religious community here. *Prestehemede c* 1250.

Preston (town, Lancashire) 'priests' village', OE *prēost*, 'priest' + *tūn*, 'village'. The name does not necessarily mean that priests lived here but that the village was an endowment for priests who served a church elsewhere. *Prestune* 1086.

Prestonpans (town, Lothian) 'priests' village with saltpans', OE *prēost*, 'priest' + *tūn*, 'village' + *panne*, 'pan'. The 'priests' were the monks of Newbattle Abbey, who laid out the saltpans here in the early 13th century. *Saltprestoun* 1587, *Prestonpans* 1654.

Prestwich (town, Greater Manchester) 'priests' farmstead', OE *prēost*, 'priest' + *wīc*, 'farmstead'. The 'farmstead' was doubtless an endowment to support a religious community. *Prestwich* 1194.

Prestwick (town, Strathclyde) 'priests' farmstead', OE *prēost*, 'priest' + *wīc*, 'farmstead'. The name is exactly the same as that of ◊Prestwich. *Prestwic c* 1170.

Princes Risborough (town, Buckinghamshire) 'prince's hill where brushwood grows', Middle English *prince* + OE **hrīsen*, 'growing with brushwood' + *beorg*, 'hill'. The name was originally just *Risborough*, but the first word was added when the Black Prince, no less, held the tenure of the place in the 14th century. *Risenbeorgas* 1004, *Pryns Rysburgh* 1433.

Princetown (town, Devon) 'prince's town'. The town arose in the first half of the 19th century round a prison for French and American prisoners taken in the Napoleonic Wars. It was named after the *Prince* of Wales, the future George IV.

Prudhoe (town, Northumberland) 'Prūda's hill spur', OE personal name + *hōh*, 'hill spur'. The 'hill spur' in question is probably the elevated site about the River Tyne here on which Prudhoe Castle stands. *Prudho* 1173.

Puddletown (village, Dorset) 'farmstead on the (River) Piddle', OE river name + *tūn*, 'farmstead'. In 1956 Dorset County Council wanted to change the name to *Piddletown*, to conform to the river name and that of ◊Piddletrenthide. Local opposition won the day, however, mainly because the present name sounds 'nicer'. The Domesday Book record is corrupt. *Pitretone* 1086, *Pideleton* 1212.

Pudsey (town, West Yorkshire) 'Pudoc's enclosure', OE personal name + *hæg*, 'enclosure'. It is possible the first part of the name may be a hill name meaning 'The Wart', from OE *puduc* in this sense. *Podechesaie* 1086.

Puffin Island (island, Gwynedd) 'island of puffins'. The name has the same meaning as that of ◊Lundy. The island is also known as *Priestholm*, 'priests' island', referring to the monastery founded here in the 6th century.

Pulborough (town, West Sussex) 'hill by the pools', OE *pōl*, 'pool' + *beorg*, 'hill'. The 'pools' would have been formed by the bend on the River Arun, by which the town stands on a hill. *Poleberge* 1086.

Purbeck (district, Dorset) 'beak-shaped ridge where snipe are', OE *pūr*, 'snipe' + **bic*, 'beak-shaped ridge'. The name refers to the Purbeck Hills, which form a ridge here. The first record of the name has a form of OE *-ingas*, 'dwellers'. *Purbicinga* 948, *Porbi* 1086.

Purfleet (town, Essex) 'Purta's stream', OE personal name + *flēot*, 'stream'. The 'stream' would have been the River Mar Dyke, which enters the Thames here. *Purteflyete* 1285.

Purley (town, Greater London) 'wood where pear trees grow', OE *pirige*, 'pear tree' *lēah*, 'wood'. This was formerly a well wooded region, and still has many individually named woods. *Pirlee* 1200.

Putney (district, Greater London) 'Putta's landing place', OE personal name + *hȳth*, 'landing place'. Putney is on the Thames. It is possible the first part of the name means 'hawk', from OE **putta*, which is also the meaning of the personal name. The overall sense would then be 'landing place where hawks are'. The Domesday Book record has *l* for *n*. *Putelei* 1086, *Puttenhuthe* 1279.

Pwllheli (town, Gwynedd) 'pool of salt water', Welsh *pwll*, 'pool' + *heli*, 'brine', 'salt water'. The second part of the name emphasizes the fact that the pool is by the sea, and not inland. *Pwllhely c*1292.

Q

Quantock Hills (hills, Somerset) 'edge', 'border', Celtic hill name. The name would probably have referred to the 'edge' of a section of the hills, not necessarily the whole chain. For a similar name, *cp* ◊Kent. The record has OE *wudu*, 'wood', added. *Cantucuudu* 682.

Queenborough (town, Kent) 'queen's borough', OE *cwēn*, 'queen' + *burh*, 'borough'. The town arose as a *borough*, or chartered town, named after *Queen* Philippa of Hainault, wife of Edward III. She died soon after the town received its charter, in 1367. *Queneburgh* 1376.

Queensbury (town, West Yorkshire) 'queen's town'. The town arose from a village known as *Queen's Head*, after an inn here. In 1863 the name was changed to its present form, after *Queen* Victoria.

Queensferry (town, Clwyd) The town, on the River Dee, was originally known as *Kingsferry*. When *Queen* Victoria came to the throne in 1837, the present name was adopted. *King's-Ferry* 1835, *Queen's-Ferry* 1868.

Quorndon (village, Leicestershire) 'hill of mill stones', OE *cweorn*, 'hand mill' + *dūn*, 'hill'. The name implies that mill stones were obtained locally. The village is also known simply as *Quorn*, and gave the name of the Quorn Hunt. *Querendon c* 1220.

R

Raasay (island, Highland) 'roe ridge island', OS *rár*, 'roe deer' + *áss*, 'ridge' + *ey*, island'. The 'ridge' is the chain of mountains in the south of the island, where red deer are still found.

Radcliffe (town, Greater Manchester) '(place at the) 'red cliff', OE *rēad*, 'red' + *clif*, 'cliff'. The name refers to the red sandstone cliff beside the River Irwell here. *Radcliffe*, Nottinghamshire, has a name of identical origin, alluding to the red loamy bank that runs down to the Trent. *Radecliue* 1086.

Radlett (town, Hertfordshire) 'road junction', OE *rād*, 'road' + *gelǣt*, 'junction'. The town lies at the point where the road from Watford joins Watling Street. *Radelett* 1453.

Radnor (district, Powys) '(district at the) red bank', OE *rēad*, 'red' + *ōfer*, 'bank', 'slope'. The name, familiar from *Radnor Forest* and the historic county of *Radnorshire*, refers to the red loamy soil found on the hill slopes here. *Raddrenoue* 1086.

Radstock (town, Avon) 'outlying farmstead by the road', OE *rād*, 'road' + *stoc*, 'outlying farmstead'. The 'road' is the ancient Fosse Way. The name was originally *Stoke*, but 'road' was added to distinguish this place from the many others of this name. *Stoche* 1086, *Radestok* 1221.

Raglan (village, Gwent) '(place) by the rampart', Welsh *rhag*, 'before' + *glan*, 'bank'. The name refers to the former castle here, dating from the 11th century. *Raghelan* 1254.

Rainham (town, Greater London) 'homestead of the Roegingas', OE tribal name + *hām*, 'homestead'. The meaning of the tribal name is uncertain. The first part of the name could also be the OE personal name *Regna*. *Renaham* 1086.

Ramsbottom (town, Greater Manchester) 'valley of the ram', OE *ramm*, 'ram' + **bothm*, 'valley'. The reference need not be to the animal but to a rock formation resembling a ram's head. The first part of the name could also be OE *hramsa*, 'wild garlic'. The valley is that of the River Irwell. *Romesbothum* 1324.

Ramsey (town, Cambridgeshire) 'island where wild garlic grows', OE *hramsa*, 'wild garlic' + *ēg*, 'island'. The town is on raised ground in the fenlands, and this is the 'island'. *Hramesege c* 1000.

Ramsgate (town, Kent) 'gap of the raven', OE *hræfn*, 'raven' + *geat*, 'gap'. The first part of the name has not been satisfactorily explained. It could be the OE personal name *Hræfn*. The 'gap' is in the cliffs here, as at ◊Margate. *Remmesgate* 1275.

Rannoch (mountain area, Highland/Strathclyde/Tayside) 'bracken', Gaelic *raineachr*, 'bracken'. The name is also familiar from *Rannoch* Moor and Forest, and from Loch Rannoch.

Rattray (town, Tayside) 'farm by the fort', Gaelic *ràth*, 'fort' + Celtic word. The second part of the name represents a word related to modern Welsh *tref*, 'farm'. *Rotrefe* 1291.

Raunds (town, Northamptonshire) '(place at the) borders', OE *rand*, 'border'. The town is located near the 'borders' or meeting point of three counties: Northamptonshire, Cambridgeshire (historically Huntingdonshire) and Bedfordshire. The OE word has a plural *s*. *Randan c* 980, *Rande* 1086.

Ravenglass (village, Cumbria) 'Glas's share', Old Irish *rann*, 'share', 'lot' + personal name. The Roman fort here was called *Glannoventa*, 'place at the bank', the 'bank' being that of the estuary of the River Esk. *Rengles c* 1180.

Rawtenstall (town, Lancashire) 'rough farmstead', OE *rūt*, 'rough' + **tūn-stall*, 'farmstead'. The second part of the name literally means 'farm site', and refers to buildings used when cattle were pastured on higher ground. The town is on the edge of high moorland. *Routonstall* 1324.

Rayleigh (town, Essex) 'clearing where roedeer are', OE *rǣge*, 'roedeer' + *lēah*, 'clearing'. The first OE word also means 'she goat', and these animals could equally have been here. *Ragheleia* 1086.

Reading (town, Berkshire) '(settlement of) Rēada's people', OE personal name + *-ingas*, 'people of'. The personal name, which could also be *Rēad*, means 'red one'. *Readingum c* 900.

Reculver (village, Kent) 'great headland', Celtic words. The *Re-* of the name means 'great', and the rest is related to modern Welsh *gylfin*, literally 'bill', 'beak'. There is no obvious 'headland' here, unless the reference is to nearby Thanet. *Regulbium c* 425, *Roculf* 1086.

Redbridge (borough, Greater London) '(place at the) 'red bridge'. The name reputedly refers to a former red brick bridge over the River Roding here. *Red Bridge* 1777.

Redcar (town, Cleveland) '(place by the) reedy marsh', OE *hrēod*, 'reed' + OS *kjarr*, 'marsh'. The name refers to the town's location on low-lying land by the sea. The first part of the name could also be OE *rēad*, 'red'. *Redker c* 1170.

Redditch (town, Hereford and Worcester) '(place by the) red ditch', OE *rēad*, 'red' + *dīc*, 'ditch'. The first part of the name could also be OE *hrēod*, 'reed'. 'Red' would have been applied to the colour of the soil, not that of the water in the 'ditch' or dyke. *La Rededich* 1247.

Redhill (district, Reigate, Surrey) '(place by the) red slope', OE *rēad*, 'red' + *helde*, 'slope'. The *-hill* is misleading, although the sense is much the same. The 'slope' is probably the one known as Redstone Hill, where the soil would have been 'red'. *Redehelde* 1301.

Redruth (town, Cornwall) '(place by the) 'red ford', Old Cornish *rid*, 'ford' + *rudh*, 'red'. The 'red ford' was probably over the small stream by which Redruth Church stands to the west of the town. It is the second part of the name that means 'red', not the first. *Ridruth* 1259.

Reigate (town, Surrey) 'roedeer gate', OE *rǣge*, 'roedeer' + *geat*, 'gate'. A 'roedeer gate' would have been an entrance to a deer park or a gap in a fence where a doe could pass with her young. *Reigata c* 1170.

Renfrew (town, Strathclyde) '(place at the) 'point of the current', Celtic words. The name represents words related to modern Welsh *rhyn*, 'point', and *ffrwyd*, 'current'. A 'point of current' is a confluence, here that of the rivers Clyde and Gryfe. *Reinfry c* 1128.

Renton (town, Strathclyde) 'Renton's (town)'. The name dates from 1782 and is that of Cecilia *Renton*, daughter of John Renton of Blackadder. The town was founded by her mother-in-law, Jean Telfer, sister of the writer Tobias Smollett (1721-71), who was born near here.

Repton (town, Derbyshire) 'hill of the Hrype', tribal name + OE *dūn*, 'hill'. The town is named for the people who gave the name of ◊Ripon. There is hardly a 'hill' here in the usual sense, but the ground rises slightly from the River Trent, near which the town stands. *Hrypadun* 730, *Rapendune* 1086.

Restormel (district, Cornwall) '(district of the) moor at the bare hill', Cornish *ros*, 'moor' + *tor*, 'hill' + *moyl*, 'bare'. The modern administrative district takes its name from the village of *Restormel*. The particular 'bare hill' has not been identified. It may have been the headland on which Restormel Castle stands. *Restormel* 1310.

Retford (town, Nottinghamshire) '(place at the) red ford', OE *rēad*, 'red' + *ford*, 'ford'. The 'red ford' would have been one with red soil over the River Idle, on which the town stands. The town is often known as *East Retford* to distinguish it from *West Retford*, over the river. *Redforde* 1086.

Rhayader (town, Powys) '(place at the) waterfall', Welsh *rhaeadr*, 'waterfall'. The town is on the River Wye, and a waterfall was prominent here until 1780, when a bridge was built. The town's Welsh name is *Rhaeadr Gwy*, 'waterfall on the Wye', and the record below relates to this. *Raidergoe* 1191.

Rhondda (town, Mid Glamorgan) '(place on the River) Rhondda', Welsh river name. The town stands stands on the Afon *Rhondda* Fawr, 'great River Rhondda', the river name itself deriving from Welsh *rhoddni*, 'noisy'. The record relates to the river. *Rotheni* 12th century.

Rhosllanerchrugog (village, Clwyd), 'moor of the heather glade', Welsh *rhos*, 'moor' + *llannerch*, 'glade' + *grugog*, 'growing with heather'. In everyday use the name is shortened to *Rhos*. The record suggests that the transcriber was English and did not understand the Welsh words. *Rose lane aghregog* 1544.

Rhos-on-Sea (town, Clwyd) 'headland by the sea', Welsh *rhos*, 'headland' + English *by the sea*. There is a small promontory here on Colwyn Bay.

Rhuddlan (district, Rhyl, Clwyd) '(place by the) red bank', Welsh *rhudd*, 'red' + *glan*, 'bank'. The reference is to the 'red' soil on the 'bank' of the River Clwyd here. *Roelend* 1086.

Rhyl (town, Clwyd) '(place by) the hill', Welsh *yr*, 'the' + OE *hyll*, 'hill'. There is hardly a hill here in the accepted sense, but the ground rises slightly to the south of the town. *Ryhull* 1301, *Hull* 1351.

Rhymney (town, Mid Glamorgan) '(place by the River) Rhymney', Welsh river name. The river name derives from Welsh *rhwmp*, 'auger', 'borer', with the suffix *-ni*. *Rempney* 1291.

Ribble (river, North Yorkshire/Lancashire) 'tearing one', OE *ripel*, 'tearing'. The name implies a river whose current has a 'scouring' action. *Rippel c* 715.

Ribchester (village, Lancashire) 'Roman fort on the (River) Ribble', OE river name + *ceaster*, 'Roman fort'. For the origin of the river name, *see* ◊Ribble. *Ribelcastre* 1086.

Richmond (town, Greater London) '(place named after) Richmond'. The original name of the place was *Sheen*, 'shelters', from OE **scēo*, 'shed'. Edward I built a palace here in the 13th century, and this was enlarged by Henry VII in the late 15th century. When it was burnt down in 1501, however, Henry renamed the place ◊Richmond, from his former title, Duke of Richmond, from the Yorkshire ◊Richmond. *Richemount* 1502.

Richmond (town, North Yorkshire) 'strong hill', Old French *riche*, 'strong' + *mont*, 'hill'. The name either refers to the town's high location or was imported by the Normans from France. It was this town that gave the name of ◊Richmond, Greater London. *Richemund c* 1110.

Rickmansworth (town, Hertfordshire) 'Rīcmǣr's enclosure', OE personal name + *worth*, 'enclosure'. The *n* of the name represents the final *r* of the personal name, to which the Domesday Book record has added an initial *P*. *Prichemareworde* 1086, *Richemaresworthe c* 1180.

Rievaulx (village, North Yorkshire) '(place in the) valley of the (River) Rye', Celtic river name + Old French *val*, 'valley'. The river name probably means simply 'stream'. *Rievalle* 1157.

Ringwood (town, Hampshire) 'wood on a boundary', OE **rimuc*, 'boundary' + *wudu*, 'wood'. The name probably refers to the location of the place near the edge of the New Forest. *Rimucwuda* 955, *Rincvede* 1086.

Ripley (town, Derbyshire) 'strip-shaped clearing', OE **ripel*, 'strip' + *lēah*, 'clearing'. The first word of the name lies behind that of the River ◊Ribble. *Ripelei* 1086.

Ripon (town, North Yorkshire) '(place in the territory of the) Hrype', tribal name. The origin and meaning of the tribal name are uncertain. The same people gave the name of ◊Repton. The Domesday Book record represents the name in a dative plural form, and this gave the modern name. *Hrypis c* 715, *Ripum* 1086.

Risca (town, Gwent) 'bank', Welsh *rhisga*, 'bank'. The town stands on rising ('banking') ground to the north of the River Ebbw.

Rishton (town, Lancashire) 'farmstead where rushes grow', OE *risc*, 'rush' + *tūn*, 'farmstead'. There are several streams and rivers in the locality. *Riston c* 1205.

Robin Hood's Bay (town, North Yorkshire) '(place by) Robin Hood's Bay'. The resort took the name of the bay, itself named after the popular outlaw, who has associations with Nottinghamshire and Yorkshire. Other places also bear his name. *Robin Hoode Baye* 1532.

Roby (town, Merseyside) 'farmstead by a boundary', OS *rá*, 'boundary' + *bý*, 'farmstead'. The boundary was probably that of a hundred here. The Domesday Book record has added an extra *l*. *Rabil* 1086, *Rabi* 1185.

Rochdale (town, Greater Manchester) '(place in the) valley of the (River) Roch', river name + OS *dalr*, 'valley'. The river name represents the first part of the original name of the place, *Recedham*, 'homestead with a hall', from OE *reced*, 'hall', and *hām*, 'homestead'. *Recedham* 1086, *Rachedal c* 1195.

Rochester (city, Kent) 'Roman fort of Hrofi', Celtic name + OE *ceaster*, 'Roman fort'. The initial *Ro-* of the name is all that remains from the original Roman name, *Durobrivae*, meaning 'walled town with the bridges', from words eventually related to English *door* and *bridge*. Remains of a Roman bridge over the Medway have been found here. *Hrofaescaestir* 731, *Rovecestre* 1086.

Rochford (town, Essex) 'ford of the hunting dog', OE *ræcc*, 'hunting dog' + *ford*, 'ford'. There was doubtless a regular crossing place for hunting dogs over the River Roach here. The river name comes from that of the town. *Rochefort* 1086.

Rockingham (village, Northamptonshire) 'homestead of Hrōc's people', OE personal name + *-inga-*, 'of the people of' + *hām*, 'homestead'. The personal name means 'rook'. *Rochingeham* 1086.

Rodings, The (village group, Essex), '(places of) Hrōtha's people', OE personal name + *-ingas*, 'people of'. The 8 villages have distinguishing additions: *Abbess* Roding was held by the Abbess of Barking, *Aythorpe* Roding was held by Aitrop, *Beauchamp* Roding was held by the De Beauchamp family, *Berners* Roding was held by Hugh de Berners, *High* Roding has a higher location, *Leaden* Roding had a church with a lead roof, *Margaret* Roding has a church dedicated to St Margaret, *White* Roding had a church with white walls.

Roehampton (district, Greater London) 'home farm where rooks gather', OE *hrōc*, 'rook' + *hām-tūn*, 'home farm'. The place was originally

Hampton, and the first part of the name was added for distinction. *Hampton* 1332, *Rokehampton* 1350.

Romford (town, Greater London) '(place by the) wide ford', OE *rūm*, 'broad', 'roomy' + *ford*, 'ford'. The 'wide ford' would have been over the River *Rom* here, whose own name comes from that of the town. *Romfort* 1177.

Romiley (town, Greater Manchester) 'wide clearing', OE *rūm*, 'broad', 'roomy' + *lēah*, 'clearing'. It is not clear where exactly the 'wide clearing' was. *Rumelie* 1086.

Romney Marsh (marshland, Kent) '(region with a) river', river name. The origin and meaning of the first part of the name are uncertain. It may represent OE *rūm*, 'broad', 'roomy'. The second part is OE *ēa*, 'river'. *See also* ◊New Romney. *Rumenea* 11th century.

Romsey (town, Hampshire) 'Rūm's island', OE personal name + *ēg*, 'island'. The 'island' is the slightly higher land on which the town arose here, away from Romsey Abbey. *Rummæsig c* 970, *Romesy* 1086.

Rona (island, Highland) 'rough island', OS *hraun*, 'rough' + *ey*, 'island'. The name refers to the island's rocky terrain.

Ross (district, Highland) 'moorland', Gaelic *ros*, 'moorland'. The secondary meanings of *ros* are 'promontory' and 'wood', and these would also be suitable for the region, now that of *Ross* and Cromarty.

Rossendale, Forest of (moorland area, Lancashire). The moorland takes its name from the valley so called, that of the River Irwell. The meaning is uncertain, but it may be 'moorland', 'wood', from a Celtic word related to modern Welsh *rhos*, 'moor', 'raised plain'. The *-dale* is the valley. *Rocendal* 1242.

Ross-on-Wye (town, Hereford and Worcester) 'hill spur by the (River) Wye', Celtic word + river name. The Celtic word that gave the main name is related to modern Welsh *rhos*, 'moor', 'raised plain'. The latter sense well suits the site of the town, on a steep hill overlooking the Wye. The river name is of Celtic or pre-Celtic origin and uncertain meaning. It may be simply 'mover', 'conveyor'. *Rosse* 1086.

Rosyth (town, Fife). The name is of uncertain origin. It may be based on Gaelic *ros*, headland', referring to the rock by the River Forth on which the town's castle formerly stood. *Rossyth* late 12th century, *Westir Rossith* 1363.

Rothbury (town, Northumberland) 'Hrōtha's stronghold', OE personal name + *burh*, 'stronghold'. The first part of the name could also represent OS *rauthr*, 'red', referring to to the colour of the local bedrock. *Routhebiria* c 1125.

Rotherham (town, South Yorkshire) 'homestead on the (River) Rother', Celtic river name + OE *hām*. 'homestead'. The river name means 'chief river'. *Rodreham* 1086.

Rotherhithe (district, Greater London) 'landing place for cattle', OE *hrȳther*, 'cattle' + *hȳth*, 'landing place'. Rotherhithe is by the Thames. An alternative version of the name, *Redriff*, was current down to at least the 19th century. *Rederheia* c 1105, *Rotherhithe, or Redriff* 1868.

Rothes (town, Grampian) '(place by the) rath', Gaelic *ràth*, 'rath'. A *rath* is a type of circular fort. An equivalent word is found in many Irish place-names. *See also* ◊Glenrothes.

Rothesay (town, Strathclyde) 'Rother's island', OS personal name + *ey*, 'island'. The name alludes to *Roderick*, son of Reginald, to whom the 'island' of Bute, on which the town is located, was granted in the early 13th century.

Rothwell (town, Northamptonshire) 'spring by a clearing', OE **roth*, 'clearing' + *wella*, 'spring', 'stream'. The town is actually on the small River Ise. *Rodewelle* 1086.

Rottingdean (village, East Sussex) 'valley of Rōta's people', OE personal name + *-inga-*, 'of the people of' + *denu*, 'valley'. The same personal name lies behind that of ◊Rutland. *Rotingedene* 1086.

Roxburgh (district, Borders) 'Hrōc's fortress', OE personal name + *burh*, 'fortress'. The name is also borne by the historic county of *Roxburghshire*. *Rokisburc* 1127.

Royston (town, Hertfordshire) 'Rohesia's village', personal name + OE *tūn*, 'village'. The name was recorded in 1184 as *Crux Roaisie*, from Latin *crux*, 'cross', and the female personal name *Rohesia*. A shortened form of the latter, with OE *tūn* added, gave the present name. The 'cross' was the stone one that Rohesia had erected at the junction of Ermine Street and Icknield Way. *Roiston* 1286.

Royston (town, South Yorkshire) 'Hrōr's farmstead', OE personal name + *tūn*, 'farmstead'. The personal name could equally be OS *Róarr*. *Rorestone* 1086.

Royton (town, Greater Manchester) 'farmstead where rye is grown', OE *ryge*, 'rye' + *tūn*, 'farmstead'. The name of ◊Ryton, Tyne and Wear, is of identical origin. *Ritton* 1226.

Ruabon (town, Clwyd) 'Mabon's hill', Welsh *rhiw*, 'hill' + Celtic god name. *Mabon* was a Celtic god of youth, reputedly the father of *Teilo*, who gave the name of ◊Llandeilo. The first part of his name has disappeared in the place-name. *Rywuabon* 1291.

Rugby (town, Warwickshire) 'Hrōca's village', OE personal name + OS *bý*, 'village'. The *-by* of the name replaced an earlier *-bury*, representing OE *burh*, 'fortified place', as shown by the Domesday Book record of the name below. *Rocheberie* 1086, *Rokebi* 1200.

Rugeley (town, Staffordshire) 'clearing by a ridge', OE *hrycg*, 'ridge' + *lēah*, 'clearing'. The town lies close to the northeastern edge of Cannock Chase, and this may have been the 'ridge' of the original. *Rugelie* 1086.

Ruislip (district, Greater London) 'leaping place where rushes grow', OE **rysc*, 'rush' + *hlȳp*, 'leaping place'. The reference would be to a point on the River Pinn where agile travellers could leap across. *Rislepe* 1086.

Rum (island, Highland) 'room', Gaelic *rúim*, 'room', 'space'. The name alludes to the island's comparative spaciousness, compared with neighbouring Eigg and Muck. The spelling *Rhum* is an artificial one introduced by the island's English owners between 1888 and 1957. *Ruim* 677.

Runcorn (town, Cheshire) 'wide bay', OE *rūm*, 'broad', 'roomy' + *cofa*, 'bay', 'cove'. The 'wide bay' is the former spacious bay that existed between Widnes and Castle Rock. *Rumcofan c* 1000.

Rushden (town, Northamptonshire) 'valley where rushes grow', OE **ryscen*, 'rushy' + *denu*, 'valley'. The terrain is generally low-lying here, and the town is only 2 miles from the River Nene. *Risedene* 1086.

Rustington (town, West Sussex) 'estate named after Rust', OE personal name + *-ing-*, 'named after' + *tūn*, 'estate'. The personal name, which may have been *Rusta*, means 'rusty', ie, 'red-haired'. *Rustinton* 1180.

Rutherglen (town, Strathclyde) 'red valley', Gaelic *ruadh*, 'red' + *gleann*, 'glen', 'valley'. The name refers to the reddish-coloured soil here. *Ruthirglen c* 1160.

Ruthin (town, Clwyd) 'red fort', Welsh *rhudd*, 'red' + *din*, 'fort'. The name alludes to the red sandstone from which the 13th-century castle was built here. *Ruthun* 1253.

Rutland (historic county, England) 'Rōta's estate', OE personal name + *land*, 'land', 'estate'. Rutland was originally a *soke*, a district having special rights. It became a county in the 13th century. *Roteland c* 1060, 1086.

Rydal Water (lake, Cumbria) 'lake of the valley where rye is grown', OE *ryge*, 'rye' + OS *dalr*, 'valley' + modern English *water*. The lake was formerly known as *Routhmere*, from the River *Rothay* ('trout stream') that flows through it. *Routhemere* 13th century, *Rydal Water* 1576.

Ryde (town, Isle of Wight) '(place by the) stream', OE *rīth*, 'stream'. The 'stream' is Monktonmead Brook, which flows through the town to the sea. *La Ride* 1257.

Rye (town, East Sussex) '(place) at the island'. The town was actually built on an island in flooded marshes. The name represents OE *īeg*, 'island', with the initial *R-* from the final letter of Middle English *atter*, 'at the'. *Ria* 1130.

Ryhope (district, Sunderland, Tyne and Wear) '(place by the) rough valleys', OE *hrēof*, 'rough' + *hop*, 'valley'. The first part of the name could also represent OE *rēfa*, 'reeve', 'bailiff'. The second part was originally in a plural form. *Reofhoppas c* 1050.

Ryton (town, Tyne and Wear) 'farm where rye grows', OE *ryge*, 'rye' + *tūn*, 'farm'. The name has exactly the same origin and meaning as that of ◊Royton. *Ritona* 1183.

S

Saddleworth Moor (moorland, Greater Lancashire) 'enclosure on a saddle-shaped ridge', OE *sadol*, 'saddle' + *worth*, 'enclosure'. The whole moor takes its name from a particular location on it. *Sadelwrth* late 12th century.

Saffron Walden (town, Essex), 'valley of the Britons where saffron is grown', Middle English *safron*, 'saffron' + OE *walh*, 'Briton' + *denu*, 'valley'. The name was originally just *Walden*, denoting a valley occupied by the Ancient Britons. The first word was added later to distinguish this Walden from others, referring to the cultivation of *saffron* for medicinal purposes. *Wealadene c* 1000, *Waledana* 1086, *Saffornewalden* 1582.

St Albans (city, Hertfordshire) 'St Alban's (town)', saint's name. The name honours *St Alban*, who was martyred here in AD 209. The records below contain OE *stōw*, 'place', and Latin *villa*, 'town'. *Sancte Albanes stow*, 1007, *Villa Sancti Albani* 1086.

St Andrews (town, Fife) 'St Andrew's (town)', saint's name. The relics of *St Andrew* were said to have been brought here in the 8th century. *Sancti Andree c* 1158.

St Austell (town, Cornwall) 'St Austol's (church)', saint's name. The name comes from the dedication of the church to *St Austol*, a 6th-century monk. *Austol c* 1150.

St Bees (village, Cumbria) 'St Bega's (church)', saint's name. *St Bega* was a 7th-century female Irish saint. The village here was originally known as the equivalent of *Kirkby*, as shown in the first record. *Cherchebi c* 1125, *Sancta Bega c* 1135.

St Blazey (town, Cornwall) 'St Blaise's (church)', saint's name. The name comes from the dedication of the church to *St Blaise*, a 4th-century martyr.

St Brides Bay (bay, Dyfed) 'St Brigid's (bay)', saint's name. The bay is named from the small village of *St Brides* here, itself named from the dedication of its church to *St Brigid* of Ireland, 6th-century Abbess of Kildare.

St Budeaux (district, Plymouth, Devon) 'St Budoc's (church)', saint's name. The 6th-century saint has a name that is the male equivalent of *Boudicca* (Boadicea). The Domesday Book record has the name meaning 'Budoc's hide', relating to a measure of land. *Bucheside* 1086, *Butshead al. Boxhead al. Budocoshide al. St Budeax* 1671.

St Columb Major (village, Cornwall) 'greater (place of) St Columba's (church)', saint's name + Latin *major*, 'greater'. *St Columba* was an obscure early martyr, known also as Columba the Virgin. The name distinguishes this place from nearby *St Columb Minor*, with a church also dedicated to her. *Sancta Columba c* 1240.

St David's (village, Dyfed), 'St David's (cathedral)', saint's name. The name is that of the saint to whom the cathedral here is dedicated.

St Edmundsbury (district, Suffolk), '(district of) Bury St Edmunds', place-name. The administrative district takes its name from an early record of the name of its chief town, ◊Bury St Edmunds.

St Helens (town, Merseyside) 'St Helen's (chapel)', saint's name. The town arose in the 17th century and takes its name from a chapel dedicated to *St Helen*. The chapel's name is recorded no earlier than 1552.

St Ives (town, Cambridgeshire) 'St Ivo's (town)', saint's name. The town is named after *St Ivo*, whose relics were discovered here in the 10th century. Its earlier name was *Slepe*, 'slippery place', alluding to its location by the River Ouse. *Sancto Ivo de Slepe* 1110.

St Ives (town, Cornwall) 'St Ya's (church)', saint's name. The town takes its name from the dedication of its church to *St Ya*, a female saint said to have come here from Ireland in the 6th century. *Sancta Ya* 1284.

St John's Wood (district, Greater London), 'St John's wood', saint's name + OE *wudu*, 'wood'. The name refers to the Knights Hospitallers of *St John*, to whom the land here was granted in the 13th century. There is no wood here now. *Boscum Prioris Sci Johannis* 1294, *Seynt Johns Woode* 1524.

St Just (town, Cornwall) 'St Just's (church)', saint's name. The name comes from the dedication of the church here to *St Just* (perhaps the 3rd-century martyr, Justus of Beauvais). *Sanctus Justus* 1291.

St Leonards (town, East Sussex) 'St Leonard's (church)', saint's name. The town takes its name from the dedication of its church to *St Leonard*. The Latin record means 'manor of St Leonard near Hastings'. *Villa de Sancto Leonardo juxta Hasting* 1288.

St Mawes (town, Cornwall) 'St Maudyth's (church)', saint's name. The town derives its name from the patron saint of the church, *St Maudyth*, a rather obscure Celtic monk. *Sanctus Maudetus* 1284.

St Monance (town, Fife) 'St Monans's (church)', saint's name. The town's name comes from the dedication of its church to *St Monans*, 6th-century Irish bishop of Clonfert.

St Neots (town, Cambridgeshire) 'St Neot's (town)', saint's name. The name is that of *St Neot*, the Cornish saint whose relics were brought here in the 10th century from *St Neot*, Cornwall. *S' Neod* 12th century.

St Pancras (district, Greater London) 'St Pancras's (church)', saint's name. The district is named for the dedication of its church to *St Pancras*, a 4th-century martyr in Rome. *Sanctum Pancratiu* 1086.

Salcombe (town, Devon) 'salt valley', OE *sealt*, 'salt' + *cumb*, 'valley'. The resort's name refers to the production of salt here, rather than simply to salt sea water. *Cp* ◊Budleigh Salterton, a town further up the coast. *Saltecumbe* 1244.

Sale (town, Greater Manchester) '(place by the) willow tree', OE *salh*, 'sallow', 'willow'. Sale is not far from ◊Salford, with its similar name. *Sale* c 1205.

Salford (town, Greater Manchester) 'ford where willow trees grow', OE *salh*, 'sallow', 'willow' + *ford*, 'ford'. The 'ford' here is over the River Irwell. The town is not far from ◊Sale, showing that willows must have been abundant in this region. *Salford* 1086.

Salisbury (city, Wiltshire) 'stronghold at Sorvio', Celtic place-name + OE *burh*, stronghold'. The meaning of *Sorvio* is obscure, but its *r* became *l* under Norman influence. The Roman fort here, at what is now Old Sarum, was called *Sorviodunum*, 'fort of Sorvio'. *Searobyrg* c 900, *Sarisberie* 1086.

Salop *See* ◊Shropshire.

Saltash (town, Cornwall) '(place by the) ash tree with salt', Middle English *salt*, 'salt' + OE *æsc*, 'ash tree'. The place was originally *Ash*. *Salt* was added later through the production of salt here. *Esse* 1221, *Saltehasche* 1302.

Saltburn-by-the-Sea (town, Cleveland) '(place by the) salt stream by the sea', OE *salt*, 'salt' + *burna*, 'stream' + modern *by the sea*. The name probably refers to the nearby brine wells, whose water was used for the brine baths opened here in the 1890s. *Salteburnam* c 1185, *Saltburn-by-Sea* 1868.

Sandbach (town, Cheshire) 'sandy valley stream', OE *sand*, 'sand' + *bæce*, 'stream in a valley'. The town is on a small tributary of the River Wheelock. *Sanbec* 1086.

Sanderstead (district, Greater London) 'sandy homestead', OE *sand*, 'sand' + *hǣm-styde*, 'homestead'. The soil is noticeably sandy here. *Sondenstede c* 880, *Sandestede* 1086.

Sandhurst (town, Berkshire) 'sandy wooded hill', OE *sand*, 'sand' + *hyrst*, 'wooded hill'. The soil is markedly sandy locally. *Sandherst* 1175.

Sandown (town, Isle of Wight) 'sandy riverside land', OE *sand*, 'sand' + *hamm*, 'riverside land'. The 'riverside land' is the flat ground between the upper reaches of the River Yar and the sea. The apparent *down* of the name is thus misleading. *Sande* 1086, *Sandham* 1271.

Sandringham (village, Norfolk) 'sandy (part of) Dersingham', OE *sand* + place-name. The village takes its name from the nearby village of *Dersingham*. Its own name means 'homestead of Dēorsige's people', with the same personal name as for ◊Dursley. *Santdersincham* 1086.

Sandwich (town, Kent) 'sandy harbour', OE *sand*, 'sand' + *wīc*, 'harbour'. The 'sand' is not that of the seashore but of the local soil, a rich sandy loam. *Sandwicæ* 710, *Sandwice* 1086.

Sandy (town, Bedfordshire) 'sandy island', OE *sand*, 'sand' + *ēg*, 'island'. The 'island' is the slightly higher ground east of the River Ivel on which the town stands. *Sandeie* 1086.

Sanquhar (town, Dumfries and Galloway) 'old fort', Gaelic *sean*, 'old' + *cathair*, 'fort'. The 'fort' is the ancient earthwork called the Devil's Dyke, to the west of the town. *Sanchar* 1150.

Saundersfoot (town, Dyfed) 'Saunders' foot (of the hill)'. The name probably refers to a site at the bottom of a hill owned by a man called *Saunders* or *Alexander*. The town is at a point where two valleys meet in an opening in the cliffs. *Sannders foot* 1602.

Savernake Forest (woodland, Wiltshire) 'district of (the River) Severn', river name + Celtic word. The name relates not to the present ◊Severn, or *Sabrina*, but to a former name of the River Bedwyn here. The final part of the name is a Celtic word meaning 'district'. *Safernoc* 934.

Sawbridgeworth (town, Hertfordshire) 'Sǣbeorht's enclosure', OE personal name + *worth*, 'enclosure'. The 'bridge' is not in the original form of the name, but happens to be appropriate for the town's location on the River Stort. *Sabrixteworde* 1086.

Sawston (district, Cambridge, Cambridgeshire) 'farmstead of Salse's people', OE personal name + *-inga-*, 'of the people of' + *hām*, 'farmstead'. The original *-ing-* of the name has disappeared. *Salsingetune* 970, *Salsiton* 1086.

Saxmundham (town, Suffolk) 'Seaxmund's homestead', OE personal name + *hām*, 'homestead'. The personal name, probably meaning 'protector of the Saxons', has not been recorded anywhere else. *Sasmundeham* 1086.

Scafell Pike (mountain, Cumbria), 'hill with a summer pasture', OS *skáli*, 'hut', 'shieling' + *fjall*, 'hill', 'mountain' + OE *pīc*, 'pike', 'peak'. The name is properly that of *Sca Fell*, a separate mountain a short distance from Scafell Pike, which is thus named after it. *Pike* denotes that it is the highest in the group.

Scalloway (town, Shetland) 'bay by the shelter', OS *skáli*, 'shelter', 'shieling' + *vágr*, 'bay'. The 'shelter' would have been set up temporarily by a summer pasture.

Scapa Flow (strait, Orkney) 'sea bay of the isthmus of the boat', OS *skalpr*, 'boat' + *eith*, 'isthmus' + *flóa*, 'flood', 'sea bay'. The 'isthmus' is the stretch of land south of Kirkwall on the eastern side of Scapa Bay.

Scarborough (town, North Yorkshire) 'Skarthi's stronghold', OS personal name + OE *burh*, 'stronghold'. The first part of the name could also represent OS *skarth*, 'gap', and the second half OE *beorg*, 'hill', giving 'hill by a gap', which in fact suits the local topography. *Escardeburg c* 1160.

Scilly Isles (islands, Cornwall). The name is ancient, and of unknown origin and meaning. It may originally have applied to a single island in the group. The *c* may have been inserted to avoid an association with *silly*. *Sully* 12th century.

Scotch Corner (road junction, North Yorkshire) 'corner to Scotland'. The junction on the Great North Road (A1) is so called bcause the main road (A66) to Scotland via Carlisle branches off here.

Scotland (country, Great Britain) 'land of the Scots'. The *Scots* were raiders who crossed from northern Ireland to what was then Caledonia (and is now Scotland) in the 5th and 6th centuries AD. The meaning of their name is unknown.

Scrabster (village, Highland) 'rocky homestead', OS *skjære*, 'rocky' + *bólstathr*, 'homestead'. Scrabster is on the rocky western shore of Thurso Bay. *Skarabolstad* 1201.

Scunthorpe (town, Humberside) 'Skúma's outlying farmstead', OS personal name + *thorp*, 'outlying farmstead'. Most places with *thorp* in their names have remained small villages, but Scunthorpe gained in size and importance after the discovery of iron ore here in the 19th century. *Escumetorp* 1086.

Seaford (town, East Sussex) 'ford by the sea', OE *sǣ*, 'sea' + *ford*, 'ford'. The 'ford' would have been over the River Ouse here before it was diverted in the 16th century to enter the sea at Newhaven. *Saforde* 12th century.

Seaham (town, Durham) 'homestead by the sea', OE *sǣ*, 'sea' + *hām*, 'homestead'. The town is a port south of Sutherland. *Sǣham c* 1050.

Seahouses (town, Northumberland) 'houses by the sea'. The resort's name is modern. *Sea Houses* 1897.

Seascale (town, Cumbria) 'huts by the sea', OS *sǣr*, 'sea' + *skáli*, 'hut', 'shieling'. The 'huts' would have been set up by a summer pasture here. *Sescales c* 1165.

Seaton (town, Devon) 'farmstead by the sea', OE *sǣ*, 'sea' + *tūn*, 'farmstead'. Many Seatons gained distinguishing additions, such as ◊Seaton Delaval. *See also* ◊Staithes. *Seton* 1238.

Seaton Delaval (town, Northumberland) 'farmstead by the sea of the de la Val family', OE *sǣ*, 'sea' + *tūn*, 'farmstead' + family name. The *de la Val* family, from *La Val*, Normandy, were here in the 13th century. *Seton de la Val* 1270.

Sedbergh (town, Cumbria) '(place by the) flat-topped hill', OS *set-berg*, 'flat-topped hill'. The name describes the hill on the slope of which the town stands. The literal meaning of the OS word is 'seat hill'. *Sedberge* 1086.

Sedgefield (district, Durham) 'Cedd's open land', OE personal name + *feld*, 'open land'. The administrative district takes its name from the village of *Sedgefield*, and it is to this that the name properly refers. The personal name could also be *Secg*. *Ceddesfeld c* 1050.

Sedgley (district, Dudley, West Midlands) 'Secg's clearing', OE personal name + *lēah*, 'clearing'. The Domesday Book record of the name has an extra *l*. *Secgesleage* 985, *Segleslei* 1086.

Sefton (district, Merseyside) 'farmstead where rushes grow', OS *sef*, 'rush' + OE *tūn*, 'farmstead'. The administrative district takes its name from the village of *Sefton*, and it is to this that the name originally applied. The Domesday Book record has letter *f* miscopied as *x*. *Sextone* 1086.

Selborne (village, Hampshire) '(place by a) stream by a (group of) willows', OE *sealh*, 'willow', 'sallow' + *burna*, 'stream'. The 'stream' of the name is *Oakhanger* Stream, now named for oaks, not willows. *Seleborne* 903, *Selesburne* 1086.

Selby (town, North Yorkshire) 'farmstead by willows', OE **sele*, 'sallow', 'willow' + OS *bý*, 'farmstead'. The first part of the name could also represent OS *selja*, with the same meaning. *Seleby* c 1030, *Salebi* 1086.

Selkirk (town, Borders) 'church by the hill', OE *sele*, 'dwelling house' + *cirice*, 'church'. The second part of the name could equally be OS *kirkja*, 'church'. The town gave the name of the historic county of *Selkirkshire*. *Selechirche* c 1120.

Selly Oak (district, Birmingham, West Midlands) 'clearing on a shelf with an oak tree', OE *scelf*, 'shelf' + *lēah*, 'clearing' + modern *oak*. A 'shelf' is a ledge of land, as on a projecting rock. The second word of the name was added in the 19th century. *Escelie* 1086, *Selvele* 1204, *Selly* 1868, *Selly Oak* 1897.

Selsey (town, West Sussex) 'island of the seal', OE *seolh*, 'seal' + *ēg*, 'island'. The reference is to the peninsula here on the beaches of which seals were formerly often seen. *Seolesiae* c 715, *Seleisie* 1086.

Sennen (village, Cornwall) '(St) Senana's (church)', saint's name. St *Senana* is the female patron saint of the church, about whom nothing is known apart from her name. *Sancta Senana* 1327.

Settle (town, North Yorkshire) 'house', OE *setl*, 'house', 'dwelling'. The name refers to a particular original 'seat' or dwelling here. *Setel* 1086.

Sevenoaks (town, Kent) '(place by) seven oak trees', OE *seofon*, 'seven' + *āc*, 'oak'. There may not actually have been 'seven oaks' here, but a group of these trees. Seven oaks were symbolically planted to the east of the town in 1955 and replaced when felled in the storms of 1987. *Seouenaca* c 1100.

Severn (river, Wales/England). The river's ancient pre-English name is of uncertain origin and meaning. *See also* ◊Savernake Forest. *Sabrina* 2nd century AD, *Sauerna* 1086.

Shaftesbury (town, Dorset) 'Sceaft's fortified place', OE personal name + *burh*, 'fortified place'. The first part of the name could also represent OE *sceaft*, 'shaft', referring to the steep hill on which the town is situated. This could have had a shaft or pole as a marker, or even been regarded as shaped like a shaft. *Sceaftesburi* 877, *Sceftesberie* 1086.

Shaldon (town, Devon) 'shallow valley', OE *sceald, 'shallow' + *denu*, 'valley'. This is the likely meaning of the name, which lacks early records. The town stands on the estuary of the River Teign. The name would not refer to this, however, but probably to an inland valley. *Shaldon* 17th century.

Shanklin (town, Isle of Wight) '(place by the) bank near the cup', OE *scenc*, 'cup' + *hlinc*, 'bank', 'ridge'. The 'cup' is the waterfall at Shanklin Chine, seen as pouring from a drinking cup. The exact location of the 'bank' is uncertain. It may have been part of the waterfall itself. *Sencliz* 1086.

Shap (town, Cumbria) 'heap (of stones)', OE *hēap*, 'heap'. The name refers to the remains of an ancient stone circle south of the town. *Hep c* 1190.

Sheerness (town, Kent) '(place by the) bright headland', OE *scīr*, 'bright' + *næss*, 'headland'. The name properly refers to the promontory on the Isle of Sheppey where the town is situated. The first part of the name could also represent OE *scear*, 'ploughshare', referring to the shape of the headland. A 'bright' headland is a broad and open one. *Scerhnesse* 1203.

Sheffield (city, South Yorkshire) 'open land by the (River) Sheaf', OE river name + *feld*, 'open land'. The river name means 'boundary', from OE *scēath*, literally 'sheath'. The Sheaf formed the boundary between Derbyshire and the historic West Riding of Yorkshire. *Scafeld* 1086.

Shefford (town, Bedfordshire) 'ford for sheep', OE *scēap*, 'sheep' + *ford*, 'ford'. The 'ford' would have been the one over the River Ivel where the Roman road (now A600) crossed it. This would have been the regular crossing place for sheep. *Sepford* 1220.

Shepherds Bush (district, Greater London) 'Shepherd's bushes', family name + modern *bush*. The first word is likely to represent a surname rather than the ordinary word *shepherd*. The second refers to bushy land formerly here. *Sheppards Bush Green* 1635.

Shepperton (village, Surrey) 'farmstead of the shepherds', OE *scēap-hirde*, 'shepherd' + *tūn*, 'farmstead'. The place would have been a site where shepherds lived, on pastures by the Thames. *Scepertune* 959, *Scepertone* 1086.

Sheppey, Isle of (island, Kent) 'island where sheep are kept', OE *scēap*, 'sheep' + *ēg*, 'island'. Islands have often been favoured as sheep pastures. *Cp* ◊Fair Isle. Modern *isle* was added when the OE word meaning this was no longer understood. *Scepeig* 696, *Scape* 1086.

Shepshed (town, Leicestershire) 'sheep headland', OE *scēap*, 'sheep' + *hēafod*, 'headland'. A 'sheep headland' is either one where sheep graze or one where sheep were sacrificed and their heads impaled. The first sense seems more likely for this high location. *Scepeshefde* 1086.

Shepton Mallet (town, Somerset) 'sheep farm of the Malet family', OE *scēap*, 'sheep' + *tūn*, 'farm' + family name. The *Malet* family held the manor here in the 12th century. *Sepetone* 1086, *Scheopton Malet* 1228.

Shepway (district, Kent) 'sheep way', OE *scēap*, 'sheep' + *weg*, 'way'. The administrative district took the name of a 'lathe' here, as one of the historic regions into which Kent was divided. A 'sheep way' is a regular route used by sheep. *Shepweye* 1227.

Sherborne (town, Dorset) '(place by the) bright stream', OE *scīr*, 'bright' + *burna*, 'stream'. The name refers to the River Yeo here, which may at one time have been called *Sherborne*. *Scireburnan* 864, *Scireburne* 1086.

Sheringham (town, Norfolk) 'homestead of Scīra's people', OE personal name + *-inga-*, 'of the people of' + *hām*, 'homestead'. The Domesday Book record of the name has *l* for *r* under Norman influence. *Cp* ◊Salisbury, where the *l* remained. *Silingeham* 1086, *Scheringham* 1242.

Sherwood Forest (forest, Nottinghamshire) 'wood of the shire', OE *scīr*, 'shire' + *wudu*, 'wood'. The name denotes that the wood was owned by the *shire* or county, either as a hunting ground or as pastureland. If the latter, it would have been for feeding pigs on acorns from the oaks. *Scirwuda* 955.

Shetland (islands, Scotland) 'hilt land', OS *hjalt*, 'hilt' + *land*, 'land'. This is the usual interpretation of the name, referring to the sword-shaped arrangement of the island group. *Haltland c* 1100.

Shifnal (town, Shropshire) 'Scuffa's corner of land', OE personal name + *halh*, 'nook'. The personal name has not been recorded anywhere else. The *n* represents its genitive ending. *Scuffanhalch* 12th century.

Shildon (town, Durham) 'shelf hill', OE *scelf*, 'shelf' + *dūn*, 'hill'. The name is appropriate for Shildon, which is on a 'shelf' or slope surrounded by hills. *Sciluedon* 1214.

Shipley (town, West Yorkshire) 'clearing where sheep are kept', OE *scēap*, 'sheep' + *lēah*, 'clearing'. The name is found elsewhere in both the north and south of England. *Scipeleia* 1086.

Shipston on Stour (town, Warwickshire) 'farmstead by the sheepwash on the (River) Stour', OE *scēap-wæsce*, 'sheepwash' + *tūn*, 'farmstead' + Celtic river name. The river name probably means 'strong one'. *Scepuuæisctune c* 770, *Scepwestun* 1086.

Shirebrook (town, Derbyshire) 'bright stream', OE *scīr*, 'bright' + *brōc*, 'stream', 'brook'. The first part of the name could also represent OE *scīr*, 'boundary', though it is not certain which boundary would be meant. *Scirebroc* 1202.

Shirley (district, Greater London) 'bright clearing', OE *scīr*, 'bright' + *lēah*, 'clearing'. A 'bright clearing' is one well cleared of trees and bushes. The name is found elsewhere, and in some cases could mean 'boundary clearing', with the first part representing OE *scīr*, 'boundary'. *Shirleye* 1314.

Shoeburyness (district, Southend-on-Sea, Essex) '(place at the) headland by Shoebury', OE place-name + *næss*, 'headland'. *Shoebury* means 'fortification providing shelter', from OE **scēo*, 'shelter', and *burh*, 'fortification'. The reference may be to an ancient camp here. The 'headland' is at the mouth of the Thames estuary. *Sceobyrig* early 10th century, *Shoberynesse* 16th century, *Shoebury-Ness* 1868.

Shoreditch (district, Greater London) 'ditch by a steep bank', OE **scora*, 'bank', 'slope' + *dīc*, 'ditch'. The 'ditch' presumably drained the 'bank', although the exact original location of either is uncertain. The bank can hardly have been that of the Thames, as Shoreditch is some way north of the river. *Soredich c* 1148.

Shoreham-by-Sea (town, West Sussex) 'homestead by a steep bank by the sea', OE **scora*, 'bank', 'slope' + *hām*, 'homestead' + modern *by sea*. The 'bank' is not that of the seashore but the steep slope of the downs east of the River Adur, at the mouth of which the town is situated. The records relate to what is now *Old Shoreham*, while Shoreham-by-Sea was known for a while as *New Shoreham*. *Sorham* 1073, *Soreham* 1086.

Shotton (town, Clwyd) 'farmstead by the steep slope', OE **scēot*, 'slope' + *tūn*, 'farmstead'. This appears to be the obvious origin of the name, but there is no 'steep slope' here, so the actual meaning may well be 'village of the Scots', with the first part representing OE *scot*, *'Scot'*.

Shrewsbury (town, Shropshire) 'fortified place of the (region of) scrubland', OE **scrob*, 'scrub' + *burh*, 'fortified place'. The first part of the name is an old district name. The present form and pronunciation of the name is due both to Norman influence and to the fact that words like 'shrew' were formerly pronounced to rhyme with 'show'. *See also* ◊Shropshire. *Scrobbesbyrig* 11th century, *Sciropesberie* 1086, *Shrovesbury* 1346.

Shrivenham (village, Oxfordshire) 'riverside land allotted by decree', OE *scrifen*, 'allotted' + *hamm*, 'riverside land'. The name implies that land beside the River Cole here was disputed, so was allotted by decree to the church. *Scrifenanhamme c* 950, *Seriveham* 1086.

Shropshire (county, England) 'shire of Shrewsbury', OE place-name + *scīr*, 'shire', 'district'. The first part of the name represents a shortening of an old form of ◊Shrewsbury. The alternative name of the county, *Salop*, in official use from 1974 to 1980, similarly represents a Norman contracted form of the county name, as shown in the records. The *r* of the original became *l*, as for ◊Salisbury. *Sciropescire* 1086, *Salopescira c* 1096.

Sidcup (district, Greater London) 'flat-topped hill', OE **set-copp*, 'seat-shaped hill'. The name implies that Sidcup arose as a place 'seated' on a hill. This is difficult to envisage now, but the ground does fall away either side of the High Street. *Cetecopp* 1254.

Sidlaw Hills (hills, Tayside) 'flat-topped hills', Gaelic *suidhe*, 'seat' + OE *hlāw* 'hill'. The name alludes to the flat-topped hills that are found at various points in the range. *Seedlaws* 1799.

Sidmouth (town, Devon) '(place at the) mouth of the (River) Sid', OE river name + *mūtha*, 'mouth'. The river name derives from OE *sīd*, 'broad', 'spacious'. *Sedemuda* 1086.

Silchester (village, Hampshire) 'Roman camp by willows', OE **siele*, 'willow', 'sallow' + *ceaster*, 'Roman camp'. According to an alternative theory, the first part of the name may be a shortened form of *Calleva*, the original Celtic name of the Roman camp here, meaning 'place in the woods', from a word related to modern Welsh *celli*, 'grove'. *Silcestre* 1086.

Silloth (town, Cumbria) 'barn by the sea', OE *sǣ*, 'sea' + OS *hlatha*, 'barn'. The first part of the name could equally be OS *sǽr*, also meaning 'sea'. *Selathe* 1292.

Silsden (town, West Yorkshire) 'Sigulfr's valley', OS personal name + OE *denu*, 'valley'. The 'valley' is that of the River Aire here. *Siglesdene* 1086, *Sighelden, or Silsden* 1868.

Silverstone (village, Northamptonshire) 'Sǣwulf's farmstead', OE personal name + *tūn*, 'farmstead'. The personal name could also be *Sigewulf*. The present form of the name has come about through false associations. *Sulueston* 942, *Silvestone* 1086.

Sissinghurst (village, Kent) 'wooded hill of Seaxa's people', OE personal name + *-inga-*, 'of the people of' + *hyrst*, 'wooded hill'. The original *x* of the name has been softened as *ss*. *Saxingherste c* 1180.

Sittingbourne (town, Kent) 'stream of the dwellers on the slope', OE *sīde*, 'slope' + *-inga-*, 'of the people of' + *burna*, 'stream'. The 'slope' is the one below the ridge on which the town is situated by Milton Creek. *Sidingeburn* 1200.

Skegness (town, Lincolnshire) 'Skeggi's promontory', OS personal name + *nes*, 'promontory'. The first part of the name could also be OS *skegg*, 'beard', referring to the shape of the promontory. The reference may be to the hook-like projection at Gibraltar Point, south of the town. *Sceggenesse* 12th century.

Skelmersdale (town, Lancashire) 'Skjaldmarr's valley' OS personal name + *dalr*, 'valley'. The present New Town developed from a village, which took its own name from the valley here. Most *-dale* names have a river name for their first part, but not this one (or ◊Wensleydale). *Schelmeresdele* 1086.

Skipton (town, North Yorkshire) 'sheep farm', OE *scīp*, 'sheep' + *tūn*, 'farm'. The *Sk-* of the name, instead of *Sh-*, is due to Scandinavian influence. *Scipton* 1086.

Skokholm (island, Dyfed) 'block island', OS *stokkr*, 'trunk', 'log' + *holmr*, 'island'. The name presumably refers to the island's shape. The first *k* may have arisen under the influence of the name of nearby ◊Skomer. *Stokholm* 1275.

Skomer (island, Dyfed) 'cloven island', OS *skalm*, 'split', 'cloven' + *ey*, 'island'. The name refers to the narrowing at the eastern end of the island, where the two inlets North Haven and South Haven almost meet at a narrow isthmus. *Skalmey* 1324.

Skye (island, Highland) 'winged (island)', Gaelic *sgiath*, 'wing'. The origin of the name is disputed. This generally accepted explanation alludes to the appearance of the island, with two mountain masses as 'wings' either side of the lower centre. *Sketis nesos* 2nd century AD.

Sleaford (town, Lincolnshire) 'ford of the (River) Slea', OE river name + *ford*, 'ford'. The river name means 'muddy stream', from a word related to OE *slīm*, 'slime'. *Cp* ◊Slimbridge. *Slioford* 852, *Eslaforde* 1086.

Slimbridge (village, Gloucestershire) 'bridge over a muddy place', OE *slīm*, 'slime' + *brycg*, 'bridge'. The 'bridge' may originally have been a causeway across muddy terrain here by the Severn estuary. The Domesday Book record is rather corrupt. *Heslinbruge* 1086, *Slimbrugia c* 1153.

Slough (town, Berkshire) 'slough', OE *slōh*, 'slough', 'mire'. The town developed on this unpromising Thames-side site through commercial considerations. *Slo* 1195.

Smethwick (town, West Midlands) 'workplace of the smiths', OE *smith*, 'smith' + *wīc*, 'special site'. The 'smiths' (metalworkers) could have worked or lived here, probably both. *Smedeuuich* 1086.

Sneinton (district, Nottingham, Nottinghamshire) For the origin of this name, *see* ◊Nottingham.

Snodland (town, Kent) 'land named after Snodd', OE personal name + *-ing-*, 'named after' + *land*, 'land'. The 'land' here would have been newly worked agricultural land by the Medway. The original *-ing-* has disappeared, and the Domesday Book record has also missed the *d* of the personal name. *Snoddingland* 838, *Esnoiland* 1086.

Snowdon (mountain, Gwynedd) 'snow hill', OE *snāw*, 'snow' + *dūn*, 'hill'. The mountain's Welsh name is *Yr Wyddfa*, 'the (place of the) cairn', from Welsh *gwyddfa*, 'mound', 'tumulus'. Mountains have long served as burial places. *Snawdune* 1095.

Soham (village, Cambridgeshire) 'homestead by a marshy pool', OE **sǣgae*, 'marshy pool' + *hām*, 'homestead'. There is no pool here now, as it was drained in medieval times. *Sǣgham c* 1000, *Saham* 1086.

Soho (district, Greater London). The name is a hunting cry. There were fields in Soho down to the 18th century. *So Ho* 1632.

Solent, The (sea channel, Hampshire/Isle of Wight). The name is pre-English and of uncertain origin and meaning. 'Place of cliffs' has been suggested. *Soluente* 731.

Solihull (town, West Midlands) 'muddy hill', OE **solig*, 'muddy' + *hyll*, 'hill'. The 'muddy hill' in question is probably the one south of St Alphege's Church. It is possible the first part of the name may represent OE **sulig*, 'pigsty'. *Solihull* 12th century.

Solway Firth (sea arm, England/Scotland) 'inlet of the pillar ford', OS *súla*, 'pillar', 'post' + *vath*, 'ford' + Scottish *firth*, 'estuary'. The 'pillar' may be the Lochmaben Stone, a granite boulder marking the end of the ford on the Scottish side. *Sulewad* 1218.

Somerset (county, England) '(district of the) settlers round Somerton', OE place-name + *sǣte*, 'settlers'. The first part of the name is a shortened form of the name of ◊Somerton. For a similar name, *cp* ◊Dorset. *Sumersæton*, 12th century.

Somerton (town, Somerset) 'farmstead used in summer', OE *sumor*, 'summer' + *tūn*, 'farmstead'. The farmstead would have been used only in summer because the land would have been wet or marshy in winter. The former marshland has been drained. *See also* ◊Somerset. *Summertone* 1086.

Sompting (village, West Sussex) '(settlement of the) dwellers by the marsh', OE **sumpt*, 'marsh' + *-ingas*, 'dwellers at'. The terrain here is low-lying although now not obviously marshy. *Suntinga* 956, *Sultinges* 1086.

Southall (district, Greater London) 'southern nook of land', OE *sūth*, 'south' + *halh*, 'nook'. The place is 'south' by comparison with ◊Northolt, although the OE word for 'nook' has developed differently there. *Suhaull* 1198.

Southam (town, Warwickshire) 'southern homestead', OE *sūth*, 'south' + *hām*, 'homestead'. It is not clear where any corresponding 'northern homestead' was. *Suthham* 998, *Sucham* 1086.

Southampton (city, Hampshire) 'southern estate on a promontory', OE *sūth*, 'south' + *hamm*, 'waterside land', 'promontory' + *tūn*, 'estate'. The original name was *Hampton*, with *South* added subsequently for distinction from ◊Northampton (although that name has a different meaning). The 'promontory' is the land between the rivers Itchen and Test. *See also* ◊Hampshire. *Homtun* 825, *Suthhamtunam* 962, *Hantone* 1086.

Southborough (town, Kent) 'southern borough', OE *sūth*, 'south' + *burh*, 'borough'. The place was originally a 'southern borough' of Tonbridge. *bo. de Suth'* 1270, *la South Burgh* 1450.

Southend-on-Sea (town, Essex) 'southern end by the sea', Middle English *south*, 'south' + *ende*, 'end' + modern *on sea*. The town arose round a location at the *south end* of the parish of Prittlewell. *Sowthende* 1481.

Southgate (district, Greater London) '(place by the) southern gate', OE *sūth*, 'south' + *geat*, 'gate'. The original 'south gate' here gave access to Enfield Chase. *Suthgate* 1370.

Southminster (village, Essex) 'southern church', OE *sūth*, 'south' + *mynster*, 'church'. It is uncertain which the corresponding 'northern church' was. It may have been the one at Steeple, 2 miles north of Southminster. ◊Upminster, with a similar name, is too far away for purposes of contrast. *Suthmynster c* 1000, *Sudmunstra* 1086.

South Molton (town, Devon) 'southern (special) estate', OE *sūth*, 'south' + Celtic word + OE *tūn*, 'estate'. The *Mol-* of the name is of uncertain origin. It may be a Celtic hill name meaning 'bald'. The town is *south* of the village of *North Molton*. *Sudmoltone* 1086.

Southport (town, Merseyside) 'southern port'. The name is a modern one, first recorded in 1798. The town is presumably called 'south' as it is on the southern side of the River Ribble estuary.

Southsea (district, Portsmouth, Hampshire) 'southern (place by the) sea'. The place grew up round the castle built by Henry VIII in 1540 at the entrance to Portsmouth Harbour. *Southsea Castle c* 1600.

South Shields (town, Tyne and Wear) 'southern sheds', Middle English *south*, 'south' + *schele*, 'shed', 'shieling'. The 'sheds' were fishermen's huts on the southern side of the River Tyne. The town was originally *Shields*, but was later differentiated from ◊North Shields. *Scheles* 1235.

Southwark (borough, Greater London) 'southern defensive work', OE *sūth*, 'south' + *weorc*, 'work'. The place arose as a defensive post on the southern side of the Thames, as an outpost to the City of London. The first record means 'fort of the men of Surrey'. *Suthriganaweorc* 10th century, *Sudwerca* 1086.

Southwell (town, Nottinghamshire) '(place at the) southern spring', OE *sūth*, 'south' + *wella*, 'well', 'spring'. The name contrasts with that of the village of *Norwell*, 7 miles northeast. The 'southern spring' itself is the Lady Well by the minster church. *Suthwellan* 958, *Sudwelle* 1086.

Southwick (town, West Sussex) 'southern farm', OE *sūth*, 'south' + *wīc*, 'farm'. Southwick depended on Kingston and lies south of it. *Sudewic* 1073.

Southwold (town, Suffolk) 'southern forest', OE *sūth*, 'south' + *wald*, 'forest'. The forest was perhaps regarded as being 'south' of Lowestoft. It is too far from *Northwold*, Norfolk, to be associated with it. *Sudwolda* 1086.

Sowerby Bridge (town, West Yorkshire) 'bridge by the farmstead on sour ground', OS *saurr*, 'sour ground', 'marshland' + *bý*, 'farmstead' + Middle English *brigge*, 'bridge'. The district here is low-lying and the soil liable to be waterlogged. The 'bridge' is over the River Calder. *Sorebi* 1086, *Sourebybrigge* 15th century.

Spalding (town, Lincolnshire) '(settlement of the) dwellers in Spald', district name + *-ingas*, 'people of'. The origin of the district name is uncertain. It may be OE **spald*, 'ditch', 'trench'. *Spallinge* 1086.

Spelthorne (district, Surrey) '(district of the) thorn tree where speeches were made', OE *spell*, 'speech' + *thorn*, 'thorn tree'. The modern administrative district took the name of a former hundred here. The 'thorn tree' would have been its meeting place, where speeches were made.

Spennymoor (town, Durham) 'moor with a fence', OE **spenning*, 'fence', + *mōr*, 'moor'. The first part of the name is conjectural, but could have the sense given, referring to a part of the moor that was fenced off or enclosed. *Spendingmor c* 1336.

Spilsby (town, Lincolnshire) 'Spillir's farmstead', OS personal name + *bý*, 'farmstead'. The personal name means 'waster', from a word related to modern English *spill*. *Spilesbi* 1086.

Spithead (sea channel, Hampshire) 'headland of the sandspit', OE *spitu*, 'sandspit' + *hēafod*, 'headland'. The name probably refers to the former sandbank called *Spit Sand*, now built over. The following record is the earliest known. *Spithead* 1653.

Spofforth (village, North Yorkshire) 'ford by a small plot', OE **spot*, 'small plot' + *ford*, 'ford'. The 'ford' would have been over the stream here, a tributary of the River Nidd. *Spoford* 1086, *Spotford* 1218.

Spurn Head (headland, Humberside) 'headland of the spur', Middle English **spurn*, 'spur' + modern *head*. The 'spur' is the projecting headland at the end of the long spit of land at the mouth of the Humber. The record means 'Ravenser spur', from *Ravenser*, a former name of the location, meaning 'Hrafn's sandbank', from an OS personal name (meaning 'raven') and *eyrr*, 'sandbank'. *Ravenserespourne* 1399.

Staffa (island, Strathclyde) 'pillar island', OS *stafr*, 'pillar' + *ey*, 'island'. The name alludes to the island's famous columns of basaltic rock.

Stafford (town, Staffordshire) 'ford by a landing place', OE *stæth*, 'landing place' + *ford*, 'ford'. The ford in question was probably at the limit of navigation on the River Sow here. This was thus a landing place. The county name, *Staffordshire*, is first recorded in the 11th century. *Stæfford* mid-11th century, *Stadford* 1086.

Staines (town, Surrey) '(place at the) stone', OE *stān*, 'stone'. The 'stone' was perhaps a Roman milestone here on the road from London to Silchester. The plural *-s* of the name is misleading, and was added later. *Stane* 11th century, *Stanes* 1086.

Staithes (village, North Yorkshire) '(place at the) landing places', OE *stæth*, 'landing place'. The record of the name shows that the 'landing places' were designed to serve nearby ◊Seaton. *Setonstathes* 1415.

Stalybridge (town, Greater Manchester) 'bridge by the wood where staves are got', OE *stæf*, 'staff', 'stave' + *lēah*, 'wood' + modern *bridge*. The original name of the place was as for ◊Staveley. *Bridge* was added much later, when the name was extended to a site across the River Tame. *Stauelegh* 13th century, *Stalybridge* 1687.

Stamford (town, Lincolnshire) '(place at the) stone ford', OE *stān*, 'stone' + *ford*, 'ford'. A 'stone ford' is one where stones are laid on a river bed to make a firmer crossing. The river here is the Welland. *Cp* ◊Stamford Bridge. *Steanford* 10th century, *Stanford* 1086.

Stamford Bridge (village, Humberside) 'bridge at the stone ford', OE *stān*, 'stone' + *ford*, 'ford' + *brycg*, 'bridge'. The village stands at a crossing of the River Derwent, where a bridge had replaced the earlier ford even before the Battle of Stamford Bridge (1066). For a 'stone ford', *see* ◊Stamford. *Stanford c* 730, *Stanfordbrycg* 1066.

Stanford le Hope (town, Essex) 'stone ford in the bay', OE *stān*, 'stone' + *ford*, 'ford' + Middle English *hope*, 'inlet', 'bay'. The town arose at a 'stone ford' (*see* ◊Stamford) on a stream near *Broad Hope*, a broad bend in the River Thames. *Staunford* 1267, *Stanford in the Hope* 1361.

Stanhope (town, Durham) 'stony valley', OE *stān*, 'stone' + *hop*, 'valley'. A 'stony valley' is one full of stones or with stony soil, in this case that of the River Wear. *Stanhopa* 1183.

Stanley (town, Durham) 'stony clearing', OE *stān*, 'stone' + *lēah*, 'clearing'. The name denotes a woodland glade with stony or rocky soil. *Stanley* 1297.

Stanmore (district, Greater London) '(place by the) stony pool', OE *stān*, 'stone' + *mere*, 'pool'. The name probably refers to a former gravelly pool here. *Stanmere* 1086.

Stansted (village, Essex) 'stony place' OE *stān*, 'stone' + *stede*, 'place'. The name may refer to a former prominent building here. *Stanesteda* 1086.

Stanwell (town, Surrey) 'stony spring', OE *stān*, 'stone' + *wella*, 'spring'. The name probably refers to the stream that flows through the town. *Stanwelle* 1086.

Stapleford (town, Nottinghamshire) 'ford (marked) by a post', OE *stapol*, 'post' + *ford*, 'ford'. Fords so marked would have been difficult or dangerous, or situated some distance from a main route. The ford here was over the River Erewash. *Stapleford* 1086.

Start Point (promontory, Devon) 'tail of land at a headland', OE *steort* 'tail', 'tongue of land' + modern *point*. The two words mean more or less the same thing. *Start Point*, Orkney, has a name of the same meaning, although there the first word represents OS *stertr*. *La Sterte* 1310.

Staveley (town, Derbyshire) 'wood where staves are got', OE *stæf*, 'staff', 'stave' + *lēah*, 'wood', 'clearing'. This name is the same as the original name of ◊Stalybridge. *Stavelie* 1086.

Steeple Bumpstead (village, Essex) 'place where reeds grow with a steeple', OE *stēpel*, 'steeple', 'tower' + *bune*, 'reeds' + *stede*, 'place'. The first word distinguishes this place from *Helions Bumpstead*, which has the name of *Tihel de Helion*, who held a manor here in the 11th century. *Bumesteda* 1086, *Stepilbumstede* 1261.

Stenhousemuir (town, Central) 'moor by the stone house', OE *stān*, 'stone' + *hūs*, 'house' + *mōr*, 'moor'. The 'stone house' would have been a distinctive building used for naming the moor, which in turn gave the name of the present town. *de Stan house c* 1200, *Stenhous* 1601.

Stepney (district, Greater London) 'Stybba's landing place', OE personal name + *hȳth*, 'landing place'. Stepney is on the Thames. The *n* represents a genitive case ending. *Stybbanhythe c* 1000, *Stibanhede* 1086.

Stevenage (town, Hertfordshire) '(place by the) strong oak tree', OE *stīth*, 'strong' + *āc*, 'oak'. The name appears to refer to a particularly robust oak tree here at some time. *Stithenæce c* 1060, *Stigenace* 1086.

Stevenston (town, Strathclyde) 'Steven's estate', personal name + OE *tūn*, 'estate'. It is not known who *Steven* was, but he must have been a landowner here in medieval times. *Stevenstoun* 1246.

Stewarton (town, Strathclyde) 'steward's estate', OE *stigweard*, 'steward' + *tūn*, 'estate'. The name refers to Walter, seneschal (high steward) to

King David I in the mid-12th century. *Stewartoun* 1201.

Stewartry (district, Dumfries and Galloway) 'stewardship'. The administrative district took the historic name for the region as a 'stewardship' of
Kirkcudbright. The steward himself was the Earl of Douglas.

Steyning (town, West Sussex) '(settlement of) Stān's people', OE per-
sonal name + -*ingas*, 'people of'. The first part of the name could equally be
OE *stān*, 'stone', so that the meaning is 'dwellers at the stony place'.
Stæningum c 880, *Staninges* 1086.

Stilton (village, Cambridgeshire) 'farmstead by a stile', OE *stigel*, 'stile' +
tūn, 'farmstead'. The 'stile' may have been over a fence here beside Ermine
Street. Travellers going to Peterborough would have needed to continue
northwards, whereas Ermine Street deviates here to the northwest.
Stichiltone 1086.

Stirling (town, Central). The town's name has never been satisfactorily
explained. It may derive from a former name of the River Forth here. Gaelic
sruth, 'stream', 'river', has been mentioned in this connection. *Strevelin
c* 1124.

Stockport (town, Greater Manchester) 'market place at an outlying settlement', OE *stoc*, 'outlying settlement' + *port*, 'market place'. The 'outlying
settlement' would have been dependent on another place. It is not clear
which this was. *Stokeport c* 1170.

Stocksbridge (town, South Yorkshire) '(place at the) log bridge', OE
stocc, 'log', 'tree trunk' + *brycg*, 'bridge'. The 'log bridge' would have
been over the Little Don here. The interpretation of the name is almost certainly correct, despite the earliest record of the name being very recent.
Stocksbridge 1841.

Stockton-on-Tees (town, Cleveland) 'farmstead at an outlying settlement', OE *stoc*, 'outlying settlement' + *tūn*, 'farmstead' + Celtic river
name. The river name, which may even be pre-Celtic, probably means
'surging river'. *Stocton* 1196.

Stoke-by-Nayland (village, Suffolk) 'religious settlement near Nayland',
OE *stoc*, 'religious settlement' + place-name. There was formerly a
monastery at this village, which is near the town of ◊Nayland. *Stoke c* 950,
Stokeneylond 1272.

Stoke Newington (district, Greater London) 'new farmstead by the tree
stumps', OE *stoccen*, 'by the tree stumps' + *nīwe*, 'new' + *tūn*, 'farmstead'.

The first word could also mean 'made of logs'. It was added to the basic name to distinguish this place from Highbury, which was formerly the manor of *Newton* Barrow. *Neutone* 1086, *Neweton Stoken* 1274.

Stoke-on-Trent (city, Staffordshire) 'outlying farmstead on the (River) Trent', OE *stoc*, 'outlying farmstead' + Celtic river name. The river name probably means 'trespasser', *ie* a river that is liable to flood its banks. The Celtic word that gave the name has its relatives in modern Welsh *hynt*, 'way', Latin *semita*, 'footpath' and French *sentier* 'path'. *Stoche* 1086.

Stoke Poges (village, Buckinghamshire) 'secondary settlement owned by the le Pugeis family', OE *stoc*, 'secondary settlement' + family name. The manor here was held by the *le Pugeis* family in the 13th century. *Stoches* 1086, *Stokepogeis* 1292.

Stone (town, Staffordshire) '(place at the) stones', OE *stān*, 'stone'. It is hard to say with any certainty what the original stones were. They may have been in or by the River Trent here. *Stanes* 1187.

Stonehaven (town, Grampian) 'stone landing place', OE *stān*, 'stone' + *hȳth*, 'landing place'. This is almost certainly the correct origin and meaning of the name, despite the location of the place on the Scottish east coast and the late dates of the earliest records. *Stanehyve* 1587, *Steanhyve* 1629.

Stonehenge (ancient stone circle, Wiltshire) 'stone gallows', OE *stān*, 'stone' + *hengen*, 'gallows', 'hanging place'. The name refers to the appearance of the trilithons, with their two upright stones and a third on top. *Stanenges c* 1130.

Stonehouse (district, Stroud, Gloucestershire) 'stone house', OE *stān*, 'stone' + *hūs*, 'house'. It is not certain what the original stone-built house was. *Stanhus* 1086.

Stony Stratford (town, Buckinghamshire) 'stony ford over a Roman road', OE *stānig*, 'stony' + *strǣt*, 'Roman road' + *ford*, 'ford'. The 'Roman road' here is Watling Street. The first word distinguishes this Stratford from others. *Stani Stratford* 1202.

Stornoway (town, Western Isles) 'steerage bay', OS *stjorn*, 'steerage', 'rudder' + *vág*, 'bay'. The precise sense of the name is not clear. Perhaps ships were obliged to manoeuvre in the original harbour here. *Stornochway* 1511.

Storrington (town, West Sussex) 'farmstead where storks are', OE *storc*, 'stork' + *tūn*, 'farmstead'. The farm may have been regularly visited by storks. *Storgetune* 1086.

Stourbridge (town, West Midlands) '(place at a) bridge over the (River) Stour', river name + OE *brycg*, 'bridge'. The Celtic or OE river name probably means 'strong one', referring to its current. There are no less than five major rivers of this name in England. *Sturbrug* 1255.

Stourport-on-Severn (town, Hereford and Worcester) 'port on the (River) Stour by the Severn'. The name is a recent one for the town at the confluence of the rivers mentioned. *Stourport c* 1755.

Stowmarket (town, Suffolk) 'place with a market', OE *stōw*, 'place of assembly', 'holy place' + Middle English *market*, 'market'. The original name of the place was simply *Stow*, here probably in the sense 'holy place'. The rest of the name was added when an important market arose. *Stou* 1086, *Stowmarket* 1268.

Stow-on-the-Wold (town, Gloucestershire) 'place on the high ground cleared of woodland', OE *stōw*, 'place of assembly', 'holy place' + *wald*, 'woodland'. *Stow* here has the sense 'holy place', as shown by the Domesday Book record of the name, which means '(St) Edward's place'. This would have been a church or chapel on the hilltop site of the Norman parish church. *Cp* ◊Wolds. *Eduuardesstou* 1086, *Stoua* 1213, *Stowe on the Olde* 1574.

Strangeways (district, Manchester, Greater Manchester) '(place by a) stream with a strong current', OE *strang*, 'strong' + *gewæsc*, 'washing', 'flood'. The name describes the original location of the place on land subject to flooding between two rivers. *Strangwas* 1322.

Stranraer (town, Dumfries and Galloway) 'plump peninsula', Gaelic *sròn*, 'peninsula' + *reamhar*, 'fat', 'plump'. The name apparently refers to the broad peninsula at the north end of the Rinns of Galloway, to the west of the town. *Stranrever* 1320.

Stratford (district, Greater London) 'ford on a Roman road', OE *strǣt*, 'Roman road' + *ford*, 'ford'. The 'Roman road' here was the one that ran from London to Colchester, and the 'ford' would have been over the River Lea. *Stratford* 1177.

Stratford-upon-Avon (town, Warwickshire) 'ford on a Roman road on the (River) Avon', OE *strǣt*, 'Roman road' + *ford*, 'ford' + Celtic river name. The 'Roman road' here joined the Roman camps at Alcester and Tiddington, and the 'ford' probably crossed the Avon near where Bridgefoot crosses it now. The river name means simply 'river'. *Stretfordæ c* 700, *Stradforde* 1086.

Strathaven (town, Strathclyde) '(place in the) valley of the Avon (Water)', Gaelic *srath*, 'valley' + Celtic river name. The river name means simply 'river'. *Cp* ◊Avon. *Strathouen c* 1190.

Strathclyde (region, Scotland) '(district in the) valley of the (River) Clyde', Gaelic *srath*, 'valley' + Celtic river name. The river name means 'cleansing one'. *Stratcluddenses c* 900.

Strathmiglo (town, Fife) '(place in the) valley of the (River) Miglo', Gaelic *srath*, 'valley' + Celtic river name. The river here now is the Eden. But its earlier name must have been *Miglo*, meaning 'marshy lake', from words related to modern Welsh *mign*, 'bog', and *llwych*, 'loch', 'lake'. *Scradimigglolk c* 1200.

Strathmore (valley, Scotland) 'big valley', Gaelic *srath*, 'valley' + *mór*, 'great'. The 'great valley' is the one that basically divides the Highlands, to the north, from the Central Lowlands, to the south.

Stratton (town, Cornwall) 'village in the valley of the (River) Neet', Cornish *stras*, 'valley' + Celtic river name + OE *tūn*, 'village'. The river name, of uncertain meaning, appears in the first record of the name below. It is now called the *Strat*, from the Cornish word that actually means 'valley'. The town is one half of the resort now known as *Bude-Stratton* (*see* ◊Bude). *Strætneat c* 880, *Stratone* 1086.

Streatham (district, Greater London) 'homestead on a Roman road', OE *strǣt*, 'Roman road' + *hām*, 'homestead'. The 'Roman road' here followed the course of what is now Streatham High Street. The Domesday Book record represents the Norman clerk's attempt to get his tongue round the awkward name. *Estreham* 1086, *Streteham* 1247.

Street (town, Somerset) '(place by a) Roman road', OE *strǣt*, 'Roman road'. The 'Roman road' of the name was the one that ran from Ilchester to the Bristol Channel coast. *Stret* 725.

Stretford (town, Greater Manchester) '(place by a) ford on a Roman road', OE *strǣt*, 'Roman road' + *ford*, 'ford'. The name is basically the same as that of ◊Stratford. The 'Roman road' here ran from Chester to Manchester, and had a 'ford' over the Mersey. *Stretford* 1212.

Stroma (island, Highland) 'island of the stream', OS *straumr*, 'stream' + *ey*, 'island'. The 'stream' is the sea current here, in the Pentland Firth. *Straumse* 1150.

Stromness (town, Orkney) 'headland of the stream', OS *straumr*, 'stream' + *nes*, 'headland'. The 'stream' is the strong sea current off the peninsula here, on Mainland. *Straumsness* 1150.

Strood (town, Kent) 'marshy land overgrown with brushwood', OE *strōd*, 'marshy land overgrown with brushwood'. Places of this name, including ◊Stroud, are usually low-lying, as here. *Strod* 889.

Stroud (town, Gloucestershire) 'marshy land overgrown with brushwood', OE *strōd*, 'marshy land overgrown with brushwood'. The name would have applied to the lower-lying land in the southern part of the town. *La Strode* 1200.

Sturminster Newton (town, Dorset) 'church on the (River) Stour by the new farmstead', Celtic river name + OE *mynster*, 'church' + *nīwe*, 'new' + *tūn*, 'farmstead'. The two words were originally the names of separate places either side of the River *Stour* (*see* ◊Stourbridge). The second name was added to the first to distinguish it from *Sturminster Marshall*, also on the Stour (and named for the *Mareschal* family there in the 13th century). *Nywentone, at Stoure* 968, *Newentone* 1086, *Sturminstr Nyweton* 1291.

Sudbury (town, Suffolk) 'southern fortified place', OE *sūth*, 'south' + *burh*, 'fortified place'. The corresponding 'northern fortified place' was probably Bury St Edmunds. *Suthbyrig c* 995, *Sutberia* 1086.

Suffolk (county, England) '(territory of the) southern people', OE *sūth*, 'south' + *folc*, 'folk', 'people'. The 'southern people' were the East Angles who occupied territory to the south of the 'northern people' of ◊Norfolk. *Suthfolchi* 895, *Sudfulc* 1086.

Sunbury (town, Surrey) 'Sunna's stronghold', OE personal name + *burh*, 'stronghold'. The same personal name lies behind those of *Sonning*, *Sunningdale* and *Sunninghill* in Berkshire. *Sunnanbyrg* 960, *Sunneberie* 1086.

Sunderland (town, Tyne and Wear) 'detached estate', OE *sundor-land*, 'detached estate'. The name can be understood as 'sundered land', meaning territory that has been separated from a main estate, perhaps as private land. *Sunderland c* 1168.

Surbiton (district, Greater London) 'southern grange', OE *sūth*, 'south' + *bere-tūn*, 'grange', 'outlying farm'. OE *bere-tūn* literally means 'barley farm'. The 'grange' here was so named by contrast with the one at ◊Norbiton. *Suberton* 1179.

Surrey (county, England) 'southerly district', OE *sūther*, 'southerly' + **gē*, 'district'. The name alludes to the district occupied by the Saxons of the middle Thames valley. They were south of the river, as distinct from the Saxons of ◊Middlesex, to the north of it. *Suthrige* 722, *Sudrie* 1086.

Sussex (county, England) '(territory of the) South Saxons', OE *sūth*, 'south' + *Seaxe*, 'Saxons'. These Saxons were south of those in the 'southerly district' of ◊Surrey. The original county is now divided into the separate counties of *East Sussex* and *West Sussex*. *Suth Seaxe* late 9th century, *Sudsexe* 1086.

Sutherland (district, Highland) 'southern territory', OS *súthr*, 'south' + *land*, 'land', 'territory'. Although in the north of Scotland, the region was so named by the Vikings as it was 'south' of their territory in Orkney and Shetland. *Suthernelande c* 1250.

Sutton (town, Greater London) 'southern farmstead', OE *sūth*, 'south' + *tūn*, 'farmstead'. The 'southern farmstead' here was so called by contrast with the one to the north at Acton. *Sudtone* 1086.

Sutton Bridge (town, Lincolnshire) 'southern farmstead by the bridge', OE *sūth*, 'south' + *tūn*, 'farmstead' + *brycg*, 'bridge'. The 'southern farmstead' here was so called by contrast with the one at *Long Sutton*, to the north. The 'bridge' is over the River Nene.

Sutton Coldfield (town, West Midlands) 'southern farmstead by charcoal workings', OE *sūth*, 'south' + *tūn*, 'farmstead' + *col*, 'charcoal' + *feld*, 'open land'. The name contrasts the 'southern farmstead' with a more northerly place. This may have been Lichfield or, more likely, Shenstone, south of Lichfield. *Sutone* 1086, *Sutton in Colefeud* 1269.

Sutton in Ashfield (town, Nottinghamshire) 'southern farmstead in Ashfield', OE *sūth*, 'south' + *tūn*, 'farmstead' + OE district name. The district name means 'open land where ash trees grow', from OE *æsc*, 'ash', and *feld*, 'open land'. It was probably a 'southern farmstead' in relation to Teversal, north of it. *Sutone* 1086, *Sutton in Essefeld* 1276.

Sutton on Sea (town, Lincolnshire), 'southern farmstead by the sea', OE *sūth*, 'south' + *tūn*, 'farmstead' + modern *on sea*. It is not clear where the corresponding northern place was. It is unlikely to have been Mablethorpe. *Sudtone* 1086.

Swadlincote (town, Derbyshire) 'Sweartling's cottages', OE personal name + *cot*, 'cottage'. The personal name could perhaps also be OS *Svartlingr*. *Sivardingescotes* 1086.

Swaffham (town, Norfolk) 'homestead of the Swabians', OE *Swǣfe*,

'Swabians' + *hām*, 'homestead'. The 'Swabians' would have settled here from *Swabia*, the former duchy that is now a district of western Germany. *Suafham* 1086.

Swanage (town, Dorset) 'farm of the herdsmen' OE *swān*, 'herdsman' + *wīc*, 'farm'. It is possible the first half of the name derives from OE *swan*, 'swan', in which case the meaning is 'farm where swans are bred'. But the former sense seems more probable, and the 'farm' would have been a dairy farm. *Swanawic* late 9th century, *Swanwic* 1086.

Swanley (town, Kent) 'clearing of the herdsmen', OE *swān*, 'herdsman' + *lēah*, 'clearing'. A meaning 'clearing where swans are' is also possible, from OE *swan*, 'swan'. However, the meaning given seems more likely. *Swanleg* 1203.

Swanscombe (town, Kent) 'enclosed land of the herdsmen', OE *swān*, 'herdsman' + *camp*, 'field', 'enclosed land'. The *-combe* of the name is misleading. *Suanescamp* 695, *Svinescamp* 1086.

Swansea (town, West Glamorgan) 'Sveinn's sea (place)', OS personal name + *sǽr*, 'sea'. The Welsh name of the town is *Abertawe*, 'mouth of the (River) Tawe'. The river's own name may mean 'dark one' or simply 'river'. *Sweynesse c* 1165.

Sway (town, Hampshire) '(place by the River) Sway', OE river name. The town takes its name from a former name of the Avon Water here, the river name itself meaning 'noisy one', from OE *swēge*, 'sounding'. Alternatively, the name could represent OE *swæth*, 'swathe', 'track', referring to a place on a regular route by the New Forest here. *Sueia* 1086.

Swindon (town, Wiltshire) 'hill where pigs are kept', OE *swīn*, 'pig' + *dūn*, 'hill'. The name is effectively 'swine down'. Old Swindon is on a noticeable hill. *Svindune* 1086.

Swinton (town, Greater Manchester), 'pig farm', OE *swīn*, 'pig' + *tūn*, 'farm'. The name is found elsewhere, for example in Yorkshire. *Suinton* 1258.

Sydenham (district, Greater London) 'Cippa's homestead', OE personal name + *hām*, 'homestead'. The present form of the name preserves a miscopying of letter *p* as *d*. The same personal name occurs for ◊Chippenham. *Chipeham* 1206, *Shippenham* 1315, *Sidenham* 1690.

T

Tadcaster (town, North Yorkshire) 'Tāta's Roman town', OE personal name + *cæster*, 'Roman town'. The personal name could equally be *Tāda*. The name of the Roman station here was *Calcaria*, 'limeworks', from Latin *calx, calcis*, 'chalk', 'lime'. *Tatecastre* 1086.

Tain (town, Highland) '(place by the) water', Celtic river name. The town is apparently named for the small stream here that flows into the Dornoch Firth. The word that gave its own name is related to Gaelic *tain*, 'water'. *Tene* 1226, *Thayn* 1257.

Talgarth (town, Powys) '(place at the) end of the hill', Welsh *tâl*, 'end' + *garth*, 'hill', 'promontory'. The town lies at the foot of the Black Mountains.

Tamworth (town, Staffordshire) 'enclosure on the (River) Tame', Celtic river name + OE *worth*, 'enclosure'. The river name is related to that of the ◊Thames, so like it, probably means 'dark one' or simply 'river'. *Tamouuorthig* 781, *Tamuuorde* 1086.

Tandridge (district, Surrey) '(special) ridge', OE *hrycg*, 'ridge', 'hill'. The administrative district takes its name from the village of *Tandridge*. The first part of its name is of uncertain origin. It may be OE *denn*, 'woodland pasture' (especially for pigs). The 'ridge' is probably that of nearby Tandridge Hill. *Tenhric c* 965, *Tenrige* 1086.

Taplow (village, Buckinghamshire) 'Tæppa's tumulus', OE personal name + *hlāw*, 'mound', 'tumulus'. The 'tumulus' is a barrow in the churchyard here. *Thapeslau* 1086.

Tarporley (village, Cheshire) 'peasants' clearing', OE **thorpere*, 'peasant', 'cottager' + *lēah*, 'clearing'. This interpretation of the name is conjectural, but possible. *Torpelei* 1086, *Thorperlegh* 1281.

Taunton (town, Somerset) 'farmstead on the (River) Tone', Celtic river name + OE *tūn*, 'farmstead'. The river name may mean 'roaring stream'. *Tantun* 737, *Tantone* 1086.

Tavistock (town, Devon) 'outlying farmstead by the (River) Tavy', Celtic river name + OE *stoc*, 'outlying farmstead'. The river name may mean 'dark one'. *Tauistoce* 981, *Tavestoc* 1086.

Tayport (town, Fife) 'port on the (River) Tay'. The name is a modern one, dating from 1888. For the origin of the river name, *see* ◊Tayside.

Tayside (region, Scotland) '(region) beside the (River) Tay', Celtic river name + English *side*. The river name may mean 'strong one' or 'dark one'. The administrative region of *Tayside* was formed in 1975, but its name was in use long before this for the land by the *Tay*.

Teddington (district, Greater London) 'estate named after Tuda', OE personal name + *-ing-*, 'named after' + *tūn*, 'estate'. This name is of the same type as ◊Paddington. *Tudintun* 969.

Tees (river, Cumbria/Durham/Cleveland). For the origin of this name, *see* ◊Stockton-on-Tees.

Teignmouth (town, Devon) '(place at the) mouth of the (River) Teign', Celtic river name + OE *mūtha*, 'mouth'. The river name means simply 'stream', 'river'. *Tengemutha* 1044.

Telford (town, Shropshire) '(town named after) Telford'. The town arose as a New Town in 1963 and was named for the engineer Thomas *Telford* (1757-1834), appointed surveyor of Shropshire in 1786 and famous for his bridges, canals and roads.

Tenbury Wells (town, Hereford and Worcester) 'stronghold on the (River) Teme with springs', Celtic river name + OE *burh*, 'stronghold' + modern *wells*. The river name perhaps means 'dark one', and is almost certainly related to that of the ◊Thames. The second word was added much later, following the discovery of saline springs in about 1840. *Tamedeberie* 1086.

Tenby (town, Dyfed) 'little fort', Welsh *din*, 'fort' + *bych*, 'little'. The name is of exactly the same origin as that of ◊Denbigh, but in a form apparently due to Scandinavian influence. The 'little fort' was on Castle Hill, where the ruins of the 13th-century Tenby Castle now stand. The Welsh name of Tenby is *Dinbych-y-pysgod*, 'little fort of the fish', alluding to its location by the sea. *Dinbych c* 1275.

Tendring (district, Essex) '(place) of the fuel gatherers', OE *tynder*, 'tinder', 'fuel' + *-ing*, 'of the'. The present administrative district adopted the name of the historic hundred here, preserved also in the name of the village of *Tendring*. *Tendringa* 1086.

Tenterden (town, Kent) 'woodland pasture of the Thanet dwellers', Celtic district name + OE *-ware*, 'dwellers' + *denn*, 'woodland pasture'. For the origin of the district name, *see* ◊Thanet. OE *denn* implies a pasture for pigs, and therefore the existence of an oak wood, furnishing the acorns that are their fodder. *Tentwardene* 1179.

Tetbury (town, Gloucestershire) 'Tette's fortified place', OE personal name + *burh*, 'fortified place'. *Tette* was a sister of King Ine of Wessex, and an abbess of Wimborne. *Tettanbyrg c* 900, *Teteberie* 1086.

Tewkesbury (town, Gloucestershire) 'Tēodec's fortified place', OE personal name + *burh*, 'fortified place'. The *d* of the personal name has disappeared from the modern place-name. *Teodekesberie* 1086.

Thame (town, Oxfordshire) '(place on the River) Thame', Celtic river name. The river name is of the same origin as that of the ◊Thames, of which it is a tributary. *Tame c* 1000, 1086.

Thames (river, England), Celtic river name. The name probably means 'dark one' or simply 'river'. Rivers with related names include the *Tame*, *Team* and *Tamar*, also possibly the *Taff* and *Teviot*. The second part of the name as the record shows gave that of the *Isis*, an alternative name for the Thames above Oxford. *Tamesis* 51 BC.

Thames Ditton (town, Surrey) 'farmstead by a ditch on the Thames', Celtic river name + OE *dīc*, 'ditch' + *tūn*, 'farmstead'. The place was originally *Ditton*, the 'ditch' being one that was excavated to drain the land and channel the standing water into the ◊Thames. The second word was added to distinguish this Ditton from *Long Ditton*, just east of it. *Ditune* 1086, *Temes Ditton* 1235.

Thamesdown (district, Wiltshire) '(district between the River) Thames and the (Wiltshire) Downs'. The administrative district is so named for its location between the *Thames* to the north and the Wiltshire *Downs* to the south.

Thamesmead (district, Greater London). The residential development on the south side of the ◊Thames arose in the 1960s. Its modern name derives from that of the river and *mead*, referring to the reclaimed marshland here.

Thanet, Isle of (region, Kent), Celtic island name. The name is of uncertain origin but may mean 'bright island', with the first part from a word related to modern Welsh *tân*, 'fire'. Perhaps there was a beacon on the peninsula here. *Tanatus* 3rd century, *Tanet* 1086.

Thatcham (town, Berkshire) 'riverside land where thatching materials are obtained', OE *þæc*, 'thatch' + *hamm*, 'riverside land'. The river here is the Kennet. The name is similar to that of ◊Thaxted. *Thæcham c* 954, *Taceham* 1086.

Thaxted (town, Essex) 'place where thatching materials are obtained', OE *þæc*, 'thatch' + *stede*, 'place'. The name is similar to that of ◊Thatcham. *Tachesteda* 1086.

Thetford (town, Norfolk) 'people's ford', OE *þēod*, 'people', 'tribe' + *ford*, 'ford'. The name alludes to a public ford or to an important one, used by many people. It would have been over the Little Ouse, which joins the Thet here. The latter river takes its name from that of the town. *Theodford* late 9th century, *Tedfort* 1086.

Thirlmere (lake, Cumbria). The name has not been traced in any early records. It may mean 'hollow lake', from OE *thyrel*, 'hole', 'opening', and *mere*, 'lake'. The 'hollow' may have been the former narrow 'waist' of the lake before it was dammed and the water level rose. *Thyrlemere* 1574.

Thirsk (town, North Yorkshire) '(place by a) marsh', OS *thresk*, 'marsh', 'lake'. The town is on low-lying land on the Cod Beck, a tributary of the Swale. *Tresch* 1086.

Thorne (town, South Yorkshire) '(place at the) thorn tree', OE *thorn*, 'thorn tree'. The original place may have been by a single such tree or a group of them. *Torne* 1086.

Thorney Island (island, West Sussex) 'thorn tree island', OE *thorn*, 'thorn tree' + *ēg*, 'island'. The name denotes an island overgrown with thorn bushes. The second word of the name was added when the sense of 'island' in the first word was no longer understood. The name is properly that of the village of *West Thorney* here. *Thorneg* 11th century, *Tornei* 1086.

Thornton Heath (district, Greater London) 'heath by a farmstead with thorn trees', OE *thorn*, 'thorn tree' + *tūn*, 'farmstead' + *hǣth*, 'heath'. The place must originally have been *Thornton*, but no early records of the name are known. *Thorneton Hethe* 1511.

Three Bridges (district, Crawley, West Sussex) '(place by) three bridges'. The place arose by bridges over the River Mole. *two bridges called the Three bridges leading from Charlewood to Crawley* 1534.

Thruxton (village, Hampshire) 'Thorkell's estate', OS personal name + OE *tūn*, 'estate'. The same personal name lies behind that of *Thirkleby*, North Yorkshire. *Turkilleston* 1167.

Thundersley (town, Essex) 'Thunor's clearing', OE god name + *lēah*, 'clearing'. *Thunor* was another name of the pagan god *Thor*, and the 'clearing' here would have been in his sacred grove. *Thunreslea* 1086.

Thurrock (district, Essex). For the origin of the name of this administrative district, see ◊Grays.

Thurso (town, Highland) '(place at the mouth of the River) Thurso', Celtic river name. The river name may mean 'bull river', from a word related to Greek *tauros* and Latin *taurus*, 'bull', and OS *á*, 'river'. A 'bull river' is one that 'roars' or has a 'headstrong' current. *Thorsa* 1152.

Tideswell (town, Derbyshire) 'Tīdi's spring', OE personal name + *wella*, 'spring', 'stream'. The name is pronounced 'Tiddzle' by some local people. *Tidesuuelle* 1086.

Tidworth (town, Wiltshire/Hampshire) 'Tuda's enclosure', OE personal name + *worth*, 'enclosure'. The present town comprises *North Tidworth*, in Wiltshire, and *South Tidworth*, in Hampshire. The first record relates to North Tidworth, the second to South. *Tudanwyrthe c* 990, *Todeworde* 1086.

Tilbury (town, Essex) 'Tila's stronghold', OE personal name + *burh*, 'stronghold'. The first part of the name could also represent *Tila*, a former stream name meaning 'useful one'. *Tilaburg* 731, *Tiliberia* 1086.

Tillicoultry (town, Central) 'hillock of the back land', Gaelic *tulach*, 'hill' + *cùl tìr*, 'back land'. The name refers to the town's location at the foot of the main ridge of the Ochill Hills.

Timperley (district, Altrincham, Greater Manchester) 'timber clearing', OE *timber*, 'timber' + *lēah*, 'clearing'. A 'timber clearing' is one where timber from the surrounding woodland is obtained. *Timperleie* 1211.

Tintagel (village, Cornwall) 'fort by the neck of land', Cornish **din*, 'fort' + **tagel*, throat', 'neck of land'. If this explanation of the name is correct, the 'fort' is the former castle on the peninsula known as Tintagel Island, and the 'neck of land' is the rocky gorge that separates it from the mainland. *Tintagol c* 1137.

Tiptree (town, Essex) 'Tippa's tree', OE personal name + *trēow*, 'tree'. The 'tree' may have been an actual tree or a constructed cross or crucifix. *Tipentrie* 12th century.

Tiree (island, Strathclyde) 'land of Ith', Gaelic *tīr*, 'land' + Celtic personal name. The identity of *Ith* is unknown. *Tir Iath c* 850, *Tiryad* 1343.

Tiverton (town, Devon) 'farmstead at the double ford', OE **twī-fyrde*, 'double ford' + *tūn*, 'farmstead'. A 'double ford' is either one with two tracks or two fords close together over different rivers. The latter is probably the sense here, over the rivers Exe and its tributary, the Loman. *Cp* ◊Twyford. *Twyfyrde* 880, *Tovretona* 1086.

Tobermory (town, Strathclyde) '(place by St) Mary's well', Gaelic *tiobar*, 'well' + *Moire*, 'Mary'. The well of the name is by the ruins of the old chapel to the west of the modern town, which arose in the 18th century. The record thus refers to the well. *Tibbermore* 1540.

Todmorden (town, West Yorkshire) 'Totta's boundary valley', OE personal name + *mǣre*, 'boundary' + *denu*, 'valley'. The 'boundary valley' is probably the one to the west of the town, on the border between West Yorkshire and Lancashire. *Tottemerden* 1246.

Toller Porcorum (village, Dorset) '(place by the River) Toller of the pigs', Celtic river name + Latin *porcorum*, 'of the pigs'. The river name, meaning 'hollow stream', was formerly that of the River *Hooke*, itself from the village so called. The second word refers to the former herds of pigs here, and was designed to distinguish this place from nearby *Toller Fratrum*, where the second word is Latin for 'of the brethren', referring to the Knights Hospitallers who owned it. The contrasting names are a nice example of medieval humour. *Tolre*, 1086, *Tolre Porcorum* 1340.

Tolpuddle (village, Dorset) 'Tola's estate on the (River) Piddle', OE personal name + river name. The personal name is that of a woman. For the river name, *see* ◊Piddletrenthide. *Pidele* 1086, *Tollepidele* 1210.

Tonbridge (town, Kent) 'bridge of the estate', OE *tūn*, 'estate' + *brycg*, 'bridge'. *See also* ◊Tunbridge Wells. The original bridge would have led over the Medway here from one part of the estate to another. *Tonebrige* 1086.

Tonypandy (town, Mid Glamorgan) 'grassland of the fulling mill', Welsh *ton*, 'grassland' + *y*, 'the' + *pandy*, 'fulling mill'. The town, in the Rhondda Valley, had its origins in the wool industry, not in coal like so many of the others here.

Tooting (district, Greater London) '(settlement of) Tōta's people', OE personal name + *-ingas*, 'people of'. The name could also be understood as 'people of the lookout place', with the first part representing OE *tōt, 'lookout'. *Totinge* 675.

Torbay (district, Devon) 'bay by (the hill called) Torre', OE hill name + Middle English *bay*, 'bay'. For the origin of the hill name, *see* ◊Torquay. *Torrebay* 1401.

Torfaen (district, Gwent) '(district of the) stone gap', Welsh *tor*, 'gap', 'break' + *maen*, 'stone'. The administrative district takes its name from that of a historic region here.

Torpoint (town, Cornwall) '(place by the) rocky headland', OE *torr*, 'hill', 'rock' + Middle English *point*, 'headland'. The 'rocky headland' lies beside the estuary of the River Hamoaze here. *Tor-point* 1746.

Torquay (town, Devon) 'quay by (the hill called) Torre', OE hill name + Middle English *key*, 'quay'. The 'quay' was built by monks from nearby *Torre* Abbey, at the foot of the hill called *Torre*. The hill name represents OE *torr*, 'tor', 'rocky hill'. *Torrekay* 1591.

Torridge (district, Devon) '(district of the River) Torridge', Celtic river name. For the origin of the river name, *see* ◊Torrington.

Torrington (town, Devon) 'farmstead on the (River) Torridge', Celtic river name + OE *tūn*. The river name means 'turbulent stream', from a word related to modern Welsh *terig*, 'rough'. *Torintona* 1086.

Totnes (town, Devon) 'Totta's promontory', OE personal name + *næss*, 'promontory'. The 'promontory' is the one on which the former 12th-century castle stood north of the Butterwalk. *Totanæs c* 1000, *Toteneis* 1086.

Tottenham (district, Greater London) 'Totta's homestead', OE personal name + *hām*, 'homestead'. The *n* represents the genitive case ending of the personal name. *Toteham* 1086.

Totton (town, Hampshire) 'estate of Tota's people', OE personal name + *-ing-*, 'of the people of' + *tūn*, 'estate'. As shown by the record, the name was originally the equivalent of modern *Tottington*. *Totintone* 1086.

Towcester (town, Northamptonshire) 'Roman fort on the (River) Tove', OE river name + *ceaster*, 'Roman fort'. The river name means 'slow one'. The name of the Roman fort here was *Lactodurum*, 'milk fort', perhaps from a former name of the Tove, referring to its milky water. *Tofeceaster* early 10th century, *Tovecestre*, 1086.

Tower Hamlets (borough, Greater London) 'hamlets of the Tower (of

London)'. The former many hamlets here were under the jurisdiction of the Tower of London. The name dates from at least as early as the 18th century.

Tow Law (town, Durham) 'lookout hill', OE **tō*, 'lookout' + *hlāw*, 'mound', 'hill'. The town stands on rising ground to the east of Wolsingham Moor. *Tollawe* 1423.

Toxteth (district, Liverpool, Merseyside) 'Tóki's landing place', OS personal name + *stoth*, 'landing place'. The 'landing place' would have been on the Mersey here. The personal name could also have been *Tōk*. The Domesday Book record has added an *s* to the initial *t* under the influence of OE *stoc*, 'place'. *Stochestede* 1086, *Tokestath* 1212.

Tranmere (district, Birkenhead, Merseyside) 'sandbank where cranes are', OS *trani*, 'crane' + *melr*, 'sandbank'. The birds must have frequented the sandbanks by the Mersey here at some time. *Tranemul* late 12th century.

Trearddur Bay (resort, Gwynedd), '(place on) Trearddur Bay', bay name. The resort took the name of the bay, itself named after a former village here. Its own name appears to mean 'Iarddur's village', from Welsh *tref*, 'village', and the personal name *Iarddur*.

Tredegar (town, Gwent) '(settlement of) Tredegar', aristocratic title. The town arose in the 19th century and took the name of the landowner, Baron *Tredegar*, whose title came from the family seat at *Tredegar*, near Newport. The name means 'Tegyr's farm', from a Welsh *tref*, 'farm', and a personal name. *Cp* ◊New Tredegar.

Tregaron (town, Dyfed) '(St) Caron's village', Welsh *tref*, 'village' + saint's name. The parish church here is dedicated to this saint.

Trent (river, England). For the origin of this river name, *see* ◊Stoke-on-Trent.

Treorchy (town, Mid Glamorgan) 'village on the (River) Orci', Welsh *tref*, 'village' + river name. The origin of the river name is uncertain.

Tresco (island, Isles of Scilly) 'farm of elder trees', Cornish *tre*, 'farm' + *scaw*, 'elder tree'. The name was originally not that of the whole island but of a farm where Tresco Abbey stands today. *Tresau* 1305.

Tring (town, Hertfordshire) '(place by the) wooded slope', OE *trēow*, 'tree' + *hangra*, 'wooded hillside'. The town is situated among hills and beech woods, and originally had a name something like *Treehanger*. The Domesday Book record is corrupt. *Treunge* 1086, *Trehangr* 1199.

Troon (town, Strathclyde) '(place at) the headland', Gaelic *an t-sròn*, 'the headland'. The town is on a prominent headland on the Firth of Clyde. *le Trone* 1371.

Trossachs, The (hills, Central), 'transverse hills', Gaelic name. The Gaelic form of the name is *Tròsaichean*, said to have been adopted from Welsh *trawsfynnyd*, literally 'cross mountain', or at least from the first part of this.

Trowbridge (town, Wiltshire) 'bridge of tree trunks', OE *trēow*, 'tree' + *brycg*, 'bridge'. The 'tree-trunk bridge' was probably over the River Biss to the west of the town centre. The Domesday Book record is highly corrupt. The Norman clerk has 'restored' what he took as a missing first letter *S*, as for a name such as *Stratford*. He has also confused OE *brycg*, 'bridge', with *byrig*, the dative form of *burh*, 'manor', 'estate'. *Straburg* 1086, *Trobrigge* 1184.

Truro (town, Cornwall) '(place of) great water turbulence', Cornish name. The interpretation is problematical. The first part of the name may mean 'great', from a word related to Cornish *tri*, 'three'. The second may be a form of *berow*, 'boiling'. The name as a whole would allude to the two rapid rivers that meet the sea here at the head of a creek. *Triueru c* 1173.

Tullibody (town, Central) 'hill of the hut', Gaelic *tulach*, 'small hill' + *both*, 'hut'. The name would have originally applied to an isolated hut or cottage here.

Tunbridge Wells (town, Kent) '(town named after) Tonbridge with a spring', OE place-name + modern *wells*. The town arose by the springs ('wells') discovered here in the 17th century, and took its name from ◊Tonbridge, 5 miles to the north. The form of the name reflects the spelling of the name of Tonbridge (with *u*) at the time of its adoption. *Tunbridge* 1771, *Tonbridge Wells* 1868.

Tunstall (town, Staffordshire) 'farm site', OE **tūn-stall*, 'farm place'. The name is found in various counties throughout England. *Tunstal* 1212.

Tweed (river, Scotland/England). For the meaning of this river name, *see* ◊Berwick-upon-Tweed.

Twickenham (district, Greater London) 'Twicca's land in a river bend', OE personal name + *hamm*, 'riverside land'. It is possible the first part of the name may represent OE **twicce*, 'river fork'. Either way, Twickenham is in a bend of the Thames at a point where the River Crane flows into it. *Tuicanhom* 704.

Twyford (town, Berkshire) '(place at the) double ford', OE *twī-ford*, 'double ford'. The 'double ford' here would have been over the rivers Loddon and Thames. *See* ◊Tiverton for a definition. *Tuiford* 1170.

Tyldesley (town, Greater Manchester) 'Tilwald's clearing', OE personal name + *lēah*, 'clearing'. It is not certain where exactly the clearing in question was. *Tildesleia c* 1210.

Tynemouth (town, Tyne and Wear) '(place at the) mouth of the (River) Tyne', Celtic river name + OE *mūtha*, 'mouth'. The river name, which could be of pre-Celtic origin, probably means simply 'river', from a basic root word meaning 'to flow'. *Tinanmuthe* 792.

Tywyn (resort, Gwynedd) '(place by the) seashore', Welsh *tywyn*, 'seashore', 'strand'. The resort is on Cardigan Bay. *Thewyn* 1254.

U

Uckfield (town, East Sussex) 'Ucca's open land', OE personal name + *feld*, 'open land'. The exact site of the original 'open land' is uncertain. *Uckefeld* 1220.

Ullapool (town, Highland) 'Olaf's dwelling', OS personal name + *ból-stathr*, 'dwelling'. All that remains of the OS word for 'dwelling' is the first syllable, altered to English *pool*. *Ullabill* 1610.

Ullswater (lake, Cumbria) 'Ulfr's lake', OS personal name + OE *wæter*, 'water'. The personal name means 'wolf'. *Ulueswater c* 1230.

Ulverston (town, Cumbria) 'Wulfhere's farmstead', OE personal name + *tūn*, 'farmstead'. The personal name could also be OS *Ulfarr*. *Ulurestun* 1086.

Unst (island, Shetland) 'abode of eagles', OS *orn*, 'eagle' + *vist*, 'dwelling', 'abode'. The island is still the home of many wild birds. *Ornyst c* 1200.

Upminster (town, Greater London) 'higher minster', OE *upp*, 'higher' + *mynster*, 'minster', 'church'. The ground rises slightly here. *Upmunstra* 1086.

Uppingham (town, Leicestershire) 'homestead of the hill dwellers', OE *yppe*, 'upland' + *-inga-*, 'of the people of', +*hām*, 'homestead'. The 'hill dwellers' would have had a good lookout point on Castle Hill, west of the town centre. *Yppingeham* 1067.

Urmston (town, Greater Manchester) 'Wyrm's farmstead', OE personal name + *tūn*, 'farmstead'. The personal name could equally be OS *Urm*. The meaning of both is 'serpent', 'dragon' (modern English *worm*). *Wermeston* 1194.

Usk (town, Gwent) '(place on the River) Usk', Celtic river name. The river name means simply 'water', and is thus related to the *Exe* of ◊Exeter.

Uttlesford (district, Essex) 'Udel's ford', OE personal name + *ford*, 'ford'. The administrative district was given the name of a historic hundred here.

Uttoxeter (town, Staffordshire) 'Wuttuc's heath', OE personal name + **hǣddre*, 'heather', 'heath'. The second part of the name falsely suggests a former Roman station, as at ◊Exeter and ◊Wroxeter, and the present form of the name may have been influenced by these two. *Wotocheshede* 1086.

Uxbridge (town, Greater London) 'bridge of the Wixan (people)', OE tribal name + *brycg*, 'bridge'. The Wixan came to settle here from elsewhere in England, perhaps the Midlands. The meaning of their name is unknown. Their 'bridge' would have been over the River Colne. *Wixebrug* c 1145.

Vale of White Horse (district, Oxfordshire). The self-descriptive name refers to the prehistoric figure of a white horse carved out of the chalk on *White Horse Hill*, west of Wantage. *The vale of Whithors* 1368.

Vauxhall (district, Greater London) 'Falkes' hall', Old French personal name + OE *hall*, 'hall', 'manor house'. The named man was *Falkes* de Bréauté, who built a manor house here in the early 13th century. *Faukeshale* 1279.

Ventnor (town, Isle of Wight) '(farm of) Vintner', family name. The name comes from that of a family called *le Vyntener*, who owned a farm here and who probably held the manor in medieval times. *Vintner* 1617.

Virginia Water (district, Surrey). The name was devised for the artificial lake here created in 1748 by the Duke of Cumberland. The name itself commemorates the pioneers who founded and settled the American colony of *Virginia*. *Virginia Water* 1749.

W

Wadebridge (town, Cornwall) 'bridge by the ford', OE *wæd*, 'ford' + *brycg*, 'bridge'. The place was originally *Wade*, but -*bridge* was added in the 15th century when a bridge was built. *Cp* ◊Fordingbridge. *Wade* 1358, *Wadebrygge* 1478.

Wadhurst (village, East Sussex) 'Wada's wooded hill', OE personal name + *hyrst*, 'wooded hill'. The surrounding area is still well wooded. *Wadehurst* 1253.

Wakefield (city, West Yorkshire) 'open land where wakes are held', OE **wacu*, 'wake' + *feld*, 'open land'. A 'wake' is a festival. The 'open land' where they were held would have been the region between the River Calder in the south and the woods of Outwood in the north. *Wachefeld* 1086.

Wales (principality, Great Britain), '(territory of the) Britons', OE *walh*, 'foreigner' 'Briton'. The form of the name represents OE *walas*, the plural of *walh*. The name was given to the 'foreigners' by the Anglo-Saxons, although the Celts (Britons) were the true natives.

Wallasey (town, Merseyside) 'island of Waley', OE island name + *ēg*, 'island'. The region here became an 'island' at high tide. *Waley* means 'island of the Welsh', from OE *walh*, 'Briton', and *ēg*, 'island'. Another *ēg* was added later, as if to mean 'Waley's island'. *Walea* 1086, *Waleyesegh* 1351.

Wallingford (town, Oxfordshire) 'ford of Wealh's people', OE personal name + -*inga*-, 'of the people of' + *ford*, 'ford'. The 'ford' would have been over the Thames. The personal name probably means 'Briton'. *Welingaforda c* 895, *Walingeford* 1086.

Wallington (district, Greater London) 'farmstead of the Britons', OE *walh*, 'Briton' + *tūn*, 'farmstead'. The name is properly *Walton*, and the misleading -*ing*- may have been introduced to distinguish this place from ◊Walton-on-Thames, 15 miles to the west. *Waletone* 1086, *Wallyngton* 1377.

Wallsend (town, Tyne and Wear) '(place at the) end of the wall', OE *wall*, 'wall' + *ende*, 'end'. The town is at the eastern 'end' of Hadrian's Wall. The Roman fort at Wallsend was called *Segedunum*, 'strong fort'. *Wallesende c* 1085.

Walmer (district, Deal, Kent) 'pool of the Britons', OE *walh*, 'Briton' + *mere*, 'pool'. There is no pool here now, but obviously there once was, and doubtless it would have been used exclusively by the Britons when they farmed the Anglo-Saxon lands here. *Walemere* 1087.

Walney Island (island, Cumbria) 'killer whale island', OS *vogn*, 'killer whale' + *ey*, 'island'. The first part of the name could equally be OE **wagen*, 'quaking sands'. *Wagneia* 1127.

Walsall (town, West Midlands) 'Walh's corner of land', OE personal name + *halh*, 'nook'. The first part of the name could also represent OE *walh*, 'Welshman'. *Waleshale* 1163.

Waltham Abbey (town, Essex) 'homestead in a forest with an abbey', OE *wald*, 'forest' + *hām*, 'homestead' + Middle English *abbeye*. The place was originally *Waltham*, the 'forest' today being represented by what remains of Waltham Forest. The second word was added when Henry II built an abbey here in the 12th century. *Waltham* 1086.

Walthamstow (district, Greater London) 'place where guests are welcome', OE *wilcuma*, 'guest' + *stōw*, 'place'. Another valid interpretation of the name is 'Wilcume's holy place', from an OE personal name (that of a woman) and *stōw* in this particular sense. Wilcume would have been the abbess of the nunnery here. *Wilcumestowe c* 1075, *Wilcumestou*, 1086.

Walton-on-Thames (town, Surrey) 'farmstead of the Britons by the Thames', OE *walh*, 'Briton' + *tūn*, 'farmstead' + Celtic river name. The original name was simply *Walton*, with the river location added subsequently for purposes of distinction. *Waletone* 1086, *Waleton super Thamis'* 1279.

Walworth (district, Greater London) 'enclosure of the Britons', OE *walh* 'Briton' + *worth*, 'enclosure'. The name is found elsewhere, for example in Co Durham. *Wealawyrth* 1001, *Waleorde* 1086.

Wandsworth (borough, Greater London) 'Wændel's enclosure', OE personal name *worth*, 'enclosure'. The River *Wandle* here took its name from the place. *Wendleswurthe* 11th century, *Wandelesorde* 1086.

Wansbeck (district, Northumberland) '(district of the River) Wansbeck', river name. The origin of the river name is uncertain. Its second half has been altered by association with *beck. Wenspic* 1137.

Wansdyke (earthwork, Berkshire/Wiltshire/Avon) 'dyke named after Woden', OE god name + *dīc*, 'ditch', 'dyke'. Either the embankment was supposed to have been built by the pagan war god *Woden*, or he was thought to preside over it. *Cp* ◊Wednesbury, ◊Wednesfield. The earthwork's name has been adopted at its western end for that of an administrative district of Avon. *Wodnes dic* 903.

Wanstead (district, Greater London) 'place by a mound', OE *wænn*, 'mound' + *stede*, 'place'. Wanstead arose on a slight hill, and this could be the original 'mound'. The first part of the name could also represent OE *wǣn*, 'wagon', giving 'place where wagons are kept'. *Wænstede c* 1055, *Wenesteda* 1086.

Wantage (town, Oxfordshire) 'place by a diminishing stream', OE *wanian*, 'to decrease' + *-ing*, 'place of'. A 'diminishing stream' is one with a fluctuating current. The 'stream' is a tributary of the River Ock. *Waneting c* 880, *Wanetinz* 1086.

Wapping (district, Greater London) '(settlement of) Wæppa's people', OE personal name + *-ingas*, 'people of'. The second part of the name could also represent OE *-ing*, giving a sense 'Wæppa's place'. *Wapping c* 1220.

Wardle (town, Greater Manchester) 'watch hill', OE *weard*, 'watch', 'lookout' + *hyll*, 'hill'. The name probably refers to Brown Wardle Hill, northwest of the town. *Wardhul c* 1193.

Ware (town, Hertfordshire) '(place by the) weirs', OE *wær*, 'weir'. There must have been frequent blockages on the River Lea here at one time. The original name is in a plural form. *Waras* 1086.

Wareham (town, Dorset) 'homestead by a weir', OE *wer*, 'weir' + *hām*, 'homestead'. The town is at the head of the River Frome estuary, where there was a fishery in medieval times. *Werham* late 9th century, *Warham* 1086.

Warkworth (village, Northumberland) 'Weorca's enclosure', OE personal name + *worth*, 'enclosure'. The name has caused speculation in the past, but this seems to be a plausible solution. *Werceworthe c* 1050.

Warlingham (town, Surrey) 'homestead of Wærla's people', OE personal name + *-inga-*, 'of the people of' + *hām*, 'homestead'. Names of this type are common throughout England, and many have remained villages. *Warlyngham* 1144.

Warminster (town, Wiltshire) 'church on the (River) Were', OE river name + *mynster*, 'church'. The river name means 'winding one'. The 'church' probably stood where the parish church of St Denys stands now. *Worgemynster c* 912, *Guerminstre* 1086.

Warrington (town, Cheshire) 'farmstead by the weir', OE *wering*, 'weir', 'river dam' + *tūn*, 'farmstead'. The 'weir' would have been on the River Mersey here. The Domesday Book record has *l* for *r*, as happened for ◊Salisbury. *Walintune* 1086, *Werington* 1246.

Warsop (town, Nottinghamshire) 'Wǽr's enclosed valley', OE personal name + *hop*, 'enclosed valley'. The allusion may be to the valley known as Warsop Vale, a mile west of the town. *Wareshope* 1086.

Warwick (town, Warwickshire) 'dwellings by the weir', OE **wǽring*, 'weir', 'river dam' + *wīc*, 'special place', 'dwellings'. The 'weir' would have been over the Avon here. The county name, *Warwickshire*, is first recorded in the 11th century. *Wǽrincwicum* 1001, *Warwic* 1086.

Wash, The (sea inlet, Lincolnshire/Norfolk) 'sandbank washed by the sea', OE *wæsc*, 'sea-washed bank'. The name was originally plural and referred to two such sandbanks which could be forded at low tide. *The Wasshes c* 1545.

Washington (town, Tyne and Wear) 'estate named after Wassa', OE personal name + *-ing-*, 'named after' + *tūn*, 'estate'. The New Town, designated in 1964, thus has an old name. *Wassyngtona* 1183.

Wast Water (lake, Cumbria) 'lake in the valley', OS *vatn*, 'lake' + *dalr*, 'valley'. The origin given here is for *Wasdale*, the valley in which Wast Water lies. The lake name thus really means 'Wasdale Water', with *Wast* a shortened form of *Wasdale*.

Watchet (town, Somerset) '(place) under the wood', Celtic words. The name derives from words related to modern Welsh *gwas*, 'servant', and *coed*, 'wood', these giving respectively *Wa-* and *-tchet*. The reference is to the cliffs behind the town, which were formerly well wooded. *Wæcet* 962, *Wacet* 1086.

Waterlooville (town, Hampshire) 'village round (the Heroes of) Waterloo (inn)', inn name + French *ville*, 'town'. The town arose in the 19th century round an inn called the Heroes of Waterloo, itself named for the soldiers and sailors who had fought at the Battle of *Waterloo* (1815) and disembarked at nearby Portsmouth on their return. *Waterloo* 1868, *Waterloo, or Waterloo Ville* 1898.

Watford (town, Hertfordshire) 'huntsmen's ford', OE *wāth*, 'hunting' + *ford*, 'ford'. The 'ford' would have been over the River Colne here. *Watford c* 945.

Watling Street (Roman road, England) 'Roman road of Wacol's people', OE personal name + *-inga-*, 'of the people of' + *strǣt*, 'Roman road'. The original stretch of the road so named was probably between St Albans and London. Hence the former name of St Albans as *Wæclingaceaster*, 'Roman fort of Wacol's people' (as if *Watlingchester*). The name was later extended to the whole road from Dover to Wroxeter. *Wæclinga stræt*, late 9th century.

Watlington (town, Oxfordshire) 'estate named after Wæcel', OE personal name + *-ing-*, 'named after' + *tūn*, 'estate'. The personal name means 'watchful one'. *Wæclinctune* 887, *Watelintone* 1086.

Waveney (district, Suffolk) '(district of the River) Waveney', OE river name. The river name probably means 'moving river', from OE *wagian*, 'to move', and *ēa*, 'river'. *Wahenhe* 1275.

Weald, The (region, England) 'woodland', OE *weald* 'woodland', 'forest'. The name is that of the region of southeast England between the North and South Downs, which were at one time well wooded. *Cp* ◊Wolds. The record of the name has the dative plural ending. *Waldum* 1185.

Wealdstone (district, Greater London) '(place by the) stone of (Harrow) Weald'. The name is a recent one, and refers to a boundary stone that separated Harrow Weald from the rest of the parish of Harrow. *Weald* here alludes to the wood near Harrow. *Weald Stone* 1822.

Wednesbury (district, West Bromwich, West Midlands) 'stronghold named after Woden', OE god name + *burh*, 'stronghold'. The name implies that the great war god *Woden* either actually made the place or that he 'reigned' over it and protected it. *Cp* ◊Wansdyke, ◊Wednesfield. *Wadnesberie* 1086.

Wednesfield (district, Wolverhampton, West Midlands) 'open land named after Woden', OE god name + *feld*, 'open land'. The pagan god *Woden* was believed to have specially favoured this land and to be its 'patron'. *Cp* ◊Wansdyke, ◊Wednesbury. *Wodnesfeld* 996, *Wodnesfelde* 1086.

Wellingborough (town, Northamptonshire) 'stronghold of Wændel's people', OE personal name + *-inga-*, 'of the people of' + *burh*, 'stronghold'. There is no obvious 'stronghold' here, but the name clearly indicates that one must have existed. *Wedlingeberie* 1086, *Wendlingburch* 1178.

Wellington (town, Shropshire) 'estate named after Wēola', OE personal name + -ing-, 'named after' + tūn, 'estate'. The personal name is speculative, even though it occurs in other places of the same name, *eg* ◊Wellington, Somerset. *Walitone* 1086.

Wellington (town, Somerset) 'estate named after Wēola', OE personal name + -ing-, 'named after' + tūn, 'estate'. This name has exactly the same origin as that of ◊Wellington, Shropshire. *Weolingtun* 904, *Walintone* 1086.

Wells (town, Somerset) '(place by the) springs', OE *wella*, 'well', 'spring'. The 'springs' here have long been known to exist and are near the east end of the cathedral. *Willan c* 1050, *Welle* 1086.

Wells-next-the-Sea (town, Norfolk) '(place by the) springs', OE *wella*, 'well', 'spring'. The name is basically the same as that of ◊Wells. The suffix is a distinguishing addition. *Guelle* 1086.

Welshpool (town, Powys) 'Welsh (place by a) pool', OE *welisc*, 'Welsh' + pōl, 'pool'. The name indicates that the 'pool' here (where the Lledin brook joins the Severn) is the Welsh side of the border. The Welsh name of the town is simply *Y Trallwng*, 'the pool'. *Pola* 1253, *Walshe Pole* 1477.

Welwyn (town, Hertfordshire) '(place by the) willow trees', OE *welig*, 'willow'. The name represents a dative plural form of the OE word, as required after *æt*, 'at'. Cp ◊Welwyn Garden City. *Welingum c* 945, *Welge* 1086.

Welwyn Garden City (town, Hertfordshire) 'garden city (near) Welwyn', OE place-name + modern *garden city*. The New Town was designated in 1948 and takes its name from the old town of ◊Welwyn, immediately north of it. It is the only town in Britain to include *Garden City* in its name. (But *cp* Hampstead Garden Suburb.)

Wem (town, Shropshire) 'marshy place', OE **wemm*, 'dirty place', 'muddy place'. The above is the most appropriate meaning for the name, referring to the marshy terrain here. *Weme* 1086.

Wembley (district, Greater London) 'Wemba's clearing', OE personal name + lēah. It is not clear where exactly the original 'clearing' was. Perhaps it was in what is now Wembley Park. *Wembalea* 825.

Wendover (town, Buckinghamshire) '(place by the) white stream', Celtic river name. The name was originally that of a stream here. Its name represents words related to modern Welsh *gwyn*, 'white', and *dwfr*, 'water'. *Wændofran c* 970, *Wendoure* 1086.

Wenlock Edge (hill ridge, Shropshire). For the origin of this name, *see* ◊Much Wenlock.

Wensleydale (valley, North Yorkshire) 'valley by Wensley', OE place-name + OS *dalr*, 'valley. The valley takes its name from the village of *Wensley* at its eastern end. The village name means 'Wændel's clearing', from an OE personal name and *lēah*, 'clearing'. Many *dale* names have a river name for their first part, but not this one. *Wandesleydale* mid-11th century.

Wentworth (district, Surrey) '(place named after Mrs) Wentworth', surname. The residential district took its name from *Wentworth* House, itself named after an early 19th-century landowner here, Mrs Elizabeth *Wentworth*.

Wessex (historic region, England), '(territory of the) West Saxons', OE *west*, 'west' + *Seaxe*, 'Saxons'. The former Anglo-Saxon kingdom, based on Winchester, is named after the *West Saxons*, so called as they lived to the west of the South Saxons of ◊Sussex and East Saxons of ◊Essex. However, unlike those territories, *Wessex* never became a county. *West Seaxe* late 9th century.

West Bridgford (town, Nottinghamshire) 'western (place by a) ford with a bridge', Middle English *west*, 'west' + OE *brycg*, 'bridge' + *ford*, 'ford'. The 'ford with a bridge' would have been over the River Trent here. The first word distinguishes the place from *East Bridgford*, 7 miles northeast of it. *Brigeforde* 1086, *Westburgeforde* 1572.

West Bromwich (town, West Midlands) 'western farm where broom grows', Middle English *west*, 'west' + OE *brōm*, 'broom' + *wīc*, 'farm'. The first word distinguishes this Bromwich from ◊Castle Bromwich, now a district of Birmingham, 8 miles to the east. *Bromwic* 1086, *Westbromwich* 1322.

Westbury (town, Wiltshire) 'western stronghold', OE *west*, 'west' + *burh*, 'stronghold'. The 'stronghold' is the Iron Age camp on the hill above the town, where there is a white horse cut out of the chalk. It was doubtless regarded as being the most westerly on Salisbury Plain. *Westberie* 1086.

Westcliff-on-Sea (district, Southend-on-Sea, Essex) 'western cliff by the sea'. The name is a modern one for the place, which is to the west of Southend proper. *Cliff* 1843, *a new village called Clifton* 1868.

West Drayton (district, Greater London) 'western farmstead at a dragging place', Middle English *west* + OE *dræg*, 'dragging place' + *tūn*, 'farmstead'. For the meaning of the basic name, *see* ◊Market Drayton. The 'dragging place' here would have been by the River Colne. The first word distinguishes this Drayton from *Drayton Green*, Ealing. *Draitun* 1086, *West Draytone* 1269.

Westerham (town, Kent) 'westerly homestead', OE **wester*, 'westerly + *hām*, 'homestead'. The name refers to the location of the town in the far west of the county, near the Surrey border. The Domesday Book record shows one way of coping with non-French *W. Westarham* 871, *Oistreham* 1086.

West Ham (town, Greater London) 'western riverside land', Middle English *west*, 'west' + OE *hamm*, 'riverside land'. The town's name is the counterpart to *East Ham*, and the two would have originally formed a single 'riverside land' along the northern bank of the Thames here. *Cp* ◊Newham. *Hame* 1086, *Westhamma* 1186.

West Kirby (town, Merseyside) 'western village with a church', Middle English *west*, 'west' + OS *kirkju-bý*, 'village with a church'. The place was originally *Kirby*, but then added the first word, presumably to denote its location near the western end of the Wirral peninsula rather than for distinction from any other Kirby. *Cherchebia* 1081, *Westkirkeby* 1289.

Westminster (borough, Greater London) 'western monastery', OE *west*, 'west *mynster*, 'monastery', 'church'. The name relates to *Westminster* Abbey, which was built in the 13th century on the site of an 8th-century monastery that lay to the *west* of London. *Westmynster c* 975.

Westmorland (historic county, England) 'district of the people west of the moors', OE *west*, 'west' + *mōr*, 'moor' + *-inga-*, 'of the people of' + *land*, 'land'. The name alludes to the people who lived to the west of the North Yorkshire Pennines. The *-ing-* has disappeared from the original lengthy name. *Westmoringaland c* 1150.

Weston-super-Mare (town, Somerset) 'western farm on the sea', OE *west*, 'west' + *tūn*, 'farm' + Latin *super mare*, 'on the sea'. The original 'western farm' lay to the west of *Westonzoyland*, southeast of it. The Latin suffix distinguishes this Weston from the many others. *Weston c* 1230, *Weston super Mare* 1349.

Westray (island, Orkney) 'western island', OS *vestr*, 'western' + *ey*, 'island'. The island lies to the west of others in the northern Orkneys.

Westward Ho! (village, Devon). The west coast village takes its name from Charles Kingsley's novel *Westward Ho!* (1855), set largely in this region around Bideford. The first building erected was the church, in 1870.

Wetherby (town, West Yorkshire) 'farm where wethers are bred', OS *vethr*, 'wether' + *bý*, 'farm'. A 'wether' is a castrated ram. *Wedrebi* 1086.

Weybridge (town, Surrey) '(place by a) bridge over the (river) Wey', river name + OE *brycg*, 'bridge'. The pre-English river name is of uncertain origin and meaning. The 'bridge' is over the Wey near its confluence with the Thames. *Cp* ◊Weymouth. *Webruge* 1086.

Weymouth (town, Dorset) '(place at the) mouth of the (River) Wey', river name + OE *mūtha*, 'mouth'. The river name is probably of the same origin as that of the Wey at ◊Weybridge, so that its meaning is uncertain. *Waimouthe* 934.

Whaley Bridge (town, Derbyshire) 'clearing by a road with a bridge', OE *weg*, 'road' + *lēah*, 'clearing' + modern *bridge*. The 'road' would have been by the River Goyt here, and the 'bridge' is over it. *Weile c* 1250, *Whaleybridge c* 1620.

Whalley (town, Lancashire) 'clearing by a round hill', OE **hwæl*, 'round hill' + *lēah*, 'clearing'. The 'round hill' in question is probably the one called Whalley Nab (from OS *nabbi*, 'knoll'). *Hwælleage* 11th century, *Wallei* 1086.

Whalsay (island, Shetland) 'whale island', OS *hvalr*, 'whale' + *ey*, 'island'. The name probably refers to the general outline of the island, which resembles a whale. *Hvalsey c* 1250.

Wheathampstead (village, Hertfordshire) 'homestead where wheat is grown', OE *hwǣte*, 'wheat' + *hām-stede*, homestead'. A name that for once means directly what it says. *Wathemestede c* 960, *Watamestede* 1086.

Whetstone (district, Greater London) '(place of) whetstone', OE *hwet-stān*, 'whetstone'. The name alludes to the provision of local stone for making whetstones (sharpening stones). *Wheston* 1417.

Whickham (town, Tyne and Wear) 'homestead with a quickset hedge', OE **cwic*, 'quickset hedge' + *hām*, 'homestead'. A 'quickset hedge' is one made of cuttings from live shrubs, especially hawthorn, which are then planted in the ground. The second part of the name may represent OE *hamm*, 'enclosure'. *Quicham* 1196.

Whimple (village, Devon) '(place by the River) Whimple', Celtic river name. The river name, originally that of a stream here, means 'white pool', from words related to modern Welsh *gwyn*, 'white', and *pwll*, 'pool', 'stream'. *Winple* 1086.

Whipsnade (village, Bedfordshire) 'Wibba's detached plot', OE personal name + *snǣd*, 'detached plot'. The OE word that forms the second part of the name means literally 'piece cut off', and is related to German *schneiden*, 'to cut'. *Wibsnede* 1202.

Whiston (town, Merseyside) '(place at the) white stone', OE *hwīt*, 'white' + *stān*, 'stone'. The 'white stone' is some local feature mentioned in early texts. *Quistan* 1190.

Whitburn (town, Lothian) '(place by the) white stream', OE *hwīt*, 'white' + *burna*, 'stream'. The 'white stream' here is either the River Almond or one of the streams that flows into it. *Whiteburne* 1296.

Whitburn (town, Tyne and Wear) 'Hwīta's mound', OE personal name + *byrgen*, 'mound', 'tumulus'. The second part of the name could also represent OE *bere-ærn*, 'barn' (literally 'barley building'). *Cp* ◊Whitburn, Lothian, as a quite different name. *Hwiteberne c* 1190.

Whitby (town, North Yorkshire) 'Hvíti's farmstead', OS personal name + *bý*, 'farmstead'. The name could also mean 'white farmstead', with the first part from OS *hvítr*, 'white'. *Witeby* 1086.

Whitchurch (town, Hampshire) 'white church', OE *hwīt*, 'white' + *cirice*, 'church'. A 'white church' is probably one built of stone as distinct from wood. The identically named town in Shropshire has a name of the same origin and meaning. *Hwitancyrice* 909.

Whitechapel (district, Greater London) 'white chapel', OE *hwīt*, 'white' + Middle English *chapele*, 'chapel'. A 'white chapel' is one built of stone (*cp* ◊Whitchurch). The chapel in question was built in the 13th century and later became the parish church of St Mary Whitechapel. *Whitechapele* 1340.

Whitehaven (town, Cumbria) 'harbour by the white headland', OS *hvít*, 'white' + *hofuth*, 'headland' + *hafn*, 'harbour'. The name was originally the equivalent of *Whitehead Haven*, alluding to the hill of white stone which formed one side of the harbour. The 'headland' was then dropped for ease of pronunciation. *Qwithofhavene c* 1135.

Whithorn (town, Dumfries and Galloway) 'white building' OE *hwīt*, 'white' + *ærn*, 'building'. The 'white building' would have been the stone church here. *Cp* ◊Whitchurch. *Hwitan ærne* 731.

Whitley Bay (town, Tyne and Wear) '(place by) Whitley Bay', bay name. The present resort took its name from the bay, which itself was named from the original village of *Whitley* here. Its name means 'white wood' or 'white clearing', from OE *hwīt*, 'white', and *lēah*, 'wood', 'clearing'. A 'white wood' is a sparse one. *Wyteleya* 12th century.

Whitstable (town, Kent) '(place by the) white post', OE *hwīt*, 'white' + *stapol*, 'post'. The original 'white post' here was probably a marker for the meeting place of a hundred. *Witenestaple* 1086.

Whitworth (town, Lancashire) 'white enclosure', OE *hwīt*, 'white' + *worth*, 'enclosure'. A 'white enclosure' was probably one with white buildings. *Whiteworth* 13th century.

Whyteleafe (village, Surrey) '(place by the) White Leaf (Field)', field name. The name is a modern one, adopted from that of a field here, itself so called because of the aspens that grew in it. *White Leaf Field* 1839.

Wick (town, Highland) '(place on a) bay', OS *vík*, 'bay'. The port is on Wick Bay. *Vik* 1140.

Wickford (town, Essex) 'ford by a vicus', OE *wīc*, 'vicus' + *ford*, 'ford'. A *vicus* is a Romano-British settlement. *Wicforda c* 975, *Wicfort* 1086.

Wickham Market (town, Suffolk) 'homestead by a vicus with a market', OE *wīc*, 'vicus' + *hām*, 'homestead' + Middle English *market*, 'market'. A *vicus* is an earlier Roman-British settlement. The name was originally *Wickham*, but added the second word when an important market was established here. The addition also distinguishes this place from ◊Stowmarket. *Wikham* 1086.

Widecombe in the Moor (village, Devon) 'valley where willow trees grow in the moor', OE *wīthig*, 'willow' + *cumb*, 'valley' + Middle English *yn the more*, 'in the moor'. The addition to the name relates to ◊Dartmoor, and emphasizes the isolated location of the village. *Widecumba* 12th century, *Wydecomb yn the More* 1461.

Widnes (town, Cheshire) 'wide promontory', OE *wīd*, 'wide' + *næss*, 'promontory'. The 'wide promontory' is the one on which the town stands by the Mersey. *Wydnes c* 1200.

Wigan (town, Greater Manchester) '(place of) Wigan', Celtic personal name. The name may originally have been Welsh *Tref Wigan*, 'Wigan's village'. *Wigan* 1199.

Wight, Isle of (county, England) '(place of the) division', Celtic placename. The name apparently refers to the location of the island between the two arms of the Solent, so that there is a 'division' of the sea channel here, obliging ships to alter course. The original word is related to modern Welsh *gwaith*, 'work', 'time'. *Vectis c* 150, *Wit* 1086.

Wigston (town, Leicestershire) 'Wīcing's farmstead', OE personal name + *tūn*, 'farmstead'. The first part of the name could also represent the OS personal name *Vikingr*. The town is also known as *Wigston Magna*, 'Great Wigston', to be distinguished from the village of *Wigston Parva*, 'Little Wigston'. The latter's name has a different meaning: 'rocking stone', from OE *wigga*, literally 'beetle', and *stān*, 'stone'. *Wichingestone* 1086.

Wigton (town, Cumbria) 'Wicga's farmstead', OE personal name + *tūn*, 'farmstead'. *Cp* ◊Wigtown, a name of identical origin. *Wiggeton* 1163.

Wigtown (town, Dumfries and Galloway) 'Wicga's farmstead', OE personal name + *tūn*, 'farmstead'. The name is identical to that of ◊Wigton. *Wigeton* 1266.

Willesden (district, Greater London) '(place by a) hill with a spring', OE *wiell*, 'spring' + *dūn*, 'hill'. The name should really be *Wilsdon* but was altered in about 1840 by the railway company to match that of neighbouring ◊Harlesden and ◊Neasden. *Willesdone* 939, *Wellesdone* 1086, *Wylsdon* 1563, *Wilsdon* 1822.

Willington (town, Durham) 'estate named after Wifel', OE personal name + *-ing-*, 'named after' + *tu*, 'estate'. This is a name of the same type as ◊Paddington. *Wyvelintun c* 1190.

Wilmslow (town, Cheshire) 'Wīghelm's mound', OE personal name + *hlāw*, 'mound'. The name does not imply that Wīghelm was buried in the mound named after him, but that his estate was associated with it. *Wilmesloe c* 1250.

Wilton (town, Wiltshire) 'farmstead on the (River) Wylye', Celtic river name + *tūn*, 'farmstead'. The river name may mean 'tricky one', referring to its habit of flooding. *See also* ◊Wiltshire. *Uuiltun* 838, *Wiltune* 1086.

Wiltshire (county, England) 'shire of Wilton', OE place-name + *scīr*, 'shire'. The county took the name of ◊Wilton, the town on which it was originally centred. *Wiltunscir* 870, *Wiltescire* 1086.

Wimbledon (district, Greater London) 'Wynnmann's hill', OE personal name + *dūn*, 'hill'. The 'hill' of the name was probably the one that is now Wimbledon Hill. The letters *b* and *l* represent the Norman pronunciation of the awkward *ns* and *ms*. *Wunemannedune c* 950.

Wimborne Minster (town, Dorset) '(place by the River) Wimborne with a monastery', OE river name + *mynster*, 'monastery', 'church'. The River *Allen* here was earlier the *Wimborne*, 'meadow stream', from OE **winn*, 'meadow', and *burna*, 'stream'. The 'monastery' was the nunnery founded here in the early 8th century. *Winburnan* late 9th century, *Winburne* 1086, *Wymburneminstre* 1236.

Wincanton (town, Somerset) 'farmstead on (an arm of the River) Cale', Celtic river name + OE *tūn*, 'farmstead'. The river name, of uncertain origin and meaning, has been prefixed by a Celtic word meaning 'white', related to modern Welsh *gwyn*, 'white'. This is the *Win-* of the place-name. *Wincaletone* 1086.

Winchcombe (town, Gloucestershire) 'valley with a bend', OE **wincel*, 'corner', 'bend' + *cumb*, 'valley'. Winchcombe is in a deep valley of the River Isbourne. *Wincelcumbe c* 810, 1086.

Winchelsea (town, East Sussex) 'island by a river bend', OE **wincel*, 'corner', 'bend' + *ēg*, 'island'. The coastline south of the town has changed since the original name was given, and there is no 'island by a river bend' now. *Winceleseia* 1130.

Winchester (city, Hampshire) 'Roman town (called) Venta', pre-Celtic place-name + OE *ceaster*, 'Roman town'. The name of the Roman town may possibly mean 'favoured place', alluding to one that was propitious for trading or the like. The OE form of the name was closer to *Wintanchester*, but the second syllable has disappeared. *Ouenta c* 150, *Uintancæstir c* 730, *Wincestre* 1086.

Windermere (lake, Cumbria) 'Vinandr's lake', OS personal name + OE *mere*, 'lake'. The personal name is actually a Swedish one. *Winandermere* 12th century.

Windsor (town, Berkshire) 'bank with a windlass', OE **windels*, 'windlass' + *ōra*, 'bank', slope'. The 'windlass' would have been a winding mechanism for hauling carts (rather than boats) up from the edge of the Thames. *Windlesoran c* 1060.

Winsford (town, Cheshire) 'Wine's ford', OE personal name + OE *ford*, 'ford'. The 'ford' would have been over the River Weaver, on the road from Chester to Middlewich. *Wyneford c* 1334.

Winslow (town, Buckinghamshire) 'Wine's mound', OE personal name + *hlāw*, 'mound'. The 'mound' would probably have been a burial one. *Cp*

◊Wilmslow. *Wineshlauu* 795, *Weneslai* 1086.

Winterton (resort, Norfolk) 'winter farmstead', OE *winter*, 'winter' + *tūn*, 'farmstead'. A 'winter farmstead' was one used in the winter months, as it could be here by the sea, on a site that is higher and drier than one inland. *Wintertun* 1044, *Wintretuna* 1086.

Wirksworth (town, Derbyshire) 'Weorc's enclosure', OE personal name + *worth*, 'enclosure'. The personal name is the same as for ◊Workington and ◊Worksop. *Wyrcesuuyrthe* 835, *Werchesworde* 1086.

Wirral (peninsula, Merseyside/Cheshire) '(place at the) corner of land where bog myrtle grows', OE *wīr*, 'bog myrtle' + *halh*, 'nook'. The name poses problems, since the Wirral is hardly a nook. Moreover it is mainly high and dry, whereas bog myrtle grows in damp places. But no better explanation for the name has yet been made. *Wirhealum* early 10th century.

Wisbech (town, Cambridgeshire) 'marshy meadow valley', OE *wisc*, 'marshy meadow' + *bece*, 'valley'. The first part of the name could also be the OE river name *Wissey* ('marshy stream'), although Wisbech is now on the Nene. The second half could equally be OE *bæc*, 'ridge', meaning the ridge of land on which the town stands. *Wisbece* 1086.

Wishaw (town, Strathclyde) 'willow wood', OE *wīthig*, 'willow' + *sceaga*, 'wood'. The first part of the name could also represent OE **wiht*, 'bend', perhaps referring to the curving hillside on which the town is situated. *Witscaga* 1086.

Witham (town, Essex) 'homestead by a river bend', OE **wiht*, 'bend' + *hām*, 'homestead'. There is a 'bend' in the River Brain to the south of the town. *Witham* late 9th century.

Withernsea (resort, Humberside) '(place by a) lake near a thorn tree', OE *with*, 'near' + *thorn*, 'thorn tree' + *sǣ*, 'lake'. The name may be Scandinavian, from similar words having the same meanings. *Widfornessei* 1086.

Witney (town, Oxfordshire) 'Witta's island', OE personal name + *ēg*, 'island'. The 'island' is the relatively high terrain on which the town is situated by marshland, in which the River Windrush divides into several branches. *Wyttanige* 969, *Witenie* 1096.

Wiveliscombe (town, Somerset) 'Wifel's valley', OE personal name + *cumb*, 'valley'. The town is in a marked valley between high hills. *Wifelescumb* 854, *Wivelescome* 1086.

Wivenhoe (town, Essex) 'Wīfa's hill spur', OE personal name + *hōh*, 'hill spur'. The 'hill spur' in question is to the north of the town. *Wiunhov* 1086.

Woburn (village, Bedfordshire) '(place by the) crooked stream', OE *wōh*, 'crooked' + *burna*, 'stream'. 'Crooked stream' is effectively a river name. *Cp* ◊Wombourne. *Woburne* 1086.

Woking (town, Surrey) '(settlement of) Wocc's people', OE personal name + *-ingas*, 'people of'. The name relates directly to that of ◊Wokingham. *Wocchingas c* 712, *Wochinges* 1086.

Wokingham (town, Berkshire) 'homestead of Wocc's people', OE personal name + *-inga-*, 'of the people of' + *hām*, 'homestead'. The personal name here is almost certainly that of the same man who gave the name of ◊Woking. *Wokingeham* 1146.

Wolds, The (upland districts, England) 'high forest land', OE *wald*, 'high forestland'. The *Wolds*, in east central and northeastern England, have a name used of high forestland that has been subsequently cleared. *Cp* ◊Weald.

Wolsingham (town, Durham) 'homestead of Wulfsige's people', OE personal name + *-inga-*, 'of the people of' + *hām*, 'homestead'. The personal name means 'wolf victory'. *Wlsingham c* 1150.

Wolverhampton (town, West Midlands) 'Wulfrūn's high farmstead', OE personal name + *hēah*, 'high' + *tūn*, 'farmstead'. The *-hampton* is misleading, since the *hamp-* represents OE *hēan*, the dative case of *hēah*, 'high'. The town stands on high terrain. The personal name was added later. It is that of the lady to whom the manor here was granted in 985, and who founded a monastery. *Heantune* 985, *Wolvrenehamptonia c* 1080.

Wolverton (town, Buckinghamshire) 'estate named after Wulfhere', OE personal name + *-ing-*, 'named after' + *tūn*, 'estate'. The personal name means 'wolf army'. *Wluerintone* 1086.

Wombourne (town, Staffordshire) '(place at the) crooked stream', OE *wōh*, 'crooked' + *burna*, 'stream'. The name, which is actually that of the stream here, is identical to that of ◊Woburn. *Wamburne* 1086.

Wombwell (town, South Yorkshire) 'stream in a hollow', OE *wamb*, 'hollow' + *wella*, 'stream'. The first part of the name could also be the OE personal name *Wamba*. *Wanbuelle* 1086.

Woodbridge (town, Suffolk) '(place by the) wooden bridge', OE *wudu*, 'wood' + *brycg*, 'bridge'. The name could also be understood to mean '(place by the) bridge near the wood', from the same two OE words. *Oddebruge c* 1050, *Wudebrige* 1086.

Wood Green (district, Greater London) 'green place near a wood', OE *wudu*, 'wood' + *grēne*, 'green'. The 'wood' here is Enfield Chase, and Wood Green Common represents a remnant of the original 'green'. *Wodegrene* 1502.

Woodhall Spa (town, Lincolnshire) 'hall by a wood with a spa', OE *wudu*, 'wood' + *hall*, 'hall' + modern *spa*. The second word of the name was added when the town became a watering place. *Wudehalle* 12th century.

Woodhouse (district, Sheffield, South Yorkshire) 'house by a wood', OE *wudu*, 'wood' + *hūs*, 'house'. The meaning is thus not 'wooden house'. *Wdehus* 1200.

Woodmansterne (village, Surrey) '(place by the) thorn tree by the boundary of the wood', OE *wudu*, 'wood' + *mǣre*, 'boundary' + *thorn*, 'thorn tree'. The Domesday Book clerk clearly had trouble with this long name. *Odemerestor* 1086, *Wudemaresthorne c* 1190.

Woodstock (town, Oxfordshire) 'woodland settlement', OE *wudu*, 'wood' + *stoc*, 'place', 'settlement'. The region round the town is still well wooded. *Wudestoce c* 1000, *Wodestoch* 1086.

Woolacombe (village, Devon) 'valley with a spring', OE *wiella*, 'spring', 'stream' + *cumb*, 'valley'. The village lies in a characteristic West Country 'coomb'. *Wellecome* 1086.

Wooler (town, Northumberland) 'spring promontory', OE *wella*, 'spring' + **ofer*, 'promontory'. The 'promontory' is the highish ground on which the town stands overlooking the River Till. *Wulloure* 1187.

Woolwich (district, Greater London) 'place where wool was loaded', OE *wull*, 'wool' + *wīc*, 'special place', 'port'. Wool would have been loaded onto and off ships on the Thames here. The first record has *uu* to render *w*, and the Domesday Book record is corrupt. *Uuluuich* 918, *Hulviz* 1086.

Wootton Bassett (town, Wiltshire) 'farmstead by a wood of the Basset family', OE *wudu*, 'wood' + *tūn*, farmstead' + family name. The *Basset* family from Normandy held the manor here in the 13th century. *Wdetun* 680, *Wodetone* 1086, *Wotton Basset* 1272.

Worcester (city, Hereford and Worcester) 'Roman town of the Weogora people', tribal name + OE *ceaster*, 'Roman town'. The folk name probably derives from a Celtic river name meaning 'winding river'. However, this is not necessarily the Severn, on which Worcester stands. The county name, *Worcestershire*, is first recorded in the 11th century. *Weogorna civitas* 691, *Wigranceastre* 717, *Wirecestre* 1086.

Workington (town, Cumbria) 'estate named after Weorc', OE personal name + *-ing-*, 'named after' + *tūn*, 'estate'. The personal name is the same as that behind ◊Worksop, although almost certainly not that of the same man. *Wirkynton c* 1125.

Worksop (town, Nottinghamshire) 'Weorc's valley', OE personal name + *hop*, 'valley'. It is not certain which valley the name refers to. *Werchesope* 1086.

Wormwood Scrubs (district, Greater London) 'scrubland by a wood where snakes are', OE *wyrm*, 'snake' + *holt*, 'wood' + **scrubb*, 'scrubland'. The first word, originally used alone, has been recently corrupted by association with *wormwood*. *Wermeholte* 1200, *Wormholt Scrubbs* 1819.

Worsley (town, Greater Manchester) 'Weorcgȳth's clearing', OE personal name + *lēah*, 'clearing'. The personal name, as quoted that of a woman, could also be *Weorchæth*, that of a man. *Werkesleia* 1196, *Wyrkitheley* 1246.

Worthing (town, West Sussex) '(settlement of) Weorth's people', OE personal name + *-ingas*, 'people of'. The name is typical of Sussex, which abounds in *-ing* names of this type. *Ordinges* 1086.

Wotton-under-Edge (town, Gloucestershire) 'farmstead by a wood below an escarpment', OE *wudu*, 'wood' + *tūn*, 'farmstead' + *ecg*, 'edge'. The 'Edge' is an escarpment of the Cotswolds at the foot of which the town lies. *Wudutune* 940, *Vutune* 1086, *Wotton under Egge* 1466.

Wragby (town, Lincolnshire) 'Wraghi's farmstead', OS personal name + *bý*, 'farmstead'. The personal name is a Danish one. *Waragebi* 1086.

Wrekin, The (hill, Shropshire) Celtic place-name. The original name is that of a hill fort here. Its meaning is uncertain, but it in turn gave the name of ◊Wroxeter.

Wrexham (town, Clwyd) 'Wryhtel's pasture', OE personal name + *hamm*, 'riverside land', 'pasture'. There is no obvious river at Wrexham now, but there clearly once was, as testified by such street names as Watery Road, Brook Street and Bridge Street. The original form of the name must have been something like *Wrightham*, and the present spelling is due to Welsh influence. *Wristlesham* 1161, *Gwregsam* 1291.

Wroxeter (village, Shropshire) 'Roman fort near the Wrekin', Celtic hill name + OE *ceaster*, 'Roman fort'. The Roman fort here was called *Viriconium*, from the same source. It is possible the hill name, alluding to its own fort, may have meant something like 'fort of Virico'. *Ouirokonion c* 150, *Rochecestre* 1086.

Wychavon (district, Hereford and Worcester) '(district of) Droitwich and (the River) Avon'. The name was devised for the administrative district established here in 1974. It is a combination of the second part of the name of ◊Droitwich in a historic form (*eg Drihtwych* in 1347) and the name of the River *Avon*. Droitwich is in the north of the district, and the Avon in the south.

Wye (river, Wales/England). For the meaning of this river name, *see* ◊Ross-on-Wye.

Wymondham (town, Norfolk) 'Wīgmund's homestead', OE personal name + *hām*, 'homestead'. The Leicestershire village of the same name has the same origin and meaning. *Wimundham* 1086.

Yarm (town, Cleveland) '(place at the) fish weirs', OE **gear*, 'fish weir'. The town lies in a loop of the River Tees, an ideal location for 'fish weirs', or traps to catch fish. The name represents **gearum*, the dative plural form of the OE word, as required after *æt*, 'at'. *Iarun* 1086.

Yarmouth (town, Isle of Wight) 'gravelly estuary', OE **ēaren*, 'gravelly' + *mūtha*, 'mouth', 'estuary'. The River *Yare* here took its name from that of the town. Its earlier name was probably ◊Freshwater, now the name of the village at the southern end of the estuary. *Ermud* 1086, *Ernemuth* 1223.

Yarmouth (town, Norfolk) *See* ◊Great Yarmouth.

Yeadon (town, West Yorkshire) '(place by the) steep hill', OE **gēah*, 'steep' + *dūn*, 'hill'. The town is on a spur of the hill ridge known as The Chevin. *Iadun* 1086.

Yelverton (town, Devon) 'village of the elder tree ford', OE *ellen*, 'elder' + *ford*, 'ford' + *tūn*, 'village'. The *-ton* was added later to the basic name, and a *Y-* was added to the original *E-* by the Great Western Railway in 1859 to reflect the local pronunciation. *Elleford* 1291, *Elverton* 1765, *Elfordtown* 1809.

Yeovil (town, Somerset) '(place on the River) Gifl', Celtic river name. The town is named from its river, originally the *Gifl*, but now the *Yeo*. The river name means 'forked river'. *Yeo* developed from *Gifl* under the influence of OE *ēa*, 'river'. *Gifle c* 880, *Givele* 1086.

Yes Tor (hill, Devon) 'eagle's hill', OE *earn*, 'eagle' + *torr*, 'hill'. The *s* of *Yes* is possessive. *Ernestorre* 1240.

York (city, North Yorkshire) 'Eburos' estate', Celtic name. The name evolved either from a Celtic personal name *Eburos* or from a Celtic word meaning 'yew tree', related to Welsh *yw*. The Roman name, *Eboracum*, was taken by the Anglo-Saxons to derive from OE *eofor*, 'wild boar', and to this they added *wīc* to give a name *Eoforwic* (see record below). The Vikings then came here and altered the last part of this to *vík*, 'bay', although there is no bay here. The blended name was subsequently smoothed and shortened to give modern *York*, with the *k* from the OS word. *Eborakon c* 150, *Eoforwic c* 1060, *Euruic* 1086.

Z

Zeals (village, Wiltshire) '(place by the) willows', OE *sealh*, 'willow', 'sallow'. The spelling of the name reflects the West Country pronunciation (as for 'Zummerzet' and the like). *Sele* 1086.

County boundaries pre-1974 (England and Wales) and pre-1975 (Scotland)

County boundaries since 1974 (England and Wales) and since 1975 (Scotland)

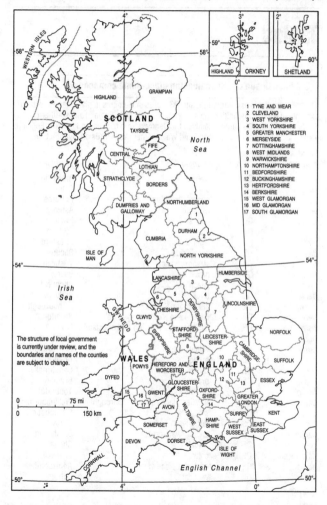

1 TYNE AND WEAR
2 CLEVELAND
3 WEST YORKSHIRE
4 SOUTH YORKSHIRE
5 GREATER MANCHESTER
6 MERSEYSIDE
7 NOTTINGHAMSHIRE
8 WEST MIDLANDS
9 WARWICKSHIRE
10 NORTHAMPTONSHIRE
11 BEDFORDSHIRE
12 BUCKINGHAMSHIRE
13 HERTFORDSHIRE
14 BERKSHIRE
15 WEST GLAMORGAN
16 MID GLAMORGAN
17 SOUTH GLAMORGAN

The structure of local government
is currently under review, and the
boundaries and names of the counties
are subject to change.

Tables

I. Old English and Old Scandinavian place-name components

The following list is of common OE and OS words or elements in place-names, with an example of each. By definition, most such places will be in England and southern Scotland, with the OS names mainly in the Danelaw, *ie* in the east and north of England, as well as in the islands of Scotland and Wales. Asterisked words are hypothetical.

Word or element	OE or OS	Meaning	Example
á	OS	'river'	Ambleside
āc	OE	'oak'	Acton
ærn	OE	'house', 'building'	Potterne
æsc	OE	'ash tree'	Ashford
æwell	OE	'river source'	Ewell
ald	OE	'old'	Oldham
alor	OE	'alder tree'	Alresford
bæc	OE	'back', 'ridge'	Bacup
bæce, bece	OE	'stream', 'valley'	Wisbech
bearu,	OE	'grove'	Beer
bēce	OE	'beech'	Bitchfield
beorc	OE	'birch'	Berkeley
beorg, berg	OE	'hill', 'mound'	Farnborough
bere-tūn	OE	'barley farm', 'outlying grange'	Surbiton
bere-wīc	OE	'barley farm', 'outlying part of estate'	Berwick
bōc	OE	'beech'	Bookham
botm	OE	'valley bottom'	Ramsbottom
brād	OE	'broad', 'spacious'	Bradford
brōc	OE	'brook', 'stream'	Carisbrooke
brōm	OE	'broom'	Bromley
brycg	OE	'bridge'	Tonbridge
burh	OE	'fortified place', 'manor', 'borough'	Wellingborough
burna	OE	'stream'	Sittingbourne
by	OS	'farmstead', 'village'	Derby
cærse	OE	'cress', 'watercress'	Carshalton
calc, cealc	OE	'chalk'	Chelsea
cald, ceald	OE	'cold'	Caldwell
camp	OE	'enclosed piece of land'	Addiscombe
cat	OE	'wild cat'	Catford

cēap	OE	'trade', 'market'	Chipstead
ceaster, cæster	OE	'Roman fort', 'Roman town'	Manchester
cēping	OE	'market'	Chipping Campden
cēse	OE	'cheese'	Chiswick
cirice	OE	'church'	Whitchurch
clif	OE	'cliff', 'slope'	Clevedon
* clōh	OE	'ravine', 'deep valley'	Clough
cniht	OE	'youth', 'servant'	Knightsbridge
cnoll	OE	'hill top', 'hillock'	Knowle
cot	OE	'cottage', 'hut', 'shelter'	Didcot
crāwe	OE	'crow'	Crawley
cumb	OE	'coomb', 'short valley'	Widecombe in the Moor
cyning	OE	'king'	Kingston
dalr	OS	'valley'	Borrowdale
denn	OE	'woodland pasture, especially for pigs'	Tenterden
denu	OE	'long valley'	Rottingdean
dēor	OE	'animal', 'deer'	Darley
dīc	OE	'ditch', 'dyke'	Diss
dræg	OE	'dragging place'	Drayton
dūn	OE	'hill', 'down'	Neasden
ēa	OE	'river'	Eton
earn	OE	'eagle'	Arnold
ēast	OE	'east'	Aston
ecg	OE	'edge'	Edgeworth
ēg	OE	'island', 'dry ground in marsh'	Pewsey
ende	OE	'end', 'district of an estate'	Gravesend
eofor	OE	'wild boar'	Everton
ey	OS	'island'	Barra
fearn	OE	'fern', 'bracken'	Faringdon
feld	OE	'open land'	Enfield
flēot	OE	'estuary', 'creek', 'inlet'	Purfleet
ford	OE	'ford', 'river crossing'	Oxford
fūl	OE	'foul', 'dirty'	Fulford
funta	OE	'spring'	Havant
gāt	OE	'goat'	Gatwick
gata	OS	'way', 'street'	Harrogate
* gē	OE	'district'	Surrey
geat	OE	'gate', 'gap', 'pass'	Reigate
gōs	*OE*	'goose'	Gosport
grāf	OE	'grove'	Gravesend
grēne	OE	'green', 'grassy place'	Greenham

hæg	OE	'enclosure'	Haywood
hǣth	OE	'heath', 'heather'	Hatfield
halh	OE	'corner of land', 'nook'	Ludgershall
hālig	OE	'holy'	Holywell
hām	OE	'homestead', 'village', 'estate'	Rotherham
hamm	OE	'enclosure', 'hemmed-in land', 'riverside land'	Buckingham
hām-stede	OE	'homestead', 'dwelling site'	Hemel Hempstead
hām-tūn	OE	'home farm', 'enclosure with a homestead'	Northampton
hēafod	OE	'head', 'headland'	Birkenhead
hēah	OE	'high', 'chief'	Henley-on-Thames
hēg	OE	'hay'	Hayford
here	OE	'army'	Hereford
hīd	OE	'hide', 'amount of land for one family'	Piddletrenthide
hlāw	OE	'mound', 'hill'	Lewes
hōc	OE	'hook', 'corner of land'	Liphook
hōh	OE	'heel of land', 'hill spur'	Houghton
holmr	OS	'island', 'raised land in marsh'	Durham
hop	OE	'small enclosed valley'	Bacup
hramsa	OE	'garlic'	Ramsey
hwīt	OE	'white'	Whitchurch
hyll	OE	'hill'	Hilton
hyrst	OE	'wooded hill'	Sandhurst
hȳth	OE	'landing place', 'harbour'	Lambeth
-ing	OE	'characterized by', 'belonging to'	Clavering
-ing-	OE	'connected with', 'named after'	West Lavington
-inga-	OE	'of the people of'	Nottingham
-ingas	OE	'people of', 'dwellers at'	Hastings
kirkja	OS	'church'	Kirkby
lacu	OE	'stream', 'water course'	Mortlake
lamb	OE	'lamb'	Lambeth
land	OE	'land', 'estate'	Cleveland
lang	OE	'long'	Langton
lēah	OE	'wood', 'clearing', 'meadow'	Purley
mǣre, gemǣre	OE	'boundary'	Mersey
mere	OE	'pond', 'pool', 'lake'	Cromer
middel	OE	'middle'	Milton Keynes
mōr	OE	'moor', 'barren upland'	Dartmoor
mūtha	OE	'river mouth', 'estuary'	Plymouth
myln	OE	'mill'	Millom

mynster	OE	'monastery', 'minster', 'large church'	Westminster
næss, ness	OE	'promontory', 'headland'	Sheerness
nes	OS	'promontory', 'headland'	Skegness
nīwe	OE	'new'	Newton
north	OE	'north'	Northampton
ōfer	OE	'bank', 'shore'	Overstrand
* ofer	OE	'flat-topped ridge'	Mickleover
ōra	OE	'shore', 'hill slope', 'flat-topped hill'	Windsor
oxa	OE	'ox'	Oxford
pæth	OE	'path', 'track'	Morpeth
pōl	OE	'pool', 'pond'	Poulton-le-Fylde
port	OE	1) 'harbour', 2) 'town', 'market', 3) 'gate'	1) Portsmouth, 2) Newport
prēost	OE	'priest'	Preston
rēad	OE	'red'	Redhill
risc, * rysc	OE	'rush'	Ruislip
sǣ	OE	'sea', 'lake'	Seaton
sǣte	OE	'settlers', 'dwellers'	Somerset
salh	OE	'willow', 'sallow'	Salford
salt	OE	'salt'	Saltash
sand	OE	'sand'	Sandown
sceaga	OE	'wood', 'copse'	Birkenshaw
scēap, scīp	OE	'sheep'	Skipton
scēat	OE	'corner of land', 'projecting piece of land'	Aldershot
scīr	OE	1) 'shire', 'district', 2) 'bright'	1) Cheshire, 2) Sherborne
* sele	OE	'willow copse'	Selborne
stān	OE	'stone', 'rock'	Stanley
stapol	OE	'post', 'pillar'	Barnstaple
stede	OE	'enclosed pasture', 'place'	Brasted
stoc	OE	'place', 'outying farmstead', 'dependent settlement'	Woodstock
stōw	OE	'place', 'place of assembly, 'holy place'	Chepstow
strǣt	OE	'Roman road'	Stratford
sūth	OE	'south'	Southampton
thorn	OE	'thorn tree'	Thornton Heath
thorp	OS	'dependent farmstead', 'secondary settlement'	Scunthorpe
thveit	OS	'clearing', 'meadow'	Bassenthwaite
toft	OS	'house site', 'homestead'	Lowestoft
torr	OE	'rock', 'rocky hill'	Torquay
trēow	OE	'tree', 'post', 'beam'	Coventry

tūn	OE	'enclosure', 'farmstead', 'village', 'estate'	Preston
wæd, gewæd	OE	'ford'	Biggleswade
wæter	OE	'water', 'river', 'lake'	Haweswater
wald	OE	'woodland', 'forest', 'high woods', 'cleared high woods'	Cotswolds
walh	OE	'Briton', 'Welshman'	Cornwall
-ware	OE	'dwellers'	Canterbury
weg	OE	'way', 'track', 'road'	Holloway
wella, wiella	OE	'spring', 'stream'	Stockwell
weorc	OE	'building', 'fortification'	Newark
wer, wær	OE	'weir', 'river dam', 'fishing enclosure'	Wareham
west	OE	'west'	Westbury
wīc	OE	'Romano-British settlement', 'specialized farm', 'trading settlement', 'harbour'	Norwich
wīd	OE	'wide', 'spacious'	Widnes
worth, worthign	OE	'enclosure', 'enclosed settlement'	Letchworth
wudu	OE	'wood', 'forest'	Northwood
wyrm	OE	'reptile', 'snake', 'dragon'	Wormwood Scrubs
yfer	OE	'edge of a hill', 'hill brow'	Hever

II. Welsh and Gaelic place-name components

The following list is of common Welsh and (Scottish) Gaelic words and elements in place-names, with an example of each. By definition, such places will be mainly in Wales and Scotland.

Word or element	Welsh or Gaelic	Meaning	Example
aber	Old Welsh	'confluence', 'estuary'	Aberdeen
ard	Gaelic	'height'	Ardnamurchan
beinn	Gaelic	'mountain'	Ben Nevis
blaen	Welsh	'highland'	Blaenau Ffestiniog
bryn	Welsh	'hill'	Brynmawr
caer	Welsh	'fortified place'	Caernarfon
caol	Gaelic	'strait'	Kyles of Bute
cill	Gaelic	'church', 'burial place'	Kilmarnock
coed	Welsh	'wood'	Betws-y-Coed
dùn	Gaelic	'fortified place'	Dundee
eaglais	Gaelic	'church'	Ecclefechan
glan	Welsh	'bank', 'shore'	Glamorgan
gleann	Gaelic	'glen', 'valley'	Glenelg
inbhir	Gaelic	'river mouth', 'confluence'	Inverness
llan	Welsh	'enclosure', 'church', 'village'	Llangollen
loch	Gaelic	'lake'	Loch Lomond
pen	Welsh	'head', 'height', 'hill'	Penmaenmawr
pont	Welsh	'bridge'	Pontypridd
ros	Gaelic	'moor', 'heath', 'promontory'	Ross
srath	Gaelic	'broad valley'	Strathclyde
tref	Welsh	'village'	Tredegar
uachtar	Gaelic	'upper'	Auchterarder

III. American place-names exported from Britain

Early colonists and settlers in America frequently named a new settlement for a place in 'the old country', either because they had come from there or for some other connection. The following is a selection of such names, with American state and British county or region. (Names adopted from people's surnames or titles, such as New York, are not included, even though these themselves came from place-names.) Some of the American spellings differ from the English, and have preserved historic forms. A good example is *Lexington*, as which the English *Laxton* was known as recently as the 19th century.

Aberdeen, Missouri	Aberdeen, Grampian
Abingdon, Virginia	Abingdon, Oxfordshire
Acton, Massachusetts	Acton, Greater London
Allerton, Massachusetts	Allerton, Merseyside
Amesbury, Massachusetts	Amesbury, Wiltshire
Andover, Massachusetts	Andover, Hampshire
Ashburnham, Massachusetts	Ashburnham, East Sussex
Attleboro, Massachusetts	Attleborough, Norfolk
Barnstaple, Massachusetts	Barnstaple, Devon
Bath, Maine	Bath, Avon
Bedford, Massachusetts	Bedford, Bedfordshire
Berks County, Pennsylvania	Berkshire
Berkshire County, Massachusetts	Berkshire
Beverly, Massachusetts	Beverley, Humberside
Bexley, Ohio	Bexley, Greater London
Biddeford, Maine	Bideford Devon
Billerica, Massachusetts	Billericay, Essex
Birmingham, Alabama	Birmingham, West Midlands
Boston, Massachusetts	Boston, Lincolnshire
Boxford, Massachusetts	Boxford, Suffolk
Braintree, Massachusetts	Braintree, Essex
Branford, Connecticut	Brentford, Greater London
Bridgewater, Massachusetts	Bridgwater, Somerset
Bristol, Connecticut	Bristol, Avon
Bucks County, Pennsylvania	Buckinghamshire
Burlington, New Jersey	Bridlington, Humberside
Buxton, Maine	Buxton, Norfolk
Cambridge, Massachusetts	Cambridge, Cambridgeshire
Canterbury, New Brunswick	Canterbury, Kent
Cardiff-by-the-Sea, California	Cardiff, South Glamorgan

Chalfont, Pennsylvania	Chalfont St Giles, Buckinghamshire
Chelmsford, Massachusetts	Chelmsford, Essex
Chelsea, Massachusetts	Chelsea, Greater London
Cheviot, Ohio	Cheviot Hills, Borders
Colchester, Connecticut	Colchester, Essex
Coventry, Connecticut	Coventry, West Midlands
Cynwyd, Pennsylvania	Cynwyd, Clwyd
Danbury, Connecticut	Danbury, Essex
Darby, Pennsylvania	Derby, Derbyshire
Darlington, South Carolina	Darlington, Co Durham
Dartmouth, Massachusetts	Dartmouth, Devon
Dedham, Massachusetts	Dedham, Essex
Derby, Connecticut	Derby, Derbyshire
Dorchester, Massachusetts	Dorchester, Dorset
Dover, Delaware	Dover, Kent
Edinboro, Pennsylvania	Edinburgh, Lothian
Edinburg, Texas	Edinburgh, Lothian
Essex, Maryland	Essex
Exeter, New Hampshire	Exeter, Devon
Falmouth, Massachusetts	Falmouth, Cornwall
Framlingham, Massachusetts	Framlingham, Suffolk
Glasgow, Montana	Glasgow, Strathclyde
Glastonbury, Connecticut	Glastonbury, Somerset
Gloucester City, New Jersey	Gloucester, Gloucestershire
Greenwich Village, New York	Greenwich, Greater London
Gretna, Louisiana	Gretna Green, Dumfries and Galloway
Groton, Connecticut	Groton, Suffolk
Guilford, Connecticut	Guildford, Surrey
Hampshire County, Massachusetts	Hampshire
Hartford, Connecticut	Hertford, Hertfordshire
Harwich, Massachusetts	Harwich, Essex
Haverford, Pennsylvania	Haverfordwest, Dyfed
Haverhill, Massachusetts	Haverhill, Suffolk
Hawarden, Iowa	Hawarden, Clwyd
Hempstead, New York	Hemel Hempstead, Hertfordshire
Hingham, Massachusetts	Hingham, Norfolk
Hull, Massachusetts	Hull, Humberside
Huntington, New York	Huntingdon, Cambridgeshire
Hurley, New York	Hurley, Berkshire
Ipswich, Massachusetts	Ipswich, Suffolk
Isle of Wight County, Virginia	Isle of Wight
Islip, New York	Islip, Oxfordshire
Kelso, Washington	Kelso, Borders

Kilsyth, West Virginia	Kilsyth, Strathclyde
Kinloch, Missouri	Kinloch, Tayside
Lancaster County, Pennsylvania	Lancashire
Leeds, Alabama	Leeds, West Yorkshire
Leicester, Massachusetts	Leicester, Leicestershire
Leominster, Massachusetts	Leominster, Hereford and Worcester
Lewes, Delaware	Lewes, East Sussex
Lexington, Massachusetts	Laxton, Nottinghamshire
Lincoln, Massachusetts	Lincoln, Lincolnshire
Litchfield, Connecticut	Litchfield, Staffordshire
London, Kentucky	London, Greater London
Ludlow, Massachusetts	Ludlow, Shropshire
Lynn, Massachusetts	King's Lynn, Norfolk
Maidstone, Vermont	Maidstone, Kent
Malden, Massachusetts	Maldon, Essex
Manchester, New Hampshire	Manchester, Greater Manchester
Marlboro, Massachusetts	Marlborough, Wiltshire
Melrose, Massachusetts	Melrose, Borders
Middlesboro, Kentucky	Middlesbrough, Cleveland
Middlesex County, New Jersey	Middlesex
Monmouth County, New Jersey	Monmouthshire
Mount Ayr, Iowa	Ayr, Strathclyde
Needham, Massachusetts	Needham, Norfolk
Newark, New Jersey	Newark-on-Trent, Nottinghamshire
Newburgh, New York	Newburgh, Fife
New Haven, Connecticut	Newhaven, East Sussex
New Kensington, Pennsylvania	Keninsington, Greater London
New London, Connecticut	London, Greater London
Newmarket, New Hampshire	Newmarket, Suffolk
Norfolk, Virginia	Norfolk
Northampton County, Pennsylvania	Northamptonshire
Norwich, Connecticut	Norwich, Norfolk
Oxford, Mississippi	Oxford, Oxfordshire
Plymouth, Massachusetts	Plymouth, Devon
Pomfret, Connecticut	Pontefract, West Yorkshire
Portland, Maine	Portland, Dorset
Portsmouth, New Hampshire	Portsmouth, Hampshire
Radnor, Pennsylvania	Radnorshire
Reading, Pennsylvania	Reading, Berkshire
Romney, West Virginia	New Romney, Kent
Rye, New York	Rye, East Sussex
St Albans, Vermont	St Albans, Hertfordshire
Salisbury, Massachusetts	Salisbury, Wiltshire

Sandwich, Massachusetts	Sandwich, Kent
Seaford, Delaware	Seaford, East Sussex
Sheffield, Alabama	Sheffield, South Yorkshire
Sherborn, Massachusetts	Sherborne, Dorset
Shrewsbury, Pennsylvania	Shrewsbury, Shropshire
Somerset County, Pennsylvania	Somerset
Southampton, Massachusetts	Southampton, Hampshire
Southwark, Pennsylvania	Southwark, Greater London
Springfield, Massachusetts	Springfield, Essex
Stamford, Connecticut	Stamford, Lincolnshire
Stockport, New York	Stockport, Greater Manchester
Sturbridge, Massachusetts	Stourbridge, West Midlands
Sudbury, Massachusetts	Sudbury, Suffolk
Sunbury, Pennsylvania	Sunbury, Surrey
Surry County, Virginia	Surrey
Sussex County, Delaware	Sussex
Swansea, Illinois	Swansea, West Glamorgan
Taunton, Massachusetts	Taunton, Somerset
Tewksbury, Massachusetts	Tewkesbury, Gloucestershire
Thames River, Connecticut	River Thames
Tiverton, Rhode Island	Tiverton, Devon
Topsham, Maine	Topsham, Devon
Torrington, Connecticut	Torrington, Devon
Truro, Illinois	Truro, Cornwall
Wallingford, Connecticut	Wallingford, Oxfordshire
Waltham, Massachusetts	Waltham Abbey, Essex
Wareham, Massachusetts	Wareham, Dorset
Wells, Maine	Wells, Somerset
Westcliffe, Colorado	Westcliff-on-Sea, Essex
Westmoreland County, Pennsylvania	Westmorland
Wethersfield, Connecticut	Wethersfield, Essex
Weymouth, Massachusetts	Weymouth, Dorset
Willingboro, New Jersey	Wellingborough, Northamptonshire
Willington, Connecticut	Wellington, Shropshire
Wilton, Connecticut	Wilton, Wiltshire
Winchester, Connecticut	Winchester, Hampshire
Windham, Maine	Wymondham, Norfolk
Woburn, Massachusetts	Woburn, Bedfordshire
Woodbridge, New Jersey	Woodbridge, Suffolk
Wrentham, Massachusetts	Wrentham, Suffolk
York County, Pennsylvania	Yorkshire

IV. Literary place-names

Some place-names are enshrined in literary quotations. The following is a memorable selection.

> Yes; I remember Adlestrop–
> The name, because one afternoon
> Of heat the express-train drew up there
> Unwontedly. It was late June.

(Edward Thomas, 'Adlestrop', 1917)

There was a rocky valley between Buxton and Bakewell ... You enterprised a railroad ... you blasted its rocks away ... And now, every fool in Buxton can be at Bakewell in half-an-hour, and every fool in Bakewell at Buxton.

(John Ruskin, *Praeterita*, 1889)

Some word that teems with hidden meaning – like Basingstoke.

(W.S. Gilbert, *Ruddigore*, 1887)

> A merry road, a mazy road, and such as we did tread
> The night we went to Birmingham by way of Beachy Head.

(G.K. Chesterton, 'The Rolling English Road', 1914)

> There's a famous seaside place called Blackpool,
> That's noted for fresh air and fun,
> And Mr and Mrs Ramsbottom
> Went there with young Albert, their son.

(Marriott Edgar, 'The Lion and Albert', 1932)

Bugger Bognor.

(George V, 1929 or 1936)

> Clunton and Clunbury,
> Clungunford and Clun,
> Are the quietest places
> Under the sun.

(A.E. Housman, *A Shropshire Lad*, 1896)

Oxford is on the whole more attractive than Cambridge to the ordinary visitor; and the traveller is therefore recommended to visit Cambridge first, or to omit it altogether if he cannot visit both.

(Karl Baedeker, *Great Britain*, 1887)

> And Cambridgeshire, of all England,
> The shire for Men who Understand;
> And of *that* district I prefer
> The lovely hamlet Grantchester.
> For Cambridge people rarely smile,

Being urban, squat, and packed with guile.

> (Rupert Brooke, 'The Old Vicarage, Grantchester', 1915)

Till Belvoir's lordly terraces the sign to Lincoln sent,
And Lincoln sped the message on o'er the wide vale of Trent;
And Skiddaw saw the fire that burned on Gaunt's embattled pile,
And the red glare on Skiddaw roused the burghers of Carlisle.

> (Lord Macaulay, 'The Armada', 1833)

War told me truth: I have Severn's right of maker,
As of Cotswold: war told me: I was elect, I was born fit
To praise the three hundred feet depth of every acre
Between Tewkesbury and Stroudway, Side and Wales Gate.

> (Ivor Gurney, 'While I Write', c 1922)

When Adam and Eve were dispossessed
Of the garden hard by Heaven,
They planted another one down in the west,
'Twas Devon, glorious Devon!

> (Sir H.E. Boulton, 'Glorious Devon', 1902)

Come open your gates, and let me gae free,
I daurna stay langer in bonny Dundee.

> (Sir Walter Scott, *Rob Roy*, 1817)

I am a stranger here in Gloucestershire:
These high wild hills and rough uneven ways
Draw out our miles and make them wearisome.

> (William Shakespeare, *Richard II*, 1595)

In Hertford, Hereford, and Hampshire
Hurricanes hardly happen.

> (Alan Jay Lerner, *My Fair Lady*, 1956)

The fields from Islington to Marybone,
To Primrose Hill and Saint John's Wood
Were builded over with pillars of gold;
And there Jerusalem's pillars stood.

> (William Blake, *Jerusalem*, 1815)

Kent, sir – everybody knows Kent – apples, cherries, hops, and women.
> (Charles Dickens, *Pickwick Papers*, 1837)

When a man is tired of London, he is tired of life; for there is in London all that life can afford.

> (Dr Johnson, Boswell's *Life of Samuel Johnson*, 20 September 1777)

Very flat, Norfolk.

(Noël Coward, *Private Lives*, 1930)

If only I could get down to Sidcup!

(Harold Pinter, *The Caretaker*, 1960)

Sing me a song of a lad that is gone,
Say, could that lad be I?
Merry of soul he sailed on a day
Over the sea to Skye.

(R.L. Stevenson, *Songs of Travel*, 1896)

Come, friendly bombs, and fall on Slough!
It isn't fit for humans now.

(John Betjeman, 'Slough', 1937)

V. Local fare

Many places in Britain have become associated with a particular type of food. The following is a selection to suit all palates.

Arbroath smokies (smoked haddock)
Bakewell tart
Banbury cake
Bath bun
Bath chap (pork cut)
Bath Oliver (biscuit)
Caerphilly cheese
Cheddar cheese
Chelsea bun
Cheshire cheese
Colchester natives (oysters)
Cornish pasty
Devonshire cream
Dundee cake
Dundee marmalade
Eccles cake

Lancashire hotpot
Melton Mowbray pie
Norfolk dumpling
Oxford sausage
Pontefract cake
Scotch broth
Scotch egg
Scotch woodcock
Stilton cheese
Sussex smokies (smoked mackerel)
Welsh rarebit (or rabbit)
Wensleydale cheese
Wiltshire lardy
Windsor soup
Worcester sauce
Yorkshire pudding

VI. Fictional place-names

Fictional places in the works of the named writers have been identified with the real places below.

Fictional place	*Writer*	*Real place*
Abbotsea	Thomas Hardy	Abbotsbury, Dorset
Aldbrickham	Thomas Hardy	Reading, Berkshire
Axe	Arnold Bennett	Leek, Staffordshire
Babington	Dorothy Richardson	Abingdon, Oxfordshire
Banbury Park	Dorothy Richardson	Finsbury Park, Greater London
Barchester	Anthony Trollope	Salisbury, Wiltshire/Winchester, Hampshire
Barset	Anthony Trollope	Somerset
Battersby	Samuel Butler	Langar, Nottinghamshire
Belford Regis	Mary Russell Mitford	Reading, Berkshire
Birchester	W.H. Mallock	Birmingham
Blackstable	W. Somerset Maugham	Whitstable, Kent
Blunderstone	Charles Dickens	Blundeston, Suffolk
Bonnycliff	Dorothy Richardson	Sandgate, Kent
Bretton	Charlotte Brontë	Bridlington, Humberside
Briarfield	Charlotte Brontë	Birstall, West Yorkshire
Brocklebridge	Charlotte Brontë	Tunstall, Lancashire
Bromstead	H.G. Wells	Bromley, Greater London
Broxton	George Eliot	Roston, Derbyshire
Budmouth	Thomas Hardy	Weymouth, Dorset
Camelton	Thomas Hardy	Camelford, Cornwall
Casterbridge	Thomas Hardy	Dorchester, Dorset
Castle Boterel	Thomas Hardy	Boscastle, Cornwall
Chalk Newton	Thomas Hardy	Maiden Newton, Dorset
Charmley	Thomas Hardy	Charminster, Dorset
Chatteris	W.M. Thackeray	Exeter, Devon
Cherryumpton	Shane Leslie	Cherry Hinton/Trumpington, Cambridgeshire
Christminster	Thomas Hardy	Oxford
Clavering St Mary	W.M. Thackeray	Ottery St Mary, Devon
Cloisterham	Charles Dickens	Rochester, Kent
Coketown	Charles Dickens	Hanley, Staffordshire
Crampsford	Samuel Butler	Langar, Nottinghamshire
Cranford	Elizabeth Gaskell	Knutsford, Cheshire
Cresscombe	Thomas Hardy	Letcombe Bassett, Oxfordshire
Creston	Thomas Hardy	Preston, Dorset

Crockham	D.H. Lawrence	Greatham, West Sussex
Darling	James Anthony Froude	Dartington, Devon
Deerbrook	Harriet Martineau	Diss, Norfolk
Downstaple	Thomas Hardy	Barnstaple, Devon
Eagledale	George Eliot	Dove Dale, Staffordshire
East Egdon	Thomas Hardy	Affpuddle, Dorset
Eatanswill	Charles Dickens	Ipswich/Sudbury, Suffolk
Emminster	Thomas Hardy	Beaminster, Dorset
Endelstow	Thomas Hardy	St Juliot, Cornwall
Entepfuhl	Thomas Carlyle	Ecclefechan, Dumfries and Galloway
Evershead	Thomas Hardy	Evershot, Dorset
Exonbury	Thomas Hardy	Exeter, Devon
Flychett	Thomas Hardy	Lytchett Minster, Dorset
Fountall	Thomas Hardy	Wells, Somerset
Gudetown	John Galt	Irvine, Strathclyde
Havenpool	Thomas Hardy	Poole, Dorset
Hillstone	Florence Marryat	Winchester, Hampshire
Hinterschlag	Thomas Carlyle	Annan, Dumfries and Galloway
Hurstley	Benjamin Disraeli	Bradenham, Buckinghamshire
Isle of Slingers	Thomas Hardy	Isle of Portland, Dorset
Ivell	Thomas Hardy	Yeovil, Somerset
Kennetbridge	Thomas Hardy	Newbury, Berkshire
Kingsbere	Thomas Hardy	Bere Regis, Dorset
Kingscreech	Thomas Hardy	Kingston, Dorset
King's Hintock	Thomas Hardy	Melbury Osmond, Dorset
Knarborough	D.H. Lawrence	Nottingham
Knebley	George Eliot	Astley, Warwickshire
Knollsea	Thomas Hardy	Swanage, Dorset
Knype	Arnold Bennett	Stoke-on-Trent, Staffordshire
Leddenton	Thomas Hardy	Gillingham, Dorset
Lew Everard	Thomas Hardy	West Stafford, Dorset
Loamshire	George Eliot	Staffordshire
Longpuddle	Thomas Hardy	Piddlehinton/Piddletrenthide, Dorset
Longshaw	Arnold Bennett	Longton, Staffordshire
Lower Binfield	George Orwell	Henley-on-Thames, Oxfordshire
Lowton	Charlotte Brontë	Kirkby Lonsdale, Cumbria
Lumsdon	Thomas Hardy	Cumnor, Oxfordshire
Lymport	George Meredith	Portsmouth, Hampshire
Mallingford	Mrs Molesworth	Knutsford, Cheshire
Manefold	Arnold Bennett	Leek, Staffordshire
Markton	Thomas Hardy	Dunster, Somerset

Marlott	Thomas Hardy	Marnhull, Dorset
Marygreen	Thomas Hardy	Fawley, Berkshire
Matchings Easy	H.G. Wells	Little Easton, Essex
Melchester	Thomas Hardy	Salisbury, Wiltshire
Mellstock	Thomas Hardy	Stinsford, Dorset
Melport	Thomas Hardy	Weymouth, Dorset
Middlemarch	George Eliot	Coventry, West Midlands
Milby	George Eliot	Nuneaton, Warwickshire
Mill Pool	Thomas Hardy	Milborne Port, Dorset
Milton	Elizabeth Gaskell	Manchester
Mirefields	Morley Roberts	Wakefield, West Yorkshire
Monkshaven	Elizabeth Gaskell	Whitby, North Yorkshire
Moorhampton	Morley Roberts	Manchester
Moreford	Thomas Hardy	Moreton, Dorset
Morton	Charlotte Brontë	Hathersage, Derbyshire
Nether Moynton	Thomas Hardy	Owermoigne, Dorset
Norbourne	George Eliot	Norbury, Derbyshire
Northbridge	Angela Thirkell	Chipping Camden, Gloucestershire
Nunnelly	Charlotte Brontë	Hartshead, West Yorkshire
Nuttall	D.H. Lawrence	Underwood, Nottinghamshire
Nuttlebury	Thomas Hardy	Hazelbury Bryan, Dorset
Oakbourne	George Eliot	Ashbourne, Derbyshire
Oniton	E.M. Forster	Clun, Shropshire
Oozewood	Thomas Hardy	Ringwood, Hampshire
Paddiford	George Eliot	Stockingford, Warwickshire
Pen-Zephyr	Thomas Hardy	Penzance, Cornwall
Polchester	Hugh Walpole	Truro, Cornwall
Port-Bredy	Thomas Hardy	Bridport, Dorset
Quartershot	Thomas Hardy	Aldershot, Hampshire
Rosseter	George Eliot	Rocester, Staffordshire
Rummidge	David Lodge	Birmingham
St Launce's	Thomas Hardy	Launceston, Cornwall
St Ogg's	George Eliot	Gainsborough, Lincolnshire
Sandbourne	Thomas Hardy	Bournemouth, Dorset
Sandyshore	Mrs Molesworth	Fleetwood, Lancashire
Sawston	E.M. Forster	Tonbridge, Kent
Scrimpton	Thomas Hardy	Frampton, Dorset
Shaston	Thomas Hardy	Shaftesbury, Dorset
Shepperton	George Eliot	Chilvers Cotton, Warwickshire
Sherton Abbas	Thomas Hardy	Sherborne, Dorset
Shottsford Forum	Thomas Hardy	Blandford Forum, Dorset
Siddermorton	H.G. Wells	South Harting, West Sussex

Silverthorn	Thomas Hardy	Silverton, Devon
Solentsea	Thomas Hardy	Southsea, Hampshire
Stickleford	Thomas Hardy	Tincleton, Dorset
Stoke-Barehills	Thomas Hardy	Basingstoke, Hampshire
Stonyshire	George Eliot	Derbyshire
Stourcastle	Thomas Hardy	Sturminster Newton, Dorset
Stratleigh	Thomas Hardy	Bude-Stratton, Cornwall
Stuffington	W.M. Thackeray	Darlington, Co Durham
Summer Street	E.M. Forster	Holmbury St Mary, Surrey
Summertune	Compton Mackenzie	Chesham, Buckinghamshire
Tercanbury	W. Somerset Maugham	Canterbury, Kent
Tevershall	D.H. Lawrence	Eastwood, Nottinghamshire
Tilling	E.F. Benson	Rye, East Sussex
Tivworthy	Thomas Hardy	Tiverton, Devon
Tolchurch	Thomas Hardy	Tolpuddle, Dorset
Tollamore	Thomas Hardy	Stinsford, Dorset
Toneborough	Thomas Hardy	Taunton, Somerset
Tor-upon-Sea	Thomas Hardy	Torquay, Devon
Trantridge	Thomas Hardy	Pentridge/Tarrant Hinton, Dorset
Treby Magna	George Eliot	Coventry, West Midlands
Tripplegate	George Eliot	Higham on the Hill, Leicestershire
Trufal	Thomas Hardy	Truro, Cornwall
Turnhill	Arnold Bennett	Tunstall, Staffordshire
Upper Mellstock	Thomas Hardy	Higher Bockhampton, Dorset
Weatherbury	Thomas Hardy	Puddletown, Dorset
Wellbridge	Thomas Hardy	Wool, Dorset
Weydon Priors	Thomas Hardy	Weyhill, Hampshire
Whittlecombe	George Eliot	Stockingford, Warwickshire
Wimblehurst	H.G. Wells	Midhurst, West Sussex
Wintoncester	Thomas Hardy	Winchester, Hampshire
Wodgate	Benjamin Disraeli	Willenhall (district of Walsall), West Midlands
Woodhouse	D.H. Lawrence	Eastwood, Nottinghamshire

VII. Gypsy place-names

English Gypsies have (or had) their own names for many places in Britain. They were collected by the writer and expert on Gypsy folklore, George Borrow. The list below is taken from his book *Romano Lavo-Lil: Word-Book of the Romany*, published in 1874.

Gypsy name	Meaning	English name
Baulo-mengreskey tem	Swineherd's country	Hampshire
Bokra-mengreskey tem	Shepherds' country	Sussex
Bori-congriken gav	Great church town	York
Boro gueroneskey tem	Big fellows' country	Northumberland
Boro-rukeneskey gav	Great tree town	Fairlop (Greater London)
Chohawniskey tem	Witches' country	Lancashire
Choko-mengreskey gav	Shoemakers' town	Northampton
Churi-mengreskey gav	Cutlers' town	Sheffield
Coro-mengreskey tem	Potters' country	Staffordshire
Cosht-killimengreskey tem	Cudgel players' country	Cornwall
Curo-mengreskey gav	Boxers' town	Nottingham
Dinelo tem	Fools' country	Suffolk
Giv-engreskey tem	Farmers' country	Buckinghamshire
Gry-engreskey gav	Horsedealers' town	Horncastle (Lincolnshire)
Guyo-mengreskey tem	Pudding eaters' country	Yorkshire
Jinney-mengreskey gav	Sharpers' town	Manchester
Juggal-engreskey gav	Dog fanciers' town	Dudley (West Midlands)
Juvlo-mengreskey tem	Lousy fellows' country	Scotland
Kaulo gav	The black town	Birmingham
Levin-engreskey tem	Hop country	Kent
Lil-engreskey gav	Book fellows' town	Oxford
Match-eneskey gav	Fishy town	Yarmouth (Norfolk)
Mi-develeskey gav	My God's town	Canterbury
Mi-krauliskey gav	My Queen's town	London
Nashi-mescro gav	Racers' town	Newmarket (Suffolk)
Pappin-eskey tem	Duck country	Lincolnshire
Paub-pawnugo tem	Apple-water country	Herefordshire
Porrum-engreskey tem	Leek eaters' country	Wales
Pov-engreskey tem	Potato country	Norfolk
Rashayeskey gav	Clergyman's town	Ely (Cambridgeshire)
Rokrengreskey gav	Talking fellows' town	Norwich (Norfolk)
Shammin-engreskey gav	Chairmakers' town	Windsor (Berkshire)
Tudlo tem	Milk country	Cheshire
Weshen-eskey gav	Forest town	Epping (Essex)

Weshen-juggal-slommo-mengreskey tem	Foxhunting fellows' country	Leicestershire*
Wongareskey gav	Coal town	Newcastle
Wusto-mengreskey tem	Wrestlers' country	Devonshire

Weshen-juggal, 'fox', literally means 'dog of the wood', and *slommo* means 'track'.